Cornish Fishing and Seafood

Cornish Fishing and Seafood

Carol Trewin

Photography **Adam Woolfitt**

Foreword **Colin Warwick, MBE**

Alison Hodge

Contents

Foreword

What's your favourite fish to eat? I wonder if, like me, you are spoilt for choice? Welcome aboard the book that tells for the first time about the industry that puts the fish into the dish. Unlike any other book, *Cornish Fishing and Seafood* gives the reader a unique insight into the fishing fraternity, their hopes and fears, and their vision of the future and how they might continue to enjoy the rich harvest of the sea.

Within these pages is also a selection of wonderful fish and shellfish recipes. Dishes to delight the taste-buds and invoke memories of Cornish harbours, where the fishing boats land their catches. Fish that tastes as fresh as the ocean breeze.

The skipper of the average fishing vessel makes more decisions in a day than the pilot of a jumbo jet. He must comply with more rules and regulations than his counterparts in any comparable industry. At times he is branded a criminal, or worse a mindless moron who has no regard for his environment. As you read this book you will, I'm sure, agree with me that nothing could be further from the truth.

The management of the UK fish stocks is done jointly by the UK Government and the EU. Who gets what of the fish pie is the outcome of a bizarre game of political football played out in Brussels every December, which usually results in the scientific view, and indeed the industry view, being swept aside to make way for a political compromise, thus leaving the industry to pick up the pieces.

It was against this background that the Duchy Fish Quota Company was formed. Our objectives are simple. We buy fish quota when it is available, which we then lease to the industry with the emphasis being on the young up-and-coming skippers. The income derived from this activity is reinvested in more fish quota, therefore slowly building up a pool of available fish for future generations to catch.

We are a non-profit company, and the directors give their time freely. Every single person who has contributed to this book shares an absolute passion for the survival of the fishing industry, not just in the short term but more importantly providing the opportunity for growth and regeneration in our ever-evolving industry.

We need your support, and in purchasing this book you will be helping to preserve the present fleet, and giving a future to young Cornish fishermen. In return they will continue to provide the delicious, fresh, quality catch that our industry is famed for.

On average, 62 fishermen are lost or seriously injured around the UK each year. Cornwall has its share of such accidents. Despite all the safety training and modern equipment, fishing is still the most dangerous peacetime job in the UK.

We would like to dedicate this book to the fishermen who sailed to harvest the bountiful sea but who sadly did not return.

Right: A young fisherman comes into Looe harbour in the late evening.

Colin Warwick, MBE
Chairman, Duchy Fish Quota Company

Introduction

'Fishing is statistically Britain's most dangerous peacetime occupation. Competing with the elements is only one part of it. It's a love-hate relationship with the sea. It can be absolutely fantastic out there, when conditions are good, there's nothing like it. But fishermen, unlike other merchant seafarers, are really a breed of hunters.'

The words of David Whitehead, who runs the Royal National Mission to Deep Sea Fishermen in Newlyn, sum up so much of what most of us don't understand in an industry that those of us who are not part of take for granted – fishing.

The Cornish fishing industry has been reported as dying on its feet, but look a little closer, scrape away the barnacles of disillusionment with bureaucracy, the grimy layer of distrust of politicians and fishermen from other countries, and there are clear signs of an industry that is taking great strides to ensure it has a healthy future. A handful of fishermen are buying new boats; onshore businesses are investing and expanding; new schemes are promoting Cornish fish and responding to consumer demands for top-quality fish, caught using sustainable fishing methods. Hardly signs of a failing industry. Despite the constant stream of negative stories in the media, in fact the waters around the Cornish coast contain a rich diversity of different species of fish and shellfish. Most of these are nowhere near being overfished, nor are stocks in danger of imminent collapse.

This book, then, is what I hope is a fairer, and more truthful reflection of the state of fishing in Cornwall and the Isles of Scilly, always taking into account that political changes can have a sudden and dramatic impact, and that much can happen in the short time between writing and publication. While I was research-ing *Cornish Fishing and Seafood*, the huge hikes in fuel prices in the summer and autumn of 2005 completely changed the mood in Newlyn, Cornwall's biggest fishing port. Many predicted that this would be the final blow for an industry that was just starting to feel as if the future was looking brighter.

A few months later the bad press started again. First there were misleading articles in national newspapers, giving the impression that all fishing vesels are giant, industrial factory ships that tow miles-long nets, endlessly scooping up everything in their way. Then Greenpeace and the Marine Conservation Society started putting pressure on the supermarkets to stop stocking certain fish species that were perceived to be at risk. What they omitted to tell the supermarket buyers

Right: Bastard, or witch, sole and wild garlic leaves (see page 219).

was that many of their arguments were based on old scientific evidence that took no account of regional variations.

Many visitors to Cornwall may believe that the county's historic fishing villages are quaint and timeless. In fact, the Cornish fishing industry is probably more cutting edge than anywhere else in Britain. It is also more closely linked to Europe, as its principal market, than almost any other British industry, and is acutely environmentally aware, pioneering schemes to protect fish stocks and the marine environment, such as the protected spawning grounds in the Trevose Head Box. Gradually getting to know them, I found that like any other businesses, the most innovative and best run were confident about their future. The general perception of the industry often lags behind the reality of its present activities.

The problems facing Cornish fishing are not confined to politics and politicians with no real understanding of how the industry ticks; just as influential are the weather, the danger of competing with the elements at sea, global geo-politics, climate change, and oil prices. The pressures and demands on both inshore and deeper waters are immense. Gas pipelines, underwater cables, water sewerage outlets, tourism and leisure activities, oil rigs, offshore windfarms, and pilot projects for other renewable energy sources all have an impact, often negative. Yet when it comes to controversy, it is often the fishermen who are first in the firing line, the easy target.

Seafood is also changing from being a cheap source of protein to a premium, healthy product, reflecting its scarcity value and the fact that it is the last genuinely wild food from a renewable, sustainable source that man cannot directly interfere with. Genetically, a pilchard is the same as it was 10,000 years ago, so is cod. But at home consumers are still reluctant to cook fresh fish regularly. So this book includes recipes from Cornish chefs, ranging from pubs and restaurants to an organic guesthouse and tearoom. All are passionate about Cornish seafood, and I hope they can convince more people that fish is one of the easiest and quickest foods to prepare and cook. They all know that the range of fresh fish and shellfish landed in Cornwall's ports and harbours is unequalled anywhere in Britain.

This book is also about the future of fishing in Cornwall and the Isles of Scilly. While fishing quotas persist, it is difficult for new entrants to get a foot on the first rung of the fishing ladder. When boats are decommissioned and sold, so is the quota, sold to the highest bidder, often leaving the county or going abroad, depriving Cornish fishermen of a future ability to catch fish in Cornish waters. *Cornish Fishing and Seafood* has been written with the financial support of many fishing organizations and businesses, so that the proceeds from sales of the book will help the Duchy Fish Quota Company to secure a future for the next generation of Cornish fishermen and, indirectly, the many onshore businesses that depend on them setting to sea for more than 200 days of the year.

Adam Woolfitt and I would like to thank all the fishermen, and those connected in whatever way with the industry, who willingly gave us their time and knowledge to help make this book a reality. Many have allowed me to use their own words, in the form of verbatim interviews, to tell their story and the story of Cornish fishing and seafood.

Carol Trewin
Horrabridge, June 2006

Author's note
The three main areas fished by Cornish boats are the Celtic Sea, which lies south of a line from Fishguard to the Irish coast down to a line parallel with Land's End (ICES Areas VIIf and VIIg, see map on page 84); the Western Approaches, which are south of the Celtic Sea down to a line south of Brest on the west Brittany coast (ICES Area VIIh); and the Western English Channel, from the Isles of Scilly east to Swanage (ICES Area VIIe).

A note on measurements
All recipe ingredients are given in metric quantities; otherwise I have used metric or imperial measurements, as seems appropriate in the context.

Acronyms
A number of acronyms are used in this book, as shown in the panel below.

ACFM Advisory Committee on Fisheries Management	**IIFSW** Invest in Fish South West
CEFAS Centre for Environment, Fisheries and Aquaculture Science	**MAFF** Ministry of Agriculture, Fisheries, and Food
CEMARE Centre for the Economics and Management of Aquatic Resources	**MCS** Marine Conservation Society
CFP Common Fisheries Policy	**MLS** minimum landing sizes
CFPO Cornish Fish Producers' Organisation	**MSC** Marine Stewardship Council
CSFC Cornwall Sea Fisheries Committee	**NFFO** National Federation of Fishermen's Organisations
Defra Department for Environment, Food and Rural Affairs	**NGO** non-governmental organization
DFQC Duchy Fish Quota Company	**RAC** Regional Advisory Committee
EEC European Economic Community	**Seafish** Sea Fish Industry Authority
EU European Union	**SWPO** South West Producers' Organisation
FSP Fisheries Science Partnership	**SWHFA** South West Handline Fishermen's Association
ICES International Council for the Exploration of the Sea	**TAC** total allowable catch

1 Cornwall on the Move

It is a cold, dark, January morning in Newlyn as the boxes of iced fish are hauled up out of the hold of the *Crystal Sea* and manoeuvred on to a trolley. Inside are lemon sole, haddock, John Dory, ray and monkfish. Stacked four high they are wheeled off into the market where a team of men is already sorting and grading the fish, weighing them and then repacking them in yet more ice. Two hours later the auction begins, and within a few more hours those fish have been loaded on to a lorry and transported away, either to a local wholesaler for processing, or to be exported to continental Europe.

For David Stevens junior, skipper of the *Crystal Sea*, there is no time even to wait for the auction to begin. Fish safely landed and accounted for, he is joined on the quayside by his father to load enough food and water for the four-man crew's next trip. The 70 ft trawler is eased back down the harbour to another berth where she is refuelled and refilled with ice. Then it's a sharp about turn and she steams quietly out of the harbour before the rest of Newlyn is even thinking of going about its day's business.

The economics of fishing are hard. Every time a boat like the *Crystal Sea* leaves Newlyn, the Stevens brothers are effectively in debt: their agent, who sells the fish on their behalf, has supplied everything on board: fuel, ice, food, gloves, any incidental equipment needed. The cost of this has to be subtracted from what the next catch earns. This particular four-day trip in January earned about £6,000, which David describes as 'not bad', but the fuel costs alone were almost £1,600. In 2005/6 higher fuel prices added an estimated £30,000–£40,000 to their overheads. After deductions for fuel, ice, the auctioneer's and agent's charges, landing dues, food and other essential boat gear, there is little left. As with other fishing boats the remaining profit is divided on a share system: for most privately owned boats, the boat takes half and the rest is shared between skipper and crew.

Right: The trawler *Crystal Sea* at work.

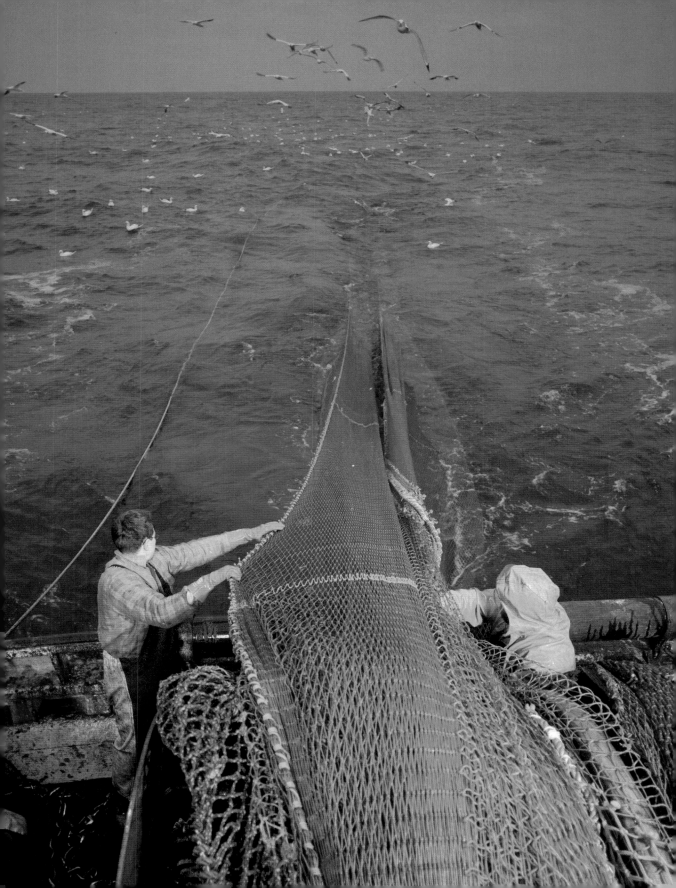

It seems a small reward for a way of life that takes no account of the hours worked, and is highly dependent on the tides and the weather. It is a working environment of extremes: little sleep, hours spent working on a cold, dark, slippery, heaving deck that pitches and rolls in every direction, washed by huge waves in bad weather. Even with the benefits of modern gear and equipment, hauling and sorting the fish is still hard work; living permanently in oilskins and sea boots, with rudimentary, if any, washing and eating facilities, this is not for the faint-hearted. When at sea all work a non-stop rota of four-hour watches, but even when not on watch there is often work to be done in the fish room, cleaning, gutting or packing fish in boxes of ice. In order to make a living while staying within the constraints of licences and quotas, the *Crystal Sea* has to fish for 280 days a year. Sea fishing is not only the most dangerous peacetime job in the world, it is the only one where normal hours of work regulations cannot apply.

Even though the bridge is bristling with the latest technology and computer screens, with sonar, echo sounders, satellite communications and GPS, David and his brother Alec still rely on their instinct and observations, learned over years of fishing in the same seas, to find the best fish and to catch them swiftly, efficiently and with a minimum of waste. These really are the last of the hunter-gatherers, pursuing the last genuinely wild food that we have.

This is a way of life for David, Alec and their two-man crew. When weather conditions permit, the *Crystal Sea* is away for a maximum of five days, fishing for carefully selected species of target fish, usually only 30 or so miles away in the waters around the Isles of Scilly. In the winter they fish for squid and whiting, and in the spring and summer change their nets to fish for lemon sole and John Dory. In the summer the boat is at sea almost constantly, with the crew changing so that each gets a few days off. 'We have learned to fish for the market, so usually we will be away a maximum of two or three days so that we can land the fish in the best condition,' explains David Stevens junior.

Their father, David Stevens senior, has stepped back from the hard physical grind of sea fishing, and although based onshore is still actively involved in the business. This is one of the more progressive businesses in the Cornish fishing industry, and the family's success is seen as proof that the industry still has a future. Yet in the last two years it has not all been plain sailing. A new gearbox and engine have set back plans to buy a new, or newer, boat by several years. Despite this the young skipper is optimistic about the future: 'I can't imagine doing anything else,' he says.

In the overall makeup of the Cornish fishing fleet these bigger vessels like the *Crystal Sea* are in a minority, and at 70 ft long cannot be compared with the giant, industrialized factory ships that are the major cause of the depletion of fish stocks around the world. In Cornwall and the Isles of Scilly the majority of the boats (71 per cent) are less than 10 metres long, often known as day boats, which means they rarely spend more than 24 hours at sea. The Cornish fleet is also set apart by its diversity. Unlike in the North Sea, where fishing is dependent on a handful of fish species, Cornish waters have a rich and diverse mix of fish to catch. On any day at either Newlyn or Looe

market, more than 20 different types will be for sale, and overall there are about 50 different fish and shellfish (see page 196) landed at 50 landing stations around Cornwall and the Isles of Scilly. These range from large, commercial harbours like Newlyn, where boats can land at any time of day or night, to tidal harbours such as Looe and Padstow, tiny coves like Penberth, or shingle beaches like Cadgwith, where the boats are winched on to the shore each day.

If there are more than 50 types of fish landed in Cornwall, then it is also true to say that there are many different ways of catching them. It is the variety of fish

On board the *Crystal Sea*.
Left: Tail end of a Force 7 gale drives the trawler along, while inside fish is gutted, cleaned, and iced.
Above: David Stevens makes up his log-book in the wheelhouse. Alec Stevens and Janis Khristianos take a break in the galley.

Top: Unloading the catch from *Crystal Sea* before dawn in Newlyn harbour. *Above and right:* Fishing vessels sail in and out of Newlyn, unload, refuel, top up stocks of ice, food and water, take on new crew members and then head straight back to sea.

species, boats and gear types that make this beleaguered industry sustainable. Among outsiders and non-fishermen the misconceptions about the types of fishing gear, and the types of boats, are considerable. Fishing methods range from handlining, to potting for shellfish, static nets, trawls and scallop dredges (see pages 200–203). In 2001 there were 599 registered vessels of all sizes fishing in Cornwall and the Isles of Scilly; only 174 were longer than 10 m, and most of these are trawlers, netters and beam trawlers working from Newlyn, Looe, Newquay, Falmouth, Polperro, Mevagissey or Padstow. The large fleet of under-10 m boats includes many small punts, also known as cove boats, no more than 16 ft long, and many other vessel types in between.

Travelling around much of the rest of the British coast it is hard to find ports and harbours with any significant numbers of fishing boats left. Cornwall, while having a smaller fleet than in the mid-1990s, still at least has enough working boats to be called a fishing fleet. Decommissioning has not had the impact here that it has in places like Peterhead or Fraserburgh, Grimsby, Fleetwood and Lowestoft. This is another of the county's unique qualities. It is the home of England's last proper fishing fleet; it has working ports and harbours that depend on fishing to make a living, and it still has fish stocks to pursue. Surrounded by the sea on three sides, and separated from the rest of the country by the River Tamar, its geographical position gives its fishermen and boats unique access to the teeming waters of the Western Channel, the Celtic Sea and the Western Approaches.

Its diverse fishing fleet, working a mixed fishery, is quite different from any other in Britain. In Scotland the bulk of the fishing fleet is mainly dedicated to white fish, nephrops (langoustines) or pelagic fish. The scale of the fishing is quite different there, with much bigger boats making, in many cases, far more money. The scale of the abuses of the fishing rules and regulations there are very much greater too. During 2005 and 2006 a series of court cases revealed just how big the black fish economy in Scotland once was.

It is hard to deny that Newlyn and the other Cornish fishing ports are a shadow of their former selves. As the fleet continues reducing, the fine balance between jobs onshore and the fish to supply those businesses has been increasingly threatened. Although they are numerically in a minority, it is the large trawlers and beam trawlers that supply the majority of the fish. Since the mid-1990s the beam-trawler fleet has been drastically reduced, and many skippers and fish processors are acutely aware that any further losses will be disastrous for the auctioneers, fuel and ice suppliers, chandlers, wholesalers, processors and transport companies who all depend on their catch being landed six days a week.

Where fishing methods and technology have changed and improved dramatically over the last 100 years, the rate of technical change (known as technical creep) has not been reflected in a similar change in the amount of fish caught. Sixty years ago boats were still using paraffin or petrol engines, nets were made from sisal or twine, crab pots were made from willow or withies and had a finite working life. Now boats have high-powered diesel engines and use monofilament nets which last much longer, and plastic-coated metal lobster and crab pots can be used all year round. Set against that is the rising cost of fuel, which in the last months of 2005 tipped the industry back into a sense of crisis that it had thought had been left behind. But then, as I discovered, fish and the fishing industry are entirely cyclical, and the cycles of boom and bust, gloom and despair versus profitability and plenty, apply as much to the business of fishing as to the fish stocks themselves. The problem is that the pattern emerges over decades rather than a handful of seasons, while politicians are very much here today, gone tomorrow, without a concern for the long term or a need to understand it.

The environmental pressures to clean up our rivers and coasts since the 1980s may have effectively taken away a major food source for juvenile fish stock. Several fishermen commented on the impact that this could have on future stocks. As more than one commented to me: 'If there's no feed the fish move on. You don't shop in a supermarket with empty shelves,' and it seems generally accepted that fish stocks are moving, perhaps more than they did historically. Build in other environmental factors and global warming, and no one should be surprised that some fish are no longer abundant in some waters but have moved to feed elsewhere.

This is not the same as a collapse of fish stocks, although some media commentators and others would have us believe that it is.

The other major imbalance that has affected the Cornish fishing industry is the consumer's lack of interest in trying unusual or different types of fish. The fact that we are becoming more adventurous is perhaps down to the influence of one man, Rick Stein. Stein's empire of restaurants and shops in Padstow may come in for some unjustified criticism, but since he opened the Seafood Restaurant in Padstow in 1975 he has become a great champion of Cornish fish and fishermen. Without his television programmes and cookery school the situation might have been far worse. 'Fishing only employs 0.3 per cent of the labour force,' he says, 'but it seems to me that it matters more, it's almost a stabilizer of life, and we ignore the soundness and dynamism of small coastal economies at our peril.'

Fishermen can be forgiven for feeling overlooked and undervalued. In sheer economic terms, measured in the value of the catch landed, they represent a very small part of Cornwall's gross domestic product (GDP). But that doesn't take into account the added value of all the shoreside jobs and their contribution to the economy and to the coastal communities, estimated in 2001 as a total industry turnover of £99 million.

Beyond the quantifiable monetary values, there is also the much more intangible effect of fishing in the county's tourism sector. Thousands of tourists are attracted to Cornwall each year as much for the coastal communities that have been shaped by centuries of fishing, as for sun, surf and good food. But this is impossible to put a value on, and sadly many of those who should know better fail to recognize this.

The Cornish fishing industry would appear to have much in its favour, yet it is under attack from all sides. Burdened to almost within an inch of its life by paperwork and bureaucracy, it is one of the most heavily regulated industries in Britain, and the future is still uncertain. This is not because of the state of its fish stocks, but because of a shortage of skilled fishermen, and a shortage of labour in the upstream processing industries. Assumptions are no longer made that the next generation will automatically continue in the business. Yet over the last few years the industry has been working hard to improve the odds stacked against it, and the revival is being led from the bottom up, by the fishermen themselves.

David Stevens junior and his brother and co-skipper, Alec, are shining examples of young fishermen who clearly believe that there is a future in fishing and are determined to make a good living out of it: 'We've been through the pain and the tough times. Stocks have improved, we're catching better fish, and technology has made gear more efficient.'

The good news for the Cornish fishing industry is that there are more like them, and they are the future.

Left: A magnet for tourists, Looe is also the second most important fishing port in Cornwall.

Andrew Pascoe
Fisherman, and Vice Chairman, South West Handline Fishermen's Association, Newlyn

Andrew Pascoe: I am the first son of Mary and Denys Pascoe, who is a fisherman, and I've got three brothers and a sister. My father has fished since he was a young boy, and my grand-father was actually a stonemason but used to fish part time, as many did in those days, they would get income from whatever was available at the time. My mother's father was the same, he was a builder but would fish during the summer months, when it was better fishing and better weather, and build in the winter, so there was fishing on both sides of my family. It was always something I wanted to do, I never wanted to do anything else. So it was in your blood as they say.

When we were still in school, me and my younger brother David had a small boat ourselves. We used to go after school, sometimes not go to school, we would be down on the boats, and in the summer holidays and weekends we started going to sea quite a bit with Dad when we were allowed to. Mum always tried to steer us away as much as possible because even then, when I left school in '86, fishing had started declining, but with the balance of fish prices going up there was still a living to be made. Then when we left school, I went to sea with Dad and my uncle on their boat for two years.

After fishing with my father, I got my own small boat and that did not quite work out, I had a lot of trouble with that one, and after a couple of years I got rid of it, did a little bit on other boats, and then started in a punt. That was about 1989–90 I would think, and during that time there weren't very many boats of that size fishing, perhaps a dozen between here and St Ives. Then it died out as the ones that were doing it originally went on to bigger and better things. When we had our second boy, Thomas, he would have been born in November '96, I was still fishing in a small boat, and I planned different types of fisheries, to try and find the best source of income for each time of the year, because nobody had ever done that in a small boat before. Punt fishing used to be in spring, summer, and most of the punts, especially around the coves, wouldn't even go to sea in the winter. It went from red mullet fishing and bass fishing in the summer, and then we had a winter mackerel fishery from November to December. Then after Christmas we started catching whiting, which is not really done in a small boat, and went on to even shooting wrecks and catching pollack and cod, from January through to the end of March. Then in the spring we would be catching mackerel again from April through to June. We also started to target spider crabs in the spring, to boost up the mackerel. Although spider crabs were a by-catch, they were never actually targeted – not from Newlyn anyway, other places were catching them with pots. So we had a very big mesh net made to tangle up big male spider crabs, because they would trundle in from deep water where they had been all winter and head for the shore to breed. I even went shark fishing in June and July, which had never been done before, although some boats were doing it for fun. They all laughed at me going out sharking in a punt, but at the time, although I had doubts, I knew there was something there. The first year I caught a few, but it was just a trial thing, and then the second year I had 33 in one day. The punt was full up that day, it was a bit chaotic, but that was a good couple of weeks during June when they came this way and it coincided with barbecues and they used to barbecue shark, so the prices were very good. We only got two or three weeks out of it, but it was another string to my bow. And then everybody started doing it, even the ones that had been laughing at me.

Well, eventually the small-boat fishing took off again, quite a lot more people started doing it, and they could see that you could make a living from it, which put more pressure on that side of it, so in 2001 James, my youngest brother, and I bought a bigger boat. It was only five years ago this March, but even then it was quite a big step. It's a 38 ft vessel, just under 12 m. So we were into the paperwork and the stuff from Defra [Department for Environment, Food and Rural Affairs] and Europe, the logbooks and the quotas and the track records, whereas if you kept under ten metres it would be not quite so bad. And it paid off because we had a good couple of years, which is what you need because you invest so much money, and because of the pressure you've put yourself under. We had a good start, but looking back, five years on, whether we would have said, 'Yes, let's go for it now,' I don't know.

We are doing what my dad and uncle were doing, more or less – crawfish, lobsters, monkfish during the summer months, using tangle nets. In the winter we change over to the mackerel fishery, and then after Christmas we're back on the white fish, we shoot wrecks with nets for pollack until the spring, when we start to go back on the turbot again. But the nets don't work on the spring tides, which is good in a way because everything gets a rest, so you get a week on and a week off with a big boat, although we have got quite a lot of work ashore mending nets and that. So the spring tides are ideal for bass on lines, so I go back to work the small boat for an income as well. That is my hobby now, it is something I enjoy and would do even if I were not getting paid for it.

" If more fish was eaten in this country, perhaps the Government would have taken more interest in the fishing industry, and we would have a far better one than we've got now. "

Before Christmas, when things are quite good, you have to put the time in. When I'm on the small boat on the spring tides and the big boat on the neap tides, it's sort of non-stop, but it pays off because we would be lucky if we get 25 to 30 days in the big boat between 1st of January and the 31st of March. During the summer we are virtually week on week off, because the weather is guaranteed, so the big boat goes virtually every day of that neap tide. With both boats I would say it's about 200, 220 days at sea, a year. It's not like a nine to five office job, and that's where with a family it's so much harder as well, because it means especially in summer time I hardly see

Andrew Pascoe arriving in Newlyn harbour on his boat Cynthia.

them at all, going to sea at 4 a.m. and coming home at 10 or 11 o'clock at night. But you have to fish that amount of time to have better money during the summer, so that when it comes to January or March you have something there as back up.

With the handline-caught bass it's all to do with marketing really, because there was so much bad press about mid-water pair trawling, and some people just stopped eating bass altogether because they were told that virtually all bass came from this method. So that's how the bass tags came about, and because we were getting very little money for them. We were getting about £4.50 a pound for bass in 1986, '87, '88, and 20 years on we are getting £8 a kilo, which is actually slightly less than we were getting then, where most other species have gone up. That's also due to imports of farmed bass, which again you can't compete with it, because if someone wants 25 portions of eight-ounce fillets they can get it exactly, plus they can supply farmed bass right throughout the year. Whereas we've got only three or four months where we can guarantee supply, so that has a major effect on the price. So we're just trying to market what we've got as a good product from a sustainable method of capture, to try and increase the price. Yes, it does seem to be working and making quite a difference

Line-caught sea bass tagged under the SWHFA's marketing scheme.

in price, 50 to 60p a kilo, which is very good because it does cost us about 12p a fish to put the tags on. Although other types of fishing catch good quality fish, this is the best, you cannot get any better than that. It's the same as free-range chickens, you get a better product with corn-fed, free-range chicken, but you pay slightly more for it because it costs more to produce. Although our fish doesn't cost more to produce, we don't catch as much.

Fish stocks are not declining any more, but there are less than there have been. I think monkfish and lemon soles and things like that have increased, and in the last three years, I've never ever seen as many sea bass, and other people have said they've never seen as much as in the last two or three years. Eight, nine years ago, at one stage we just didn't think there was any bass left, it was that bad. One season at the Runnelstone it just wasn't viable to go there, and now you are seeing as many as a hundred a day, some days. And that is a complete turn around, I don't know where they came from or whatever happened, but that's just fishing and the way it happens sometimes. I think a lot of it could be to do with warmer water temperatures and climate change because bass are not really a cold-water fish as such, but they feed better, they grow faster in warm water, and the bass are going much farther north than they ever did. And not only that, with the higher water temperature, the survival rate of the young bass is much higher, because they get to grow faster and get past each predatory stage quicker.

The biggest factor for finding fish is water temperature, as I've built up from my observations. Not many fishermen used to go on that, but when I first started targeting blue sharks, 13.5 degrees centigrade was when I started catching the sharks. So whether that was the 28th of May or the 8th of June it wasn't the date I went by, it was when I saw 13.4, 13.5 degrees then I would know. It took two or three years to get a picture of that. So because the temperature only gets to about 18 degrees in our waters, one degree temperature rise in the sea is a phenomenal amount of difference. That to me is the only calendar the fish have got, they don't know that it's the 1st of January or the 26th of March, they know that the water temperature's right and they'll be moving with that. And a lot of the feed fish, the pilchards, sardines, sand eels and everything the bigger fish chase, and things that we're targeting, are affected by that.

There's definitely a future in fishing. I don't think I could do anything else now, actually. I probably would if I had to, but as long as I can make a living I will. But there's boats tied up because there's not enough crew to take them to sea any more. And that's all down really to a lack of the next generation wanting to go fishing. Because the fishing industry is generally made up of sons of fishermen, it's not the type of thing that you go to the job centre and say, 'I am going to be a fisherman,' or you see a careers person in school and say, 'I want to be a fisherman.' It's something that either your friend was into and you grew up with it, or your family was part of it and you learned that way. But once that dries up, then you've lost the whole of the future of the industry completely, because there is going to be nobody. The experience you get growing up until you leave school is priceless, because you are already trained, you are virtually ready to go to sea as soon as you leave school. You just have all that instinctive knowledge about handling boats, and what to do with the weather, you've got over your sea sickness if you had it. We were the last large amount of younger generation who left school, around '86 to '88, about 20 or 30 of us, the last to go into it because it was starting to decline, and most of them are still fishing. I suppose the rest were steered away by their mothers who did a better job steering their sons to another, safer job than our mothers did on us.

I just think it's been very poorly managed over the years. As far as the Government was concerned, the fishing industry didn't mean that much to the country, there wasn't that many votes in it. Whereas in France and Spain, because they eat a lot more fish, fish and fishing and fishermen are very important because of the money they make and bring into the area, and they are treated in a different fashion than we are in this country. But they eat most of the fish they catch, whereas in this country we're cod and chips, and it shows in the exports. It all goes to France and Spain and abroad. And it's a shame, if we saw more fish being eaten in this country perhaps the Government would have taken more notice, and more interest in the fishing industry, and we would have had a far better one today than we've got now.

Rick Stein
Seafood Restaurant, Padstow

Rick Stein (photographed in front of a painting by Danka Natiorkowska) opened the Seafood Restaurant in Padstow in 1975. Through his restaurants, fish and chip shop, cookery school, books and television programmes he has been a great champion of Cornish fish and seafood.

Rick Stein: I had a childhood upbringing of eating lots of Cornish fish. My parents had a holiday house just outside Padstow, and I used to spend most of every summer there, and my father had a share in a lobster boat in Padstow, so we had plenty of fish when I was young, and it sort of stuck. And when Jill and I opened the restaurant in 1975, it seemed like the obvious thing to do was to concentrate on seafood.

It wasn't an original idea. I remember there was a place called Mark's Seafood Bar, which is still there in Falmouth, which was then owned by somebody I knew. I remember going there, this was in about '74, I think, to this little hole-in-the-wall place in Falmouth, where he was getting high court judges, captains of industry coming and sitting down at kitchen tables and eating grilled lobster, and Dover sole, and oysters. It seems obvious now, but the idea of selling fresh seafood in a place like Falmouth or Padstow was quite new then. There was a good restaurant in Padstow at the time called The Blue Lobster, but they tended to specialize in gratins of things, whereas this place took very fresh sole or lobster and grilled them, and that was very much more my style of food. So that's why I opened really.

In some species, there was significantly more fish then; I'm thinking particularly of sea trout, salmon peel and salmon, and also shellfish, we had a lot of crawfish then, which have virtually been fished out. But generally there hasn't been any diminishment, it seems to me, of the availability of all the other fish. We can still get things like large turbot, big conger eels, the only fish that I'm conscious of now being in very short supply are crawfish and shark, funnily enough, porbeagle shark. I think the porbeagle shark was affected by the big enthusiasm for sport fishing for them in the '60s and '70s. We do our best, and certainly we wouldn't sell porbeagle shark any more, and we wouldn't sell blue-fin tuna, but if there's a clear suggestion that any species is in danger of extinction we won't sell them.

I think the quality and variety of fish have got better in the last 30 years. I do remember in the very early days it was really hard to actually get fish apart from the stuff from the boats in Padstow, but simply because the whole infrastructure of delivery from Newlyn market or Plymouth was not brilliant. So we tended to rely on Padstow fish, and just changed the menu to whatever we could get. And in those days we weren't open in the winter, because there wasn't any business, so generally we could use local fish. We had a bit of a supply from a fish merchant in Port Isaac then, Dennis Knight, but that was about it. The supply of fresh fish has just got better and better, and so we generally use Matthew Stevens, but as far as I know he'd buy from Newlyn, Looe, and probably Plymouth as well.

We've always had this fairly strict rule that we'll only use Westcountry fish, but I break it for halibut occasionally and langoustine, because there's really no regular fishery for them here, but there could be if they could get it together. I'm not quite sure why they haven't managed to, but occasionally they land langoustine at Newlyn and we're very grateful, but it would be nice if they could land some more. I'm not sure of the economics, it's either langoustine or hake as far as I can work out.

Generally as far as Cornwall's concerned the change has been in the quality and the realization of the value of Cornish fish. If you want to sell fish in London, it's almost *de rigueur* that you have line-caught Cornish sea bass, because there is a distinct suggestion of quality in both expressions, 'line-caught' and 'Cornish'. So we are just very lucky to be where we are really, and inshore fish is what we tend to buy. As far as I am aware there is no real shortage of any of the species we use in Cornwall. But we're not on the North Sea, and I don't think people really understand the regionality of shortages, you know.

For the fish and chip shop, it just seemed it would be setting a very bad example to use local cod, and actually Icelandic cod is extremely good, because they've got plenty of stock. But it's a brilliant product, and we do get through an awful lot of cod in that restaurant, so it was probably the right thing to do. You definitely get the picture that the general public think that stocking any fish with a concern about it is committing a serious crime.

> " *One of my arguments was that maybe if we all ate a much bigger variety of fish, we wouldn't be targeting a specific species.* "

Last summer some customer harangued me just outside here about selling cod in the fish and chip shop, you know it didn't even occur to them that it might not be local cod, let alone the Icelandic cod that it was. People get very hysterical, and you can appreciate why, because fish in general is not in a healthy state.

Everybody I've talked to is catching bass, but you have to be so careful because you'll talk to fishermen about the shortages, and they'll say, 'Shortages, what shortages?' because they've got a vested interest in it. But at the end of the day, I can say that in the last 30 years of having the restaurant, apart from the fish species I've mentioned, I've not noticed any shortage. And I haven't noticed any sort of massive increase in price – obviously the price of fish has increased significantly over that period, but so has the price of beef as well.

Last summer, a portion of turbot was costing something like £12 to put on the plate, but it's come down. It does. I'm quite proud in a way that now it costs us up to £8.50 a kilo for gurnard, and that was partly because I was saying, 'Hey, this is a great fish, it shouldn't be just lobster bait, you know.' One of my arguments was that maybe if we all ate a much bigger variety of fish, we wouldn't be targeting a specific species.

Rick Stein's popular fish and chip shop in Padstow.

But I have to say I made this big mistake of mentioning grey mullet, and apparently grey mullet is incredibly tricky, I'm not quite sure what it is, but I don't think they reproduce particularly fast or in large numbers. So I got a right wrap over the knuckles for that, but I think fish like megrim sole, witch sole, gurnard, even John Dory are fetching a big price now, they're worth talking about because they are bloody good fish and people should be aware of them.

A lot of fish in this country is quite badly cooked, and I think that doesn't help, and also a lot of fish in this country is not as fresh as it could be. You can see in the cookery school that people are amazed working with the sort of raw materials that we get in Cornwall. It's terribly gratifying that they're knocked out by it, but not realizing just how lovely fish can taste.

I periodically go and buy fish in supermarkets, just to see what people can buy, and sometimes I'm just appalled by the quality, and no wonder people don't want to eat fish if what they're buying is stale and pricey as well. You probably know we made this TV series in France, and spending some time in somewhere like France you get this impression of the enormous uphill task it is for a country like Britain, that hasn't had a great enthusiasm for seafood, to get to where the French are. You can buy wonderfully fresh fish in virtually any city in the whole of France, and you know you can go to the market in Toulouse, which is a fair way from the sea, and find beautiful fish both from the Atlantic and from the Mediterranean, in a market. It's almost like you might as well give up, just stick to selling fish in Cornwall.

It's wonderful that a lot of Cornish food is now synonymous with quality, and it's surprising how easy it has been to do. I think that's probably because Cornwall is largely rural anyway, and the produce has always been good. It's just a question of pointing it out to people really, nothing more so than fish. We've got a fish counter in the deli and basically we're doing well there because we don't permit any stale fish, because if it doesn't sell in the deli we put it in the restaurants while it's still fresh. I think people find it quite frightening, I suppose the word is, how expensive it is, but if you say to them, 'Well it is expensive because it is the best.' That's one of the things that the Cornish fishermen have understood is to look after their fish; day-boat fish, well looked after, commands a great premium and bloody well it should too. I think because we have such a history of expecting food to be cheap, it's extraordinary to people when they see how much things cost. From time to time we do put Scottish langoustine on in the deli, but it's still alive and you know it is the same price as lobster, but it tastes as good as lobster if it's alive. I don't see any reason for feeling guilty about charging for what good food costs.

Even if, dare I say, EEC and local initiatives are allowed to work then things could be all right, but there is just so much pressure. I think the problem of the CFP – Common Fisheries Policy – is that it has to be all things to all Common Market countries. I'm not aware that local fishermen have the same *laissez-faire* attitude towards black fish any more, I mean they certainly used to in the '80s and early '90s, they'd all argue that they couldn't make a living out of quota fish, but whatever you think about the fish quota system to actually abuse it is not a good idea for anybody.

I did a programme about five years ago, with a guy called David Taylor, about the Cornish fishing industry, and tried to understand what the CFP meant. I think we ended up with the feeling that really, certainly patrolling inshore waters should be entirely left to the locals. Although fishermen are tarred with this brush of being hunter-gatherers they still have got their own livelihoods to consider. And I think one of the quite optimistic indications is that when you talk to fishermen they are perfectly aware of the need to conserve stocks. It's just they want a fair hearing really for what stocks mean and they're very dubious about various scientists' views of what the stocks are, and who's to know? We'd probably be better spending our money on correct patrolling of our waters rather than banning species or closing down whole areas of the North Sea. I would have said the Cornish fishing industry is a well-developed and well-policed operation if left to its own devices, I think it could well prosper, and when you meet fishermen now conservation is very much on their minds.

Padstow is a major centre for shellfishing in North Cornwall.

2 'Little fishes they call pylchards'

The pilchard (*Sardina pilchardus*) is a small, silvery fish. Most of us associate it with tins and tomato sauce, but it is becoming fashionable again through its renaissance as the Cornish sardine (a sardine is an immature pilchard) and, for those interested in reviving regional, gastronomic specialities, as a salted and cured fish. Although one of the strengths of Cornish fishing for more than 500 years has been the diverse number of fish species available, this unassuming fish was the driving economic force that dominated the industry for much of that time, providing not just employment but food, oil, fertilizer and an income. It linked Cornwall with the rest of the world, and it epitomized the boom and bust, cyclical patterns that occurred throughout Cornish fishing. Fishermen have become an integral part of these, responding as much to abundance or lack of fish as to the tides, weather and political imperatives.

Almost every historian writing about Cornwall comments on the county's relationship with the sea, which for centuries was the main source of food, transport, defence, trade and contact with the outside world. The earliest inhabitants in the Mesolithic age, although semi-nomadic, would have been hunters and fishermen. More than 6,000 years ago they used natural, rocky pools as elementary fish weirs that trapped the fish as the tide ebbed away. They would also have used traps, spears and hooks in the rivers, and lines on the beaches, to fish for salt and freshwater fish such as salmon, peal and trout. In their search for food and wealth they were developing the hunter-gatherer skills that were later to pit man against one of our most dangerous, unpredictable and fundamental elements, the sea.

The long coastline and the county's geographical isolation meant that the Cornish were mostly outward looking. They traded tin, copper, saffron, wine and fish with, among others, the Phoenicians and other Mediterranean peoples long before links were developed with the rest of England. Fishing and, to a lesser

Right: How we Caught the Pilchards, Charles Napier Hemy, 1885.

extent, mining and farming, were for hundreds of years the county's main occupations, often overlapping.

The first records of commercial fish trading come from Marazion, where in 1070 the monks of Mont St Michel were granted a licence to hold a weekly market (most likely a fish market) – a reward from Robert, Count of Mortain, who was granted extensive estates in Cornwall by William the Conqueror after the Battle of Hastings. In 1246 Saltash was granted a borough charter which included the right for fishermen to sell fish from their boats when moored in the River Tamar. Foreign fishing boats were working in Cornish waters as early as the thirteenth century, after King John granted licences to French merchants from Bayonne to fish for conger, hake and whales along the south-west coast from St Michael's Mount to Dartmouth. By the late fourteenth century, fish were being sent to Exeter from Mousehole, Penzance, Fowey and Looe. This was a vital trade given the tiny resident population in Cornwall, recorded in 1377 at around 34,000 compared with more than 49,000 in Devon and over 56,000 in Somerset.

By the sixteenth century, the pilchard fishery was well established as one of the main drivers of Cornish fishing, as William Camden recorded in *Britannia* in 1586. He noted that curing was the most efficient way of preserving these fish before transporting them thousands of miles to Catholic Europe, where they were consumed in their millions by the rural poor, in place of meat on religious fast days and during Lent.

> *'They make likewise a gainful trade in those little fishes they call pylchards which are seen upon the sea coasts, as it were in great swarms, from July to November. These they catch, garbage, salt, smoak, barrel, press, and so send them in great numbers to France, Spain and Italy where they are a welcome commodity and named Fumados.'*

As Sir Richard Carew started his *Survey of Cornwall* in the late 1500s, he found a great range of fish and shellfish caught in Cornish waters. His list of more than 45 different species, most of them familiar today, shows that the twenty-first-century abundance is nothing new. He also found many different fishing methods in place, ranging from fish weirs (a fenced area at the low tide mark which trapped salmon, trout and peal as they swam in on the tide) to fixed nets in the estuaries and at low water marks, and seine, trammel and tuck nets. Hook-and-line fishing was used for bass and whiting; mussels and limpets were gathered by hand, and crabs would be pulled out from their rocky hiding places using a 'long crook of iron'. At low tide locals could wade into the river estuaries and catch plaice and sole with their bare hands. These would no doubt have formed part of the tithes of one-tenth of the catch which were paid to the landowners, churches and monasteries up until the Dissolution of the monasteries in 1536. Tithes continued to be collected until the middle of the nineteenth century, a cause of great resentment given the large number of staunchly non-conformist Methodist fishermen in Cornwall, and that the tithes were mostly not used for ecclesiastical purposes.

While pilchards were the most important fish, Carew records that hake was also exported, and that in 1582 there were 2,000 seafaring men in Cornwall. Many of these sailed as far as Newfoundland, chasing cod, or followed the herring shoals to Ireland, setting a pattern of nomadic, distant-water fishing that would continue until Britain joined the Common Market in 1973.

By the early seventeenth century the busiest Cornish harbours were Padstow, St Ives and Looe. Vessels from these ports, and ships from Saltash, Fowey, Mevagissey, Falmouth, St Mawes, St Keverne, and Penzance were among the 200 Westcountry boats engaged in the Newfoundland trade. It was a hard way to earn a living: the fishermen were usually away for more than a year and, depending on the international politics of the day, often vulnerable to attack from pirates, or French or Spanish boats. The catch would be dried and salted in Newfoundland, and was usually sold to Mediterranean countries when they returned.

Almost 150 years after Carew, the great Cornish natural historian Dr William Borlase, in his 1758 treatise *The Natural History of Cornwall*, describes abundant fish stocks with more than 35 different types of fish, and at least 12 types of bivalve and shellfish appearing each season, providing good year-round fishing. He also notes the benefits of the inshore seine fishery for pilchards that had continued developing during the eighteenth century:

Above: Fishermen hauling a rope, study, Charles Napier Hemy

> *'It employs a great number of men on the sea, training thereby*
> *to naval affairs; it employs men, women, and children at land,*
> *in salting, pressing, washing, and cleaning the fish. In making boats,*
> *nets, ropes, casks, many other trades are dependent on the same; the*
> *poor is fed with the offal of the captures, the land with the refuse of*
> *the fish and salt, the merchants find the gain of commission and honest*
> *commerce, the fishermen, the gains of the fish.'*

Thanks to Daniel Defoe, who visited Cornwall in 1724, we know that herrings were another important catch, particularly on the north coast:

'*The chief business on this shore, is the herring fishing; the herrings, about October, come driving up the Severn Sea, and from the coast of Ireland, in prodigious shoals, and beat all up on this coast as high as Biddeford, and Barnstable, in Devonshire, and are caught in great quantities by the fishermen, chiefly on account of the merchants of Falmouth, Foy, and Plymouth, and other ports on the south.*'

At about the same time fishermen on the Isles of Scilly were trading great quantities of cod, ling, pollack, mackerel, scad, sole, plaice, turbot, conger, mullet and wrasse to Italy, France and Spain, much of it dried or salted. Scilly ling had a particularly high reputation. In 1803 Admiral Lord Nelson wrote from Toulon to a friend in Plymouth, thanking him for a present of Scilly ling, which he had 'much enjoyed'.

For several hundred years the pilchard was a vital part of the Cornish fishing industry, and when a shoal was spotted whole villages took part in landing and processing the fish. The seine started with the huer – a watchman situated high up on the cliffs – who would spot the shoals and direct the boats. Once the huer had signalled that a shoal of pilchards was nearby, at least two boats, crewed by several men, would row out rapidly and cast the seine net around the fish. The net would then be drawn inshore, and the fish held in shallow waters until they could be transferred onshore. There are many well-known paintings showing the seas literally frothing with the small, silvery fish as the fishermen use tuck nets to transfer them into baskets. It was not unknown for millions of pilchards to be landed in record catches, such as in 1868 when 16.5 million pilchards were caught in a single seine. Only three years later huge catches led to a glut of fish, prices fell, and many hundreds of hogsheads of pilchards exported to Italy were returned unwanted.

Once the catch had been landed the entire community was involved in preserving the fish. This took place in specially built pilchard cellars (also known as pilchard palaces). Here the fish were cleaned, gutted, salted, piled up and pressed for their oil. Several weeks later they were washed and packed in barrels, pressed further, and most were exported. The work was non-stop, all day and all night, often continuing ceaselessly for days on end when there were record catches to be cured.

Many writers and historians have commented on the all-pervading smell and terrible working conditions for the women, children and the elderly engaged in this task.

Below: It was the huers who alerted fishermen when a shoal of pilchards was approaching the shore, c. 1900, L.E. Comley.

In 1851 Wilkie Collins and Charles Dickens visited St Ives and saw the pilchard palaces, where the women worked for 3d per hour, receiving a tot of brandy and some bread and cheese every six hours. The importance of the pilchard cannot be underestimated. In addition to generating a valuable export income it provided much of the staple diet of the poor, who preserved the fish for winter in large stone jars, known as *bussas*, when they could afford the salt needed to cure them.

Pilchards remained the keystone of the fishing industry right through the eighteenth and nineteenth centuries, with St Ives becoming the fishery's acknowledged centre. Between 1829 and 1838 around 30 million fish (9,000 hogsheads) were exported to Catholic Mediterranean countries each year. In addition to the European trade, a new market had also been found in the West Indies.

Top: The Newlyn fishing fleet of luggers in Mount's Bay, with families on shore sorting the catch for sale, *c.* 1880, Gibson. *Above:* A cart laden with nets on Smeaton's Pier, St Ives, *c.* 1900, L.E. Comley.

During the second half of the nineteenth century, drift netting took over from seining as the prevalent way of catching pilchards, and at the end of the century a Spanish method of curing was introduced, which probably left the fish looking and tasting better. Here the pilchards were salted and left in tanks or vats for up to three weeks before being packed. Even then they remained the staple diet of most rural people who rarely had access to fresh meat.

By the late nineteenth century a pattern was established where Cornish boats would work different fisheries throughout the year. Some were in local waters, others further away, either in distant waters or pursuing herring as the shoals moved around the British coast. When this fishery was at its peak ports like St Ives would send off 100 boats, crewed by up to 800 men. They would land fish at ports all around the coast, often fishing around Ireland or as far north as Scotland. Then they would use the Forth and Clyde Canal to cross to fish in the North Sea, berthing in Yorkshire ports such as Whitby and Scarborough, and sailing south via Grimsby and Lowestoft as they made their way home.

While pilchards continued to be preserved in bulk and exported, the introduction of the railway, with the completion of Brunel's Royal Albert Bridge over the River Tamar in 1859, led to a boom in the mackerel fishery. The railway, and access to ice, meant that fresh mackerel could be sent to the London markets overnight. Until then they had mostly been sold by the fishermen's wives, or jousters, who hawked the catch around the nearest towns and villages. The London train left Penzance at 2 p.m., arriving in London 12 hours later. In the first half of 1861, 1,063 tonnes of fish were sent away by rail – a figure that increased by 30 per cent the following year. However, it was not until 1866 that there was a direct rail link to London. Until then goods had to be transferred from the standard-gauge West Cornwall railway to Brunel's broad-gauge line at Truro. By 1893 trains from Penzance were carrying 9,000 tonnes of mackerel a year. The downside was that the railway also made access to the markets easier for boats from Brixham and Plymouth, and attracted a fleet of drifters and trawlers from Lowestoft and Yarmouth. Some of these had been fishing in Cornish waters for about 20 years before the railway was built, but by the late 1870s hundreds of these east-coast boats, known as Yorkies, arrived each season.

There had been disagreements between the 'foreigners' and St Ives fishermen from the mid-1870s, which broke out over the outsiders' lack of observance of the Sabbath. Until that time Cornish boats would not fish on Sundays, but the bigger, faster, east-coast boats had no such scruples about cashing in on the market advantage of fishing on Sundays. Fish landed on a Monday could sell for up to 16s (80p) per 100 fish, compared with 5s (25p) on the Tuesday market. This came to a head in May 1896, in the now infamous Newlyn riots, when the furious Newlyn fishermen attacked the east-coast boats as they attempted to land their fish, and dumped an entire catch of 100,000 mackerel in the harbour. The rioting spread to Penzance, with Penzance men fighting alongside the meagre police force against the Newlyn fishermen. Eventually three naval gunboats were sent to Mount's Bay, and 350 soldiers of the Royal Berkshire regiment were brought in to try to settle the dispute. No lasting agreement was reached, and as memories of the conflict faded away changes gradually crept in, and in the twenty-first century many Cornish fishing boats will sail on a Sunday if conditions dictate.

Above: Jousters in Newlyn, from an engraving by J.T. Blight, c. 1860.

The real change in the industry came with motorized boats. At the turn of the century many luggers were laid up because the Cornish could not afford to buy the new steam drifters, giving more fishing opportunities to the east-coast and French boats. It took Cornish fishermen ten years to follow their east-coast rivals into steam-powered drifters, even though the Cornwall Sea Fisheries Committee (CSFC)'s records show that a steam-powered drifter had been trialled in Mevagissey in 1864, but the experiment 'did not prove a success and as a consequence the engines were removed and the boat converted into a sailing lugger.' The switch to steam engines was probably delayed because of the difficulty of getting coal. The east-coast men had easy access to the Midlands coalfields, whereas the Cornish depended on coal from south Wales. The first Cornish-owned, steam-powered drifter probably went into service in about 1906.

It was at about the same time that the spring and summer mackerel fishery became more important, and shellfishing and long lining also became more prominent fisheries. But even before the start of the First World War there was concern about the decline of the industry. Two government inquiries were held, in 1913 and 1914, the first specifically to investigate the state of fishing in Devon and Cornwall. One of the outcomes was a loan scheme to help convert Cornish fishing boats into more efficient motorboats. This helped the industry to develop during the war years as there were few boats working from other British ports, so there was a good market for fish caught off the Cornish coast.

Above: Fish sale on the quay at St Ives, 1920s, L.E. Comley.

Although by the 1920s seining for pilchards had more or less died out, inshore boats were drift netting for mackerel, pilchards and herring, long liners were catching skate, turbot and ray, and others were fishing for crabs, lobsters and crawfish. By the mid-1920s there were growing concerns about French and Belgian trawlers working the offshore fishing grounds. These boats were using nets with very small mesh sizes and flooding the market with small fish, and it was

Above: The Pilchard Works museum in Newlyn, which closed in 2005, showed the history of the pilchard industry and how the fish were salted and packed for export, mostly to Catholic countries, especially Portugal.

widely believed that this indiscriminate trawling was having serious effects on fish stocks. This in turn forced the small, inshore boats, which made up the majority of the Cornish fleet, further out to sea into areas that they were ill-equipped to fish safely. Many simply gave up.

The 1928 minutes of the CSFC record that there were fewer than 60 east-coast boats and 20 Cornish boats working the mackerel fishery, compared with 108 east-coast steam drifters and 300 Cornish drifters working out of various ports in 1907. Other fishing methods, such as long lining, were also threatened by the trawlers.

Looking back over 500 years of close observations of the fishing industry, the same cycles and sense of boom and bust exist now as they did then. From 1747 to 1756 an average of 90 million fish were dispatched each year from four main Cornish ports – Fowey, Falmouth, Penzance and St Ives – valued at £50,000 per year. Several years of poor catches and failure followed, but the industry was revived in 1790 by huge catches exceeding all expectations. Later the same patterns emerged as the herring fishery became more important. It disappeared and reappeared, in between being replaced by large shoals of mackerel, ultimately culminating in the mackerel boom of the late 1970s and early 1980s.

In the 1930s history repeated itself, as a new threat to the Cornish fishing industry appeared – Belgian motor trawlers equipped with modern diesel engines, which were far more efficient than Cornish steam trawlers and drifters. When the east-coast boats arrived in Mount's Bay in the nineteenth century they had had a severe impact on the mackerel fishery, and eventually were influential in forcing the Cornish fleet to modernize. The Belgian trawlers were to have the same effect. They not only developed beam trawling, which many years later was to become the backbone of Newlyn's fishing economy, but initially they put extreme pressure on the small Cornish inshore boats, whose only protection was the three-mile territorial waters limit. During this inter-war period, the industry struggled as many of the younger fishermen looked for alternative employment. Many emigrated and, according to the Cornish historian Claude Berry, the exodus was so great that 'four out of every ten boats, and three out of every ten fishermen, dropped out of this industry. ... At Padstow and Port Isaac, Newlyn and Mevagissey, one of every four boats was either laid up or sold.'

In 1936 the Cornwall Sea Fisheries Officer, W.H. Barron, reported that only 157 boats were being insured by the Cornish Fishing Vessels Insurance Society, compared with the 600 or so when it was first set up in 1915. 'Many of the above mentioned boats have been sold out of the country, and a few have been wrecked and lost, but the majority have been withdrawn from the Society because the owners are unable to pay the necessary premiums.'

Seining for pilchards may have died out in the early twentieth century, but the drift netters somehow carried on until the Italian invasion of Abyssinia in 1935 abruptly ended exports to one of the key markets, Italy. At that time there were 17 curing houses in Newlyn, and numerous merchants, many of them Italian, buying pilchards from Mevagissey, Cadgwith, Portscatho, Falmouth, Coverack, Porthleven, Polperro and Looe. Most of them stopped trading for good. This, followed by the Second World War, looked like the end for the pilchard industry. But not quite, as in 1874 a canning factory had been set up in Mevagissey, and after the Second World War further factories were built in Looe and other ports. These could cope with the feast or famine pattern of pilchard fishing by processing other fish when pilchards were scarce.

The fishery almost died out altogether, although there are mixed views about whether this was because the pilchards disappeared or because fishermen were turning to different, more efficient and perhaps more profitable types of fishing. By the early 1970s Shippams, in Newlyn, was the last remaining canning and curing business. It took Nick Howell, an innovative and imaginative incomer, to spot the possibilities of rebranding the pilchard as the Cornish sardine. A handful of highly skilled and innovative fishermen have responded to this, and are catching large numbers by ring netting, a technique that is similar to seine netting, although it is not shore based. Thus they have revived the fortunes of an abundant fish that is caught by highly sustainable methods, and needs no fishing quota.

Nick Howell
The Pilchard Works, Newlyn

Nick Howell's Pilchard Works in Newlyn is Britain's last traditional pilchard curing company. Nick is the man who rebranded the Cornish sardine.

Nick Howell: I was born in Hong Kong, 1951, and the family came back to the UK in 1960. Went to school in Berkhamsted and left there in '69. After a multitude of part-time jobs I took a holiday in Cornwall – it was the beach buggies and surfing in Perranporth that was the attraction – and when I ran out of money I thought I'd better go and work in a hotel as a waiter, barman and anything else they could offer. It was quite a fun industry, so I carried on and enrolled for hotel management and catering at Ealing College. Six months I lasted on that, couldn't stand it, too slow.

Mother then found me a job with Thomson newspapers in London, working on the *Scotsman* and the *Newcastle Journal* selling advertising space, putting features together. Daily commuting on the train dressed in a three-piece suit; just what mothers like! That was '72, and the following year the first oil crisis came, which was interesting, because the first thing people did was cut their advertising. Up until then filling the papers had been easy, but all of a sudden everybody had to sell. I managed to sell a half-million-pound campaign to the Indian Tea Board, who'd never advertised in newspapers, with a tea-tasting idea that I gave them for double-decker buses going round the North East, stopping off in high streets to offer different types of tea. Back in the office they couldn't believe it: 'Half a million, you must be kidding, you can't have sold that much.' That got me thinking about the whole organization. It was super-inefficient, so I worked out a proposition with my father, who'd retired by then, to sack ten of the managers and 28 of the sales staff, and I reckoned the same revenue would come in with massive cost savings. Being only 22 at the time, I naïvely gave it to the London sales controller, who was basically the guy who had allowed this situation to develop, and of course it went down like a lead balloon. So it was decision time, and as I couldn't stand the commuting or London I thought, 'I'll get as far away from here as possible.' So it was either Land's End or John O'Groats, and knowing Perranporth I thought it had to be warmer and sunnier in Cornwall. Before I left I used the marketing department's target group Index files to see what business was like in Cornwall, and it was mainly fishing or tourism, so I thought I'd go into fishing.

I was due five weeks holiday from Thomson, so I went back to Perranporth and it was actually dear old Jack Batchelor, who owned the Ponsmere Hotel, who gave me the idea. He was a tough businessman, but he told me that Newlyn market had gluts of fish when the price would be really cheap. He bought his fish from a man called Garsie Johns, who had started with a horse and cart, and eventually had a van. Garsie would ring Jack and say, for instance, 'Prices are on the deck this week for lemon soles, they are 7s 6d [38p] a stone,' and he would supply Jack at the same price, 7s 6d, but charge him £5 a week for the privilege of that market information. So I went down to Newlyn and on to the market and I just listened. It was hard enough understanding the language, but people also thought I was from MAFF [Ministry of Agriculture, Fisheries and Food] or I was the taxman, because I wanted to know all this information. With my *Observer Book of Fishes* I was working out which fish was which, and so I went up to Newquay and went round different hotels and said, for instance, 'I can supply you with cod at £1.50 a stone or lemons [lemon sole] at £1.80 a stone.' They didn't believe it at first, but when I told them that was what they sold for that morning on the market and they asked how I was going to make a profit I said I'd charge them £10 a week, £15 a week, £20 a week, whatever I thought the hotel would pay. This was late summer, and after two weeks I had a group of hotels signed up for the next year. The charges worked out at £280 a week, for just delivering fish to Newquay, and I was only earning £62 a week in London! Fantastic, I can make a fortune here.

Went back to London, handed in my notice at Thomson's and thought I'd better learn a bit more about fish, so early one morning I went to Billingsgate Market before going into the office, and asked stallholders, 'Can you teach me about fish, I'm going to start my own business in Cornwall?' The responses were quite short, like, 'Who do you think we are, a bloody training agency?' Eventually I found a guy who said he would teach me filleting but not pay me anything. That was Ronnie Taylor from John Liscombe's, and so I worked there during October, November and December, freezing cold, alongside the river, in a building that was open to the outside, filleting fish from four o'clock in the morning, while staying in a mate's flat, sleeping on his sofa. It was good experience, and I came down to Cornwall just after Christmas in 1975 and just went on the market every day, listening, until Easter. It was classic young enthusiasm really – I thought I knew everything about fish by then but didn't, because of course at Billingsgate the species came in as fillets or occasionally whole, and here I was back in Newlyn and there were some species that never went to Billingsgate, I had never seen them before but I just went there every morning, talking to people, feeling like a twit.

> " *You can find 'pork from Jack Jones' farm' and it'll tell you the breed's a Gloucester Old Spot, but fish is just labelled 'Cornish fish'. The label won't say 'fish from Andrew Pascoe', or 'Ian Mitchell' or 'Stefan Glinski'. Why not?* "

Of course, by the end of the first year all the hotels closed, and by the end of October we would have no business until Easter. I hadn't banked on that, I'd thought hotels would be open all year round. So I decided I'd better start wholesaling, and started with a group of guys in Cadgwith and sold to my old contacts in Billingsgate. The Cadgwith men were quite a cagey lot really, and it was hardly surprising because they used to go out and catch conger [eels] or a few monktails [monkfish] and put

Sea-birds are a constant companion of the Cornish fishing fleet.

them in the back of their vans, go out the next day and catch another lot, and add them to the van, and then maybe drive it all down to Newlyn; with no ice in sight. The excuse was that it wasn't worth driving to Newlyn with just a couple of stone of monkfish. So I said I would pick the fish up from them all and bring ice for the fish when they landed it. A couple of them reluctantly went along with the idea, and actually started getting better money for their fish. The next year 13 boats were landing to me and we had progressed to a store up by the ice works.

In 1978 we started exploring the export markets. The main merchants were selling to the best French processors, and I'd noticed that some of the French merchants were selling on to Spain, so I thought I'd go to see what Spanish customers actually wanted. Megrim soles were one of the species I found there, but I couldn't believe the prices they were making. In Newlyn they sold for £1.50 a stone as crab-pot bait. It was one of those instances when you'd think your calculator was playing up, trying to convert all these pesetas, or there must be a decimal point in the wrong place. But the price was right so we started off dealing with a company in San Sebastian, and over the following 15 years we built up a great relationship. Basically, I listened to what they wanted, how their market judged quality, how the fish should be gutted, and how they wanted fish presented. Properly graded and packed in polystyrene boxes were the main criteria, so we bought a small grading machine and in three years we had built up the business so that we needed a much larger premises, so we bought an £80,000 grading and batch-weighing machine, and that moved up to Stable Hobba industrial estate, where we fitted out the building to be the first supermarket-approved fresh fish processors in Cornwall. And we made good money for a few years by seeking new customers, asking what they wanted and matching it. The Newlyn beamers [beam trawlers] all turned to catching megrims, the netters started landing good quantities of hake and ling, and Newlyn grew to be the largest megrim-landing port in the UK.

I bought the Pilchard Works as a rather run-down salt-fish business in 1981. We streamlined it, modernized some of the processing, but kept its historical character and introduced some new product lines. By 1990, when new regulations and quotas started to have an impact on catches, we were at a crossroad. If we wanted to expand further we would have to start sourcing more fish from around the country, and get a new tier of management in place. After discussions with our customers we agreed that I would sell the fresh fish business to our Belgian customers, and keep the Pilchard Works. So after two years I stepped out of fresh processing back into salting at the Pilchard Works. Some of the ideas to diversify included capitalizing on the business's 90-year heritage by making part of it into a museum, and the other was to re-look at pilchards and find out why people didn't buy them fresh. It was an interesting exercise in how to respond to market research. We found that people didn't particularly like pilchards, but they did like sardines; the two species had images of tins, tomato sauce, school and horrible taste; or beaches, barbecues, Spain and sunshine. As a pilchard is just a mature sardine, we decided to re-brand the pilchard as the 'Cornish sardine' in 1997.

That bit of marketing has really made a difference to the Cornish catch. With other merchants and boats capitalizing on the idea, landings have gone from about seven tonnes a year to 1,400 tonnes in 2005. And Defra still estimates the sardine and pilchard stock around Cornwall are between 600,000 and 800,000 tonnes. Of course, to drive that demand it was crucial to work closely with the major retailers, and M&S [Marks & Spencer] have been fantastic in developing recipes and ideas. They were the leaders in pushing the Cornish sardine that other multiples have followed.

In 2001 we looked back at why tinned pilchards weren't more popular. Though some people loved them, there was an awful lot of the population who hated the bloody things. It was mainly the sludgy taste of most of the product that was on the shelves, coupled with memories of school dinners or even the war. So we found out how to make them taste better, and to make the tin appealing we put a Newlyn School painting on the front. We aimed the taste and look to appeal to a Waitrose-type customer, and they were very helpful and launched the new line in 2002. We've added a smoked variety since then, and are launching a special tomato one soon.

When I look back 30 years to when I was 24 and first came to Newlyn, and to what's changed today, the answer is very little. The boxes on the market are plastic now instead of aluminium, the market's 20 feet wider, and the man shouting still has a pencil, and the buyers still stand around the fish boxes, which are still on the floor. That's about it apart from the 'new' Mary Williams pier down the middle of the harbour. Some of the boats are still the same, still fishing, boats left over from the war. Where would a 24-year-old start? Where's the premises for him to operate from? And yet Newlyn's location, in a European context, is next to the best fishing grounds in Europe. Past our doors every day go the Belgians, the Dutch, the Danes, sometimes even the Norwegians, out to the Western Approaches and they all make their way back home again, and still make a living. And our guys are saying it's awful hard. There are some sectors of the industry that have a simplistic view of 'a new boat doesn't catch more fish.' New boats have more efficient engines, and they're built to withstand working in bad weather so they catch more. The lack of investment both on and off shore is what has driven Newlyn down.

We've only got about eight thinking fishermen in Newlyn, they're the developers and innovators, the ones who try new techniques, the ones who can see the advantages of new equipment and new boats, the ones who make a living. Those are the guys who've learned from their fathers and their own observations of what has happened with the currents, and how that affects the feed and consequently the patterns of fish.

These sharp guys, who've also now started to understand the benefits of marketing, need better facilities to expand and capitalize on their skills. The existing fish auction, and the way fish is distributed dilutes their efforts by losing their identity. Sea fish doesn't arrive on the restaurant counter or the shop counter accredited to the person that caught it. You can find 'pork from Jack Jones' farm', and it'll tell you the breed's a Gloucester Old Spot, but the fish is just labelled 'Cornish fish'. The label won't say 'fish from Andrew Pascoe', or 'Ian Mitchell' or 'Stefan Glinski'. Why not? When they make all the effort to go out when the weather is bad, and they've been clever enough to find a species at the beginning of the season, and take sufficient ice to sea to maintain the quality for days, they don't get the financial benefit. If the end consumer likes the product, you want them to go back to the shop and buy it again. At last we've made a start with the line-caught bass tags, which identify the catcher, but there's no reason why it shouldn't apply to all fish landed. It separates out the arguments, who is industrial fishing, who is line-caught fishing, and whether their techniques are environmentally friendly. Newlyn's future is in dedicated traceability and focused marketing.

3 On Secret Service: Something Fishy

One June evening in 1942 a brightly coloured French fishing boat slipped quietly away from her moorings in New Grimsby harbour on Tresco. Except this was no fishing boat but part of a Secret Intelligence Service operation to rescue top-secret wartime plans and information from southern Brittany, including the head of one of the most important Free French intelligence networks, Colonel Gilbert Renault and his family. Four days later the boat, her crew and passengers returned to the Isles of Scilly, and the colonel was whisked away to Falmouth on a motor gunboat, taking with him key documents that he had obtained in France, including the Nazis' blueprint for what were known as the Atlantic Wall defences. The plans were to be vital for the successful planning of the D-Day invasion in 1944.

During the Second World War many Cornish fishing boats were requisitioned by the Navy to be used as auxiliaries for maritime duties, for undercover work, and for Dunkirk , although in the end it is unclear how many took part in the rescue operation. Small fishing vessels, or boats disguised as such, manned mostly by young naval and Free French officers, were one of the most effective means of moving secret agents, equipment and information to and from occupied France without arousing the suspicion of the German forces in Brittany. These covert operations took place from the Isles of Scilly, Newlyn, the Helford River, Mylor and Falmouth, but each time a mission finished the vessels resumed their naval grey uniform for work in British waters.

Although the Second World War had a severe impact on the Cornish fishing industry, fishing did not cease altogether. While many of the fittest fishermen were already members of the Royal Naval Reserve, or joined the armed forces shortly after war was declared, others, particularly the inshore and cove fishermen who knew the coastline well, were put on mine-sweeping and anti-submarine duties. This left the youngsters and their grandparents to continue catching fish, although at first this was only permitted during daylight hours, so was restricted to

Above: Fishing boats come in on the tide at Padstow on the North Cornwall coast.

inshore fishing. Some beaches were mined, and coils of barbed wire and anti-tank devices protected most of them, making fishing close inshore very hazardous. The biggest run of barbed wire in the Penwith area was said to be from Newlyn harbour to Marazion. Cornwall was seen as a relatively safe haven for other fishing fleets. Lowestoft, on the East Anglian coast, was closed to all but naval traffic, so several of the east-coast motor trawlers were based in Padstow or Newlyn; it was French and Belgian fishing boats taking refuge in Newlyn that kept the port going, continuing with some limited inshore trawling, as most of the bigger Newlyn boats had been called up for service.

Under emergency wartime powers the Government controlled all fish sales, and most of the fish landed was sent to Billingsgate each day by train from Penzance. Shell fishermen were particularly badly affected by this, as they were no longer allowed to sell their catches themselves and there were barely any merchants officially registered to handle shellfish. Many of the hitherto important markets, such as France for crawfish, disappeared overnight. The shortage of Cornish caught and landed fish led to a heavy reliance on imported fish – tuna from Spain; salt-cod from the Faeroe Islands and Iceland, and whale meat and snoek (a Southern hemisphere fish, in this case probably imported from South Africa) – which British families found hard to develop a taste for. Billie Stevenson, in his book *Growing Up with Boats*, comments that 'Eleven million half pound cans of this fish were imported, but once tasted the rest remained unsold.'

At the end of the war the Cornish fishing industry was in a poor state, and over the next few years a number of government initiatives were set up to revive it, not least to ensure a steady supply of cheap protein to feed the growing UK population. As early as 1945 the Inshore Fishing Industry Act gave the Ministry of Food the power to make loans and grants for purchasing boats, motors and other essential gear. However, rising costs for everything from long-line hooks to ropes, twine and drift nets undermined any attempts to revitalize the industry. A subsidy of 10d (4p) was paid on every stone of white fish landed (much to the dismay of the shell fishermen who were excluded from the scheme). The Herring Industry Board had been set up in 1935 to reorganize, regulate and develop the dwindling herring fishery, and this was followed in 1951 by the White Fish Authority, with a remit to do anything needed to boost the industry. The authority also offered grants and loans to encourage more people to go fishing, and this was funded by the fish buyers who paid a levy of 1/2d (0.4p) per stone on all landings except shellfish. Both organizations were later replaced by the Sea Fish Industry Board, now known as the Sea Fish Industry Authority, or Seafish.

So few new boats were being built during the immediate post-war years that ports and harbours were falling into disrepair. According to Commander William

Luard, Chairman of the CSFC at the time, 'Creeping paralysis is seeping through the whole industry, and hope, so long deferred, is undermining the staunchest will-power and resolution'. His prophetic words, written in 1952 with the memories of war, and the bombing of Hiroshima still very strong, could just as well have been written 50 years later:

> 'The men who still number approaching one third of the total fishing personnel of the country, are the last smallholders of the sea, individualists, fine seamen, the crews of lifeboats. The fishing ports, coves and villages in which they live, an essential part of our island heritage, are now in danger of degenerating into full scale tourist centres, catering for the ephemeral needs of holiday makers instead of forming a far-flung chain of strategic centres from which intensive fishing could be carried out in any future emergency that would certainly see all the deep sea trawlers requisitioned for naval service, or rather those that escaped the certain atom bombing of the major fishing ports.'

Above: Penberth, one of Cornwall's smallest working fishing coves.
Below: Mr Moore was first licensed to sell fish from a handcart in East Looe in the 1960s (see page 159).

In 1952 Norway introduced an exclusion zone for foreign vessels, to protect its inshore fishing grounds. Six years later came the start of what were to become the Cod Wars, when Iceland introduced territorial limits on some of its fishing grounds, banning the British distant-water trawlers from fishing there. As C.H.B. Richards, the Cornwall Sea Fisheries Officer at the time, ruefully noted, Cornish fishermen needed the same protection for their inshore waters if they were to have any chance of making up for the volume of fish previously caught in these distant waters:

> 'What a difference it would have made to several Cornish fisheries had similar protective measures been introduced by our own government after the last war. Unless the fishing grounds bordering our present three mile limit are given better protection against over-fishing, our inshore fishermen will find it most difficult to earn their livelihood in the near waters.'

Meanwhile foreign vessels were continuing to clean up Cornish fish stocks just as they had between the two wars. Richards warned that: 'The adverse effect of the operations of foreign vessels is again being felt in several fisheries and quick action is needed to save these fisheries from extinction.'

By 1954 the entire Cornish fishing fleet had dwindled to 383 boats employing 816 men, whereas only 30 years earlier, in 1924, the comparative figures were 953 fishing vessels crewed by 3,110 men. The territorial limit on Cornish coastal waters was eventually extended from three to six miles in 1966, which gave the inshore fishery a little more protection, but did nothing to diminish competition from French and other foreign vessels who would fish right up to the limit whenever possible.

Writing this book it has been curious, but perhaps not unexpected, to find that the same issues have dogged the industry for hundreds of years: from managing predators such as cormorants, shags and seals to consumer likes and dislikes. For instance, in 1952 there were concerns that bass and mullet were not selling well 'probably due to the consumers' lack of information on the best methods of cooking the fish'. The CSFC committee resolved to ask the Ministry of Food for help with this before the next bass and mullet season.

The conflicts of 100 years earlier are repeated, between fishermen using fixed gear such as crab pots and nets and those using mobile gear, usually trawling; concerns over foreign vessels putting pressure on inshore stocks; using the wrong mesh sizes, and what would now be classified as illegal fishing methods. Then there was the issue of succession. Where was the encouragement for the next generation to go fishing? Such was the dire state of the crew numbers in the mid-1950s that many skippers asked for their crew's national service to be deferred, and one vessel owner, William Stevenson, paid his men an incentive to go to sea in addition to any income they earned from his boats' catches.

Above: Sorting fish in Newlyn market, early 1960s. The metal boxes were later replaced with plastic ones.

The poor state of Cornish fishing in general was shown in 1953 in places like Padstow, where there was consternation when the east-coast boats failed to appear. Despite the rivalry, their presence each year brought valuable income to the small fishing village.

As the inshore pilchard and mackerel fisheries continued their slow decline, some of the South East Cornwall ports, particularly Looe, switched to shark sport fishing during the 1960s. Elsewhere, catching crawfish was booming – with pots, tangle nets or caught by skin divers working in inshore waters. This boom continued through the 1970s until the stocks were fished out. They have not really recovered to the same extent. A classic example of unregulated overfishing destroying a fishery.

It was the influence of one Cornish fishing family that led to the development of a new form of fishing, beam trawling, setting up one of Newlyn's most important fisheries. W. Stevenson & Sons was established in the mid-nineteenth century, and has played a major role in the development of Newlyn as England's premier fishing port. The company was the first to own an 80 ft diesel-engined fishing boat, the *Efficient*. Originally built for long lining and to catch herring, in 1939 she was converted to trawling. During the late 1940s and 1960s the Stevenson family built up its trawler fleet in Newlyn, buying Admiralty motor fishing vessels, which

had been built to replace war losses, and refitting them as fishing boats. W. Stevenson & Sons became the first Cornish firm to introduce beam trawling, in 1972. The Dutch had practised this form of fishing after the Second World War; it was copied by the Belgians and then in Brixham. Unlike conventional stern trawling, beam trawlers use a pair of trawl nets, one on each side of the boat, their mouths held open by a beam. Initially developed for inshore shrimp fishing, beam trawlers became an efficient way of catching bottom-dwelling fish such as megrim sole, monkfish and plaice. By the early 1990s the Newlyn beam-trawler fleet was one of the biggest privately owned fleets in the country, and megrim sole became a major catch for Newlyn, with the beam trawlers responsible for increasing landings of high-quality flat fish.

Despite recently undergoing a significant restructuring, W. Stevenson & Sons remains unique as the owner of England's biggest privately run fishing fleet, working 16 beam trawlers, one trawler, one netter and four other support vessels. The family-run company also runs a number of shore-side businesses, including their Newlyn fish auction, fish merchants, fish retailers, chandlery suppliers and boat agents.

It took almost 50 years from the end of the Second World War to expose the flaws of the post-war policies of encouraging expansion and pursuing fish as a cheap form of protein to feed the nation. After the deprivations of rationing and food shortages it is easy to understand why fish and chips regained its former popularity, and families started to eat much more processed fish in the form of fish fingers and canned and frozen fish. But there has been a recognition that, as with highly intensive farming, industrializing a wild source of food can only be detrimental and lead to serious problems – whether depletion of stocks, in the case of fishing, or creating animals and poultry that are devalued, with no taste, and which require too many artificial feeds and medicines to be honestly described as coming from a genuinely sustainable production system.

The history of Cornish fishing illustrates why we need a significant culture shift towards understanding the real cost of our food. There is no such thing as cheap food, and the fishing industry illustrates that, not in terms of the daily prices we pay for fish, but in terms of the gradual and long-term decline of coastal fishing communities. These are the hidden costs that consumers neither see nor understand, but they are very real nonetheless. As Chapter 4 shows, these emerging issues and concerns became more contentious, and Cornish waters and fish stocks came under far greater pressure, when Britain joined the Common Market.

Top: The *Admiral Blake*, a typically configured beam trawler, puts out of Newlyn harbour.
Above: Some of a beam trawler's gear. The average length of each net is about 16 m (see page 200.)

The Isles of Scilly

Visitors to Scilly sense the islands' special nature immediately. In addition to their being an Area of Outstanding Natural Beauty and a Heritage Coast, the crystal-clear seas around these 200 low-lying, granite islands and rocks have Marine Park status. Fishing has continued in these waters since the islands were first occupied over 4,000 years ago, but it is a shadow of what it was in the late seventeenth and early eighteenth centuries, when fish was one of the islands' primary exports (see Chapter 2).

Commercial fishing, while subject to the same regulations as the rest of the Cornish fishing industry, is also distinctly different here, and is probably closest to the ideal of a sustainable, inshore, mixed-species fishery. Around 30 boats work in these unpolluted waters, many selling a mixture of fish and shellfish direct to the islands' pubs, hotels and restaurants. This includes lobster, crab and crawfish, grey mullet, pollack, wrasse, mackerel, whiting, turbot, conger eels, red mullet, John Dory, monkfish, and flat fish such as brill and plaice.

The Scillonian fishing fleet is almost exclusively made up of vessels that are less than 10 m long – with one exception, the netter *Victory of Helford*, which is 10.37 m. Steve Watt, the Isles of Scilly Maritime Officer, believes that a balance has been found between vessel numbers and resources: 'The numbers are much less than 30 or 40 years ago, when there was quite a big fishing fleet. Now it's a workable number, but it is difficult to make a full-time living from fishing.'

Two boats fish full time, and less than ten people earn their living solely from fishing. The rest are part-time. Some stop fishing in November, or when poor sea conditions make it unsafe; others carry on until Christmas and start again in the spring.

'We don't have as much shelter as in Cornwall, and we're much more exposed to the tides and weather,' explains Mark Pender, who probably fishes for nine or ten months of the year. 'We have to push it to make a living.'

The fishermen switch between potting for shellfish, netting, inshore trawling and handlining. The high environmental value of the sea-bed is protected by a local by-law limiting scallopers to two dredges per side. By making it uneconomic, they are deterred from fishing for scallops in the waters inside a four-mile limit.

Most of the Scillonian vessels work from St Mary's, the largest inhabited island, while each of the so-called off-islands supports only three or four boats. Occasionally vessels from Cornwall and elsewhere fish in Scillonian waters, but they are limited by size and tonnage (less than 11 m long and 10 tonnes) if they are to fish within the six-mile limit managed by the Isles of Scilly Sea Fisheries Committee. The lack of modern landing facilities means that for many of these outsiders it is easier to steam 42 miles back to Newlyn than to land on St Mary's. While catches can be landed here, there are no processing facilities for fresh fish, and the small harbour's limited facilities have

only recently been upgraded, including installing a chill store and ice-making facilities. Any fish sent on to Newlyn from the Scillies usually sells for a lower price and is known as 'overlanded' fish. Shellfish is sent to specialist merchants in Cornwall and Devon.

So it is clearly in fishermen's interests to develop local markets. The most progressive have also recognized that to make a living they have to find ways of earning more from their catch before selling it on to others. For some this means gearing their trade almost entirely to the tourist season, which effectively stops between November and March, often the worst time of the year for bad weather in this exposed archipelago. Bad for business, but good for the fish. The stocks are well managed by the small size of the fleet and the seasonality of fishing effort.

Most of the part-timers have other jobs. When the Scillonian flower industry was at its height, many would fish in the summer and pick flowers in the winter. Now the range of part-time employment varies. One fisherman on St Martin's is also the post-man, another runs a fish and chip shop every evening, selling the fish he has caught that day. Others, such as Mark Pender (who also fills the role of honorary patrol officer for the Sea Fisheries Committee), and his father and uncle on Bryher, also process their catch. Mark's father Mike catches crabs and lobsters, while his brother Johnny does the processing. Much of their fresh, hand-picked crab goes straight to the Hell Bay Hotel, only 200 yards away, or to the island's other cafés. On St Martin's, Mark and his wife Suzanne have set up a mail-order business selling shellfish; Toby Tobin-Dougan, the island's baker, smokes freshly caught grey mullet and Atlantic salmon; on St Mary's the Scillonian Shellfish Company sells cooked and dressed crab and lobster, and crab paté.

The men who fish these clear, unpolluted waters are convinced that they produce some of the best fish and shellfish in the world. 'It is outstanding quality because we take such care of the water,' says Mark Pender.

The Isles of Scilly should be the answer to every foodie's dream, eating fresh fish and shellfish caught a few hours earlier from the sea just a few yards away. While many of the fishermen and shell fishermen sell direct to the cafés, pubs and hotels, the sad truth is that this small number of boats cannot meet demand at the height of the tourist season, and some catering outlets buy in fresh fish, mostly from mainland Cornwall. For those who know where to find it, however, Scillonian fish and shellfish are hard to beat.

Top: Fishing in the unpolluted waters of the Isles of Scilly.
Middle: Mark Pender.
Above: Crab and lobster pots on Bryher.

John Moor
Boat builder, Mevagissey

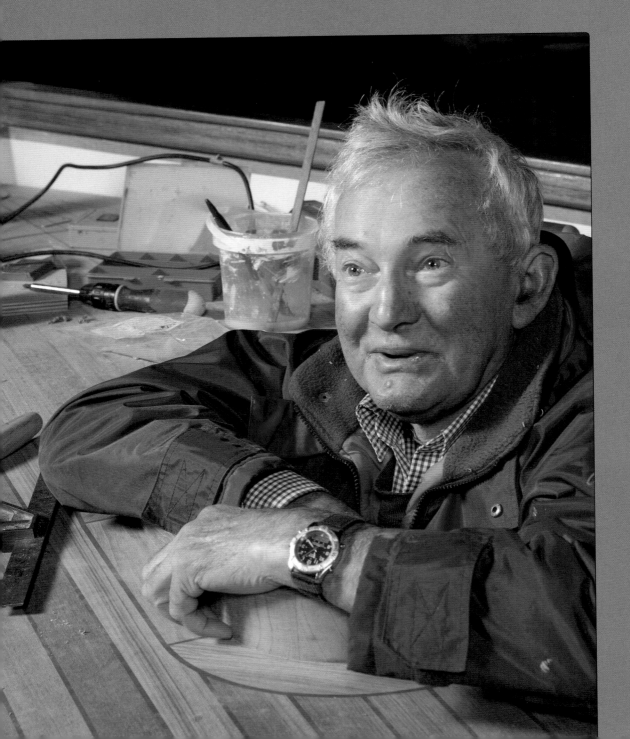

John Moor: I started boat building in Cadgwith, I worked with my uncle then, working with the family. I left when I was 19 and came up here to finish my apprenticeship at Percy Mitchell at Portmellon. Then I was two years in the RAF on national service – the best years of your life they say, but it depends on what you are doing. If it's the cook-house it's not very good. I was lucky, I was on the operational side, the flying side of it.

When I came out of the RAF I went to the dockyard, then spent two years when there was not much boat-building work, '56–57. I was married by then, and come here and went back to Mitchell's again, for the next four or five years. There was not a lot of work after that, so I went building and just thought, 'What the hell am I doing here?'

Then a chap from Padstow I was friendly with came over one night and asked if I'd like to build him a boat. I said, 'At the moment I've no yard or anything… .' He left it go one year, and came back saying he wanted a 48 ft boat for passengers.

So I built it in a field at the top of the hill here, opposite the school, I built a shed in the field without planning permission. When we launched the boat they had to close the road so that we could get the boat up. And I've been building boats ever since.

We moved from the top of the hill to Charlestown for about 12 years, but I wasn't able to buy any of the property there, so we bought this site when it came up.

This site had always been a boatyard, so there was no problem with planning, it goes back to the 1790s. So ever since then I've been building boats for people all round Cornwall, even to Scotland and Wales.

I had to go in hospital for a while, there were about two or three of us here then, so I said to my son, 'We'd better start something,' so we laid a boat down, a 28 ft crabber. We had the boat half built and advertised it in *Fishing News*, and a bloke rang up from the Western Isles and said, 'Can you keep it until I'm down in a fort-night?' So then when I next heard from him he was at Torquay and getting the train and could I pick him up? So when we got back here I opened the shed doors, he just said, 'Right, where's the paperwork?' You see if you get a good name for it, the name's everything. He sent down a lump of money, and we got on with he and he eventually had that boat.

There've been some changes from when I was in Cadgwith in the late 1940s – then two men could easily make a living from 150 crab pots. Now one man has to have 500 pots to make a living. The way of life has changed, everyone wants so much. A few years ago you would have an ounce of baccy and a pint of beer, and you lived in an estate house, now they all have mortgages to pay.

Fishing is finished really, a number of boats have packed up, there's no more than a dozen proper boats here. When I first came here they all fished from Polperro, Mevagissey, Falmouth, Newlyn, St Ives and all round the coast.

When the mackerel were here 30 years ago, we had a wave of new boats, we had a waiting list. Each boat used to catch up to 200 stones of mackerel a day in the mackerel boom time, they've had nothing like that this year. There's no waiting list for fishing boats now, they reckon on the network that there's a lot of boats for sale.

It's not so much the boats that have changed, it's the catching power in them, then there's sonar, echo sounders plus all the other equipment, plus the amount of gear they carry. The fitting out finish is very different – the ring netters put their fish straight into tanks now.

I aren't over confident about the future, particularly with fuel being a big factor, for every 100 horse power of engine they burn four gallons an hour. There's been some changes in engines. When I lived in Cadgwith all they had was 15 horse power max, and now we're talking about building about 350 horse power, for crabbing or netting.

I've built anything that a customer wanted, but I've always liked building fishing boats because you think fishing boats will be used to give people a living, when yachts are tied up in a marina for 12 months of the year.

> ❝ *If you are going out to sea in it, you want to know that it's made right.* ❞

We bought this place and opened the yard in 1976, so we've been here for 30 years – my son, who used to work for Pendennis shipyard, lots of yachts made there in Falmouth, he'll carry on after, but there's no grandson to carry on, only granddaughters. I suppose I've built about 50 or 60 boats. When we were building large boats we had seven or eight men, you know. Now it's just me and my son and I'm 73, I like to be involved still but I'm not doing so much. I do think there's a future for the boat builders when they're well known, there's a lot of leisure craft being built.

The old museum here shows how this yard was all open, it used to build schooners and things like that. Where the museum is now was a workshop.

I don't like fibreglass, wood is much better. We work a lot in Burma teak. Little boats can be built of larch or oak, which is very good for boat building, it's durable, strong you know. Larch is one-sixth of the price of teak, teak is £90–£100 per cubic foot. Over the years when building fishing boats we've used iroko, but I wouldn't use it again now.

We use a lot of oak for the frame, following the grain of the wood, you run the grain in the shape you want, so that gives you the strength, if you use short-grained wood it breaks up. You're looking at a life for a boat of 40 to 50 years, then it can go on after that. We've also built gigs, three of them, for Cadgwith and for Mevagissey as well.

It takes about 12 months from start to finish on most of the boats we build here. We do take great care over it and the detail, it's got to be right if they are spending a big lump of money on it. If you are going out to sea in it, you want to know that it's made right.

In contrast to John Moor & Son, Cygnus Marine in Penryn make commercial and leisure boats from steel, aluminium and fibreglass, which they sell worldwide. This 40 ft hull, the biggest the company makes, was destined for the Northern Ireland fishing fleet.

4 From Bonanza to Brussels

'There were times when we would steam out and we would start hitting the shoal about three miles off the coast, and you would steam all day with the echo sounder on and you'd never get out of the mark. One day, our best day, we came into Falmouth with 814 stone of mackerel. The leg holes were under water, we had mackerel tails bunged into the leg holes to stop water coming in. Because it's a fairly old fashioned boat the rudder is external, and it's got a slot in the transom where the tiller can move through and that was dipping under the water, and so we had every rag and shirt that was available stuffed in there and the rudder held central, because we couldn't steer the boat, so we used the mizzen [sail] then to steer the boat. We offset the mizzen so we could make Falmouth in a straight line. It was crazy really.'

The mid-1970s were heady times for inshore fishermen like Chris Bean, here recalling the enormous shoal of fish that appeared off the Cornish coast, and which for many Cornish fishermen marked a turning point in an industry that had been struggling to sustain itself. Prior to the mackerel boom there was little fishing, the pilchard industry was in its death throes, and many fishermen had quit in the 1950s and 1960s to find more lucrative employment elsewhere.

However, many other nations were soon cashing in on this fishing bonanza. Almost the entire Scottish pelagic fleet sailed down to fish in Cornish waters. Then there were also boats from all the northern and east-coast ports – Grimsby, Hull, Fleetwood and Lowestoft – which after 1976 could no longer fish in Icelandic waters, and other pelagic boats that had lost the herring fishery in the North Sea. All were in search of new fish to catch, and the Cornish mackerel boom was it. Many of them landed their catch in Plymouth, Penzance or Milford Haven. They were joined by Russian and Eastern European factory ships, and vessels from any

Right: Most of the mackerel landed in Cornwall is caught by handline fishermen.

other country that had a pelagic fishing fleet. These would all fish outside the 12-mile limit of the UK's territorial waters while the local boats tried to fish inside the three-mile limit. What went on in between sounded like maritime mayhem. Between 200 and 300 boats were fishing out of Looe, Falmouth and Newlyn, and at the height of the boom catches each season were estimated at 100 tonnes per man. The trawlers would transfer millions of tonnes of mackerel to the bigger, factory ships, known as Klondikers, which were moored up in Falmouth Bay or Weymouth Bay. There were tales, apocryphal or otherwise, of almost being able to walk on the mackerel as the shoal was so dense. There were also no minimum sizes, no limits to catches or restriction on fishing effort. This record-breaking shoal of mackerel sat off the Cornish coast from the Eddystone lighthouse, off Rame Head in South East Cornwall, down to the Isles of Scilly for several winters. The scale was something never before seen, with some scientists describing it as the biggest shoal of mackerel on the planet.

From 1973 to 1975 the Cornish handline fishermen had had this fishery almost exclusively to themselves, but by 1977 they were competing with the larger trawlers and factory ships, and the Chief Sea Fisheries Officer at the time, Broundand S. Tonkin, expressed the concerns that must have been growing across the entire Cornish fishing community about the long-term effects of this unprecedented bonanza:

> 'I cannot say if the fishing effort now taking place will deplete stocks to an uneconomic level, but it is apparent that the South West mackerel fishery is playing an increasingly important role in the UK fishing industry and should, therefore, be the subject of a very comprehensive scientific examination in the very near future. Worldwide experience proves that fish are not limitless, and it would be tragic if this mackerel fishery was ravished to a point of non-recovery.'

But still it went on. In one winter quarter in 1978, 675,000 stones of mackerel, worth £500,000 were reported as being landed, although much of this fish was not sold for human consumption but was processed into fishmeal. Restrictions were introduced in 1976 and 1977 to limit the amount of fishing and the length and capacity of boats and mesh sizes, and by the end of 1978 a mackerel quota was introduced. But in each case all these were either ignored or exceeded. What this meant was that many of the bigger boats transhipped all the over-quota fish on to the Klondikers to be frozen, canned or processed. As these were outside the territorial waters limit they completely disregarded the regulations. Another downside was that the new restrictions led to tonnes of mackerel being discarded,

Left: Fish market in progress at Looe, with the Moby Clock (see page 76).

leading to stories of the sea-bed being carpeted with dead fish. Even after the South West Mackerel Box was introduced in 1981 (see Chapter 6), mackerel was still permitted to make up 15 per cent of a vessel's catch. This meant that the bigger boats fished on regardless, while the small, inshore boats and handline fishermen, who had spent years rebuilding this fishery, lost out because the glut forced prices down and they believed that the bigger boats stopped the mackerel from shoaling in the shallower, inshore waters.

Something had to give, and it was the fish, but even now opinions are divided about whether they were fished out. Many scientists believe that this massive shoal was not self-sustaining, that like a dinosaur it was bound to expire due to a lack of natural resources to sustain it, or simply the mackerel had moved on in search of new sources of feed.

Above: Things became very heated in the Cod Wars, with frequent physical contact between Royal Naval ships, sailing with British trawlers, and Icelandic gunboats.

If the early 1970s were the time when the abundance of mackerel was just becoming apparent, they were also critical years for the fishing industry, not just in Cornwall but across the whole of the British Isles. Two major political events took place which led to fundamental changes affecting both inshore fishermen and the distant-water fleet. One was joining the Common Market, or European Economic Community (EEC – since 1993 the European Union, or EU) in 1973, the other was the escalation of the Icelandic Cod Wars.

The Cod Wars had started in 1958, when Iceland extended her territorial limits from four to 12 miles from the Icelandic coast, excluding many British trawlers from what they saw as fish-rich Arctic waters. In 1972 that limit was extended to 50 miles, along with agreements allowing British boats to fish in some limited areas inside the 50-mile limit. In 1975 the dispute intensified when the agreement ran out, and the Icelandic government declared that it was extending the territorial waters limit, thus excluding foreign vessels, to 200 miles. Britain came very close to declaring war on Iceland, and in the interim period until the new limits came into place, British vessels fished accompanied by Royal Navy frigates. Although few shots were fired there were several incidents in which Icelandic coastguard boats cut the British trawlers' nets and rammed several British ships. Eventually a compromise was reached, but only after NATO (the North Atlantic Treaty Organization) had intervened to resolve the conflict. The British trawlers gained a further six months to withdraw gradually from Icelandic waters. From the end of 1976, only Icelandic boats could fish inside Iceland's 200-mile limit.

The impact was felt all around the British coast, as trawlers that had successfully fished as far north as the Arctic Circle turned instead to home waters. Steve Farrar, of Bluesail Fish in Looe, believes this caused far-reaching economic difficulties. Here's how he assesses the impact:

> 'Ports have been driven out of business because in the last 30 years boats have been denied their traditional fishing grounds. They can't go and fish off Iceland, they can't go and fish off the coast of Norway. So as soon as Iceland declared UDI [Unilateral Declaration of Independence] and as soon as we were subject to the rule of Europe, unfortunately that meant that the days of the fishing industry's free ability to roam the North Sea and the Arctic Sea were savagely curtailed.'

Above: Former Prime Minister Edward Heath, seen here caricatured in a 1974 protest, remains a central hate figure for fishermen for abandoning their industry to Europe.

If the Cornish fishing industry had been struggling during the 1960s, the effects of joining the EEC in 1973 were to make an even greater impact, which more than 30 years later shows no sign of diminishing. The most important issue was what eventually became the CFP. Edward Heath, the Conservative Prime Minister, agreed that as part of the conditions for Britain's membership there should be equal access to a shared resource – in this case the fish-rich seas around the British Isles. These negotiations opened up rights to fish in Britain's territorial waters, where 65 per cent of European fish stocks were to be found, apart from within three miles of the shore, which remained more or less exclusively the preserve of British boats. Although at that time the EEC had only six member states – France, Germany, Italy, Luxemburg, The Netherlands and Belgium – the fact that Denmark and Ireland joined in the same year was enough to increase considerably the numbers of boats fishing, particularly in the North Sea. Interestingly, Norway declined to join the EEC for the opposite reasons – to protect its fish stocks and its fishing communities.

For French, Belgian, Dutch and Danish boats new access to British waters was the start of a fishing free-for-all. Overnight, the British had gone from having exclusive fishing in the waters up to six miles from the coast to sharing everything except the seas within three miles of the coast, although this was later revised to six miles. Even though fishing inside this limit should have been the exclusive reserve of UK vessels, some boats, particularly the French and Belgian, had what are known as grandfather rights, which entitled them to continue fishing up to the six-mile limit as they had prior to Britain joining the EEC. The EEC extended the territorial limit to 12 miles when it finally introduced the CFP in 1983, handing control of fisheries policy to the bureaucrats in Brussels.

What was to become the CFP had its origins in 1976, when exclusive fishing arrangements for all EEC member states were set at an outer limit of 200 miles of EEC coastlines. Within those 200 miles, the fisheries would be accessible only to member states, and would be managed under a common fisheries policy, although Spanish fishing vessels were already working in UK waters long before Spain was granted membership. It took seven years of wrangling to agree the CFP, and by the time it was in place it was already fundamentally flawed. Good prices for fish and generous EEC grants meant that fishing fleets in many member states were expanding, putting more pressure on fish stocks.

The net result was that a far greater number of fishing vessels were fishing in UK waters, so by the time Spain and Portugal joined in 1986, the EEC had recognized that fish stocks were being over exploited, and that conservation measures were badly needed. To put the impact of the Spanish accession into perspective, the most recent EU figures show that the Cornish fleet, with 733 vessels, makes up 0.9 per cent of the total EU fishing fleet; the total UK fleet is 751 boats (7.8 per cent of the total). Compare this with the Spanish fleet of 13,658 vessels, or about 15.9 per cent of the total EU fleet.

Fish quotas and what are known as total allowable catches (TACs), were finally introduced as a result of the 1983 CFP. These were set for selected fish species, such as cod and haddock, which the scientists assessed as being in danger of being overfished, but initially the limits were set so generously that most boats failed to catch their quota each year. For other species, such as squid, pilchards or red mullet, there were no quotas, and fishermen were free to pursue them as actively as they wished, which of course they did.

It was not until the mid-1990s, and even the early years of the twenty-first century, that severe measures were introduced to conserve the exploited fish stocks, including decommissioning grants to scrap boats, and drastic cuts in quotas. Reformed twice, in 1992 and 2002, the CFP has essentially failed in what it set out to do. There is almost universal agreement across the industry that quotas are the

Right: Early morning market at Newlyn.

wrong tool for managing fish stocks, and for areas such as Cornwall and the Isles of Scilly are a totally inappropriate way of managing a multi-species fishery.

The CFP was reviewed and revised again in 2003, by which time scientists' assessments of North Sea cod stocks suggested they were on the point of collapse, and at one-tenth of their levels in 1970. This is the kind of headline that has been used consistently by the media and environmentalists as proof of the dire state of the entire fishing industry and the UK's fish stocks, but which significantly fails to take into account regional differences. Fishing in the North Sea is largely for four species: cod, plaice, langoustines (confusingly called prawns, but also known as nephrops or Dublin Bay prawns) and haddock, and it is the North Sea that has been under more pressure from more vessels from more EU member states than any other UK fishery.

Although the events of 1973 were a watershed for the British fishing industry, this should be seen in context. For hundreds of years British, including Cornish, fishermen had thought nothing of sailing hundreds of miles to work in other nation states' territorial waters, and the majority of the sea fish caught by Cornish boats is exported to European markets, where consumers are far more discerning than many British buyers.

The handline mackerel fishery had been almost wiped out, and quotas were in place for so-called pressure stocks such as cod, so in the early 1980s the more innovative fishermen turned to other fishing methods, such as long-lining for conger eels and some static gill netting. Initially this was very successful, landing huge quantities of spur dogs and hake. It too was completely unregulated. 'There were no controls whatsoever, none whatsoever. It was like, "hey this is good," but you could see that there was going to be an end to it,' was how one fisherman described this new mini-boom. That was followed by an expansion of the hake fishery and fishing on wrecks, again seen as a good time for the industry, but not so good for fish stocks, followed by a revival of tangle netting (see page 201) for monkfish and turbot.

The 1990s were the time when bureaucrats, politicians and scientists watched with dismay as the CFP failed to save fish stocks, and fishermen of all nations were perceived to be finding ways of getting round many of the regulations (see Chapter 5), which turned out to be a very broad-brush approach, taking no account of the variations between different fishing areas and communities. Many saw the tough measures brought in as being too little too late, effectively squeezing the future life-blood out of the industry. What all were agreed on was that quotas were a catastrophe: completely ineffective both for conservation and as a way of ensuring the future livelihood of Cornwall's fishermen. Demoralized and despairing, this was a time when many decided they could no longer see a future in the industry, which given the legislative pressures they were under is hardly surprising.

Paul Trebilcock

**Chief Executive, Cornish Fish Producers'
Organisation, Newlyn**

The Cornish Fish Producers' Organisation (CFPO), based in Newlyn, represents all Cornish fishermen.

Paul Terbilcock: I was born and grew up in Newquay, my dad and grandfather were fishermen, so it was very much a Cornish fishing background. I started off with a small punt, or a tender you would call it down here, ferrying fishermen to and from their moorings in Newquay harbour for 10p a ferry ride. That was ice-cream money as I remember. Gradually me and my brother started to work a few pots for lobsters and crabs outside the harbour, within sculling distance. Then we bought a 16 ft cove boat and we worked some sole nets, caught some mackerel, lobsters, crabs, a bit of everything really, just in and around Newquay bay. That was all through school, but most mornings, evenings, school holidays, odd 'unofficial' days off, I was at sea messing around or working that boat with my brother.

Then I went to Hull University, it would have been 1994 and I would have been 17 or 18. I did Marine Biology with Fisheries Management, and it's certainly been useful to get that degree. I was working in summers and other holiday times aboard various boats in Newquay, for whoever needed a deckhand or extra hand. It took me through till the end of university, came back for a little while, just doing the same sort of thing, working various boats. Then I got a job in Scotland, working for the Scottish Fisheries Protection Agency, so if you like poacher turned gamekeeper, in a place called Kinlochbervie, which I'd never heard of until I got there, and it was certainly a culture shock. It's a fishing village, a landing station probably you'd call it, right in the northwest tip of Scotland, about as far as you could get. A single-track road in. I probably wasn't the best fisheries officer in the world, because I couldn't morally justify some of the stuff which I was supposed to do. But what it did do was give me an understanding, an insight into the enforcement side of the fishing industry, something which I'd never really appreciated. It's difficult, they're not the policy-makers but they have to enforce what I think they would freely admit are sometimes ludicrous or nonsensical regulations.

At the time it was a big fleet of white-fish trawlers, 80 ft plus, landing into Kinlochbervie on a regular basis. And because I don't seem to be able to stay on dry land for too long, in my free time I went to sea. I did three or four trips out of Kinlochbervie, white-fish trawling in the west of Scotland, what they call the Butt of Lewis, which was totally different to anything I'd seen or done down here. So I got a taste of how that Scottish white-fish fleet worked. I lasted up there for 12 months. I was never going to fit in, so that was the end of that.

I came back then to work in Hull with Seafish as a training adviser, where I organized and helped to run gear technology courses. And that was a taste of the world of a sea fishery quango, NGO [non-government organization], which was supposed to be working for the industry yet still answered to the Government, because it was set up by the Government. I was in Hull for about 18 months, two years, and then after that it was over the Humber to Grimsby, where I had two years or maybe 18 months with the NFFO, the National Federation of Fishermen's Organisations. It was initially more of a safety and training officer person, but in reality it became a far more general position, because of the nature of that organization, similar to this one in some respects, dealing with whatever the issue of the day might be, but as a national organization, working for fishermen from all around the country. Then in May 2002, I came here. I was one of those people that the more I found out the more I wanted to know, the more I wanted to try and influence certain things, people I'd seen on that journey. I thought I could make a difference for the good, for the Cornish fishermen. I'd got a taste of the whole picture from catching to enforcement, to safety and training, to the political lobbying side, back to here, where I've taken on the role of quota management representative, which hopefully I've done pretty well for the last three or four years.

The CFPO was set up about 25 years ago, and it's 100 per cent funded by fishermen. There's no government, no European, no external funding, it's membership funded, that's it. There are about 19 POs in the country, and the nearest one is the South West PO, which represents Brixham and Devon. Cornwall is the biggest PO in England, Wales and Northern Ireland, second biggest in the country. There are two main functions: one is quota management and one is representational lobbying.

" Brussels just cannot manage an industry which is regionally diverse. It's a static sort of monster managing a dynamic industry, and those two aren't compatible. "

Quotas started off in the North Sea only, and then Area VII [main fishing area for Cornish boats, see page 84] came on later. It began with mackerel back in the late '70s, early '80s, and then from there it became the broader quotas for the dozen or so species we're managing. For a while, as with all things when they came in, quotas were pretty much unrestricted. But gradually as the fleet grew, but also knowledge of stock assessment and fishery science improved, it became necessary from a government point of view and from a European point of view, to manage those stocks in some way, because just letting people go to sea and do what they want was going to lead down the path of no fish.

The quotas are basically based on historic track records of what boats caught. And all the boats put their quota into a pool, which has the benefit of if you've got things on that track record that you don't catch, somebody else will, and vice versa, which is almost a sharing system, and it gives the most possible flexibility in quota management. We manage it on a monthly basis, and each month we send out a PO bulletin – basically a list of the quota species, and what each boat can catch per month. We also engage in international swaps through Defra. So for many years we were involved in an ongoing swap with France, where we swapped away whiting, which we didn't catch much of, for cod, which we catch a lot of. Unfortunately, that's stopped now because of the restrictions on cod. The trouble with quota management is each year is different. It is very complicated, I suppose, and it's a little bit of risk and intuition … obviously you can't afford for the PO to go over on any species, and you can't afford to let boats catch away. But at the same time, my own opinion is the name of the game for a PO is to keep its members fishing for 12 months of the year with maximum fishing opportunity, and that's what hopefully we do. Touch wood, I haven't closed any fishery early in the four years I've been here, and I don't intend to in the next however many years.

The trouble is that the management system ended up being so complicated and being developed by people who didn't understand the complexities of the fisheries they were dealing with, who weren't fishermen, who were actually either civil servants or European equivalents to civil servants. The system may well have worked in theory, but in practice and the reality of the fishing industry, it never did work, and never will. There is a recognition of that in Europe and Westminster now, and they are trying to improve it. And maybe as a result of some of the head banging we do, there is a move away from central management towards that regional management through what they call the Regional Advisory Councils, which is something that had to happen if the fishing industry was going to continue. But I think it has yet to be proven. Brussels giving up that power is going to be more difficult than setting up the Regional Advisory Council. A centrally managed, unresponsive thing like Brussels just cannot manage an industry which is regionally diverse. It's a static sort of monster managing a dynamic industry, and those two aren't compatible. Everybody realizes that now.

Yes, we've had an improving situation. Over a period of time we've been involved in the FSP – Fisheries Science Partnership – which was government-funded, and remains government-funded, and in essence is CEFAS [Centre for Environment, Fisheries and Aquaculture Science] scientists, which are independent supposed government scientists, going aboard our boats and doing some stock assessment work. And for the past three years we've been involved in partnerships on monkfish, on sole, on cod, and last year we've done some selectivity stuff with the gill-netters and hake. And we see them as ongoing projects, because after a period of time those trends become more and more scientifically credible. But just because you're doing the science and helping the science doesn't mean you get the answer you want. We've had cuts in cod quota, but a lot smaller than suggested, and we've had some minimal cuts in sole in certain areas, but big increases in others.

I think everybody knew that in the South West the stocks are nowhere near as bad as are being portrayed in the rest of the country, and nowhere near as bad as perhaps some of the environmental groups or angling groups may lead people to believe. We know because things like the levy, which is collected off boats from their grossings, has been consistent for five, six, seven years; landings of our key species have been consistent, there is no big drops or anything like that. There is no doubt that the fish are there, and of course in the South West probably about 40 per cent of what we catch is non-pressure stock anyway, is non-quota species, which by definition means it's fairly healthy, so that's a slight advantage we work at. That's not to say there's not things we can improve, we all want more fish in the sea, and to be able to land more, but in terms of what's there, we're lucky in one sense, we could say we were incredibly good in another sense.

The other bit is, I guess, the political bit, and there are two or three things we've done there. One of them is we more or less started a regional advisory council before the EU Commission even thought about it. Basically, six or seven years ago, we started transnational meetings with organizations like this one that exist in France, Spain and Ireland, with people who fish alongside our boats and fish in the same area, we arrange meetings where we sit down and talk about issues. We worked on the Trevose closed area, we worked on advice coming out on times when it was bad, hake recovery plan, general fisheries management stuff which affects all of us who fish in the area we fish.

There are several conservation measures going on, including the Trevose Head Box. It's the single conservation measure which will have the most benefit of anything in the entire CFP, and the reason for that is because it's come from fishermen, and it started here and went on to this transnational thing, so now we have French, Irish, Belgians involved. And it is using the fishermen's knowledge, backed up by scientific evidence from CEFAS and their equivalents in France. It's primarily cod that the closures are based on, but the area is a prolific spawning ground, prolific nursery area for haddock, soles, whiting, any number of species. And the fishermen eventually got what they asked for, 3,500 square miles are closed to fishing during February and March, the spawning time when fish are aggregated there. So it is a real biggy, and hopefully going to pay some dividends in the future.

There are a lot of things we are trying to do as a science partnership: we have used these things called benthic release panels in beam trawls. The basic theory is that a lot of the benthic things drop right out of the trawl net before it comes to the top, so your starfish, your little crabs, urchins, just drop back into the sand [see page 112]. And we found that reduced the amount of benthics coming up in the beam trawls by about 80 per cent. It's a double winner for us, it means there's less work on the deck, it means the fish is less scuffed up if you're towing for two hours, and from an environmental point of view, putting that stuff back where it is, they love it. So we're quite keen on that one.

We've been involved in things like the Code of Practice for inshore boats, which came about because of concerns about porpoises and gill nets. So two years ago we introduced a voluntary code for our netters which last year we rolled out around the coast. And basically it's just what we call best practice, commonsense: don't shoot when you know porpoises are around, if you catch them let other people know.

The environmental lobby has grown considerably, and so if we want to continue our fishing operations we have to try to work with them. There will only be one loser if we take on the environmentalists, and that will be us, the fishermen. So things like IIF – Invest in Fish – things like the Trevose closure, things like benthic release panels, voluntary codes, are all important in two ways. One, we don't want to take on environmentalists head on, but secondly to ensure that people keep buying our fish and they should buy Cornish fish because it is, in my opinion, the most environmentally sound fish to buy.

We have to take steps to ensure that there's long-term, environmentally sustainable fishing, and I still believe that the Cornish fleet, because of its diversity, is in the position to do that. There is no one particular bit of ground, no one species, no one area that's hit hard all the time. It's that diversity that enables us to operate in that way, and I think that our fishermen have acknowledged that there is a growing environmental angle to everything we do in fisheries management and we are, I would have to say, pioneers.

We still have a problem with public perception of what we do, and what we're about, and that may be our own fault, or maybe it's just a fact that sometimes the media are just not interested in the positive side. But we're doing a lot which is not just cosmetic, it's a bit more meaningful than that. Government scientists making stock assessments, looking at alternatives to fisheries management which take into account all stakeholders and the long-term environment and sustainability. If you'd spoken about those sorts of things ten years ago, you'd have been laughed out of any fishing port in the country. But the political world, the public perception world has changed, and if the fishing industry doesn't change with it, then we'll be a thing of the past. We'll be the thing getting laughed at or drummed out. I don't want to see that happen, and I'm fairly determined to make sure it doesn't happen.

Steve and Carole Farrar
Fish merchants, Looe

Steve Farrar is a fish merchant, and with his wife Carole owns Bluesail Fish.
He is also a partner with Heugh Symons in Looe Fish Selling Ltd., which
runs the electronic fish auction in Looe.

Steve Farrar: Bluesail Fish Company was set up in 1982, and came to Looe in 1987.
Before that I worked for a Scottish company who had an office in the South West
managing the sales of very large volumes of mackerel. And before that I managed a
fishing co-operative in Cornwall, and before that I ran a shellfish hatchery in Galicia in
North West Spain. I've never fished professionally, although I go out in the boats every
so often for a day out.

   Looe Fish Selling is the auction house, it is not allowed to trade fish, it is only
allowed by its remit to auction fish on behalf of the boats – under quite tight control
parameters set by consensus here between the boats, the merchants and, importantly,
the harbour commissioners, and the auction house itself.

   I set up Bluesail with Heugh in Plymouth in 1982, when the Scottish mackerel
fleet departed – they were here between about '76 or '77 and '82 – because essentially
the Scottish fleet had taken the best bit out of the local mackerel fishing, and it wasn't
economic for them to come down and fish any more. Killed it in other words. I think the
mackerel are all right now, although they have never really recovered to the 1970s stock
levels, probably because of heavy fishing in other areas and environmental changes.
The hook-and-line quota for the South West is currently just under 2,000 tonnes for the
entire South West. A significant proportion of that is caught by the Looe fleet, probably around about half the total quota I would have thought. To put it into some level
of comparison, when I managed Flushing and Falmouth Fishermen's Co-operative in
1975, the fishing co-operative in Flushing alone landed 2,200 tonnes of mackerel, in
one season, just that village, let alone Looe, Polperro, Mevagissey, Penryn, Falmouth,
Newlyn, and so on. So my guess is it was probably seven, eight or nine thousand
tonnes landed at that time by hook-and-line fishermen in Cornwall, possibly more.

   We came to Looe in '87 because the fishermen of Looe had previously had their
catches sold on Plymouth fish market, and in 1985 and '86 they started a movement to
re-create their old fish auction market here. It was opened in '87, and we were granted
one of two auction licences then. A year or so later, the other company collapsed and
Looe Fish Selling took over responsibility for all the auction market. Shortly afterwards
we promoted the construction of fish packing units here to back up what had become a
successful new market. At one particular meeting I remember saying to them, 'You're
reliant on lorries coming in, have you ever thought what would happen if the lorries
don't come?' 'Ah, well no, not really.' 'Well, how about you get some nice, indigenous
buyers here, who are paying you rent and aren't going to go away?' So the fish packing
units back up the fish market very significantly indeed, and there are a number of successful fish merchants in the port, and a good number of very successful boats.

Carole Farrar: Looe Fish Selling Company has an electronic auction system, and basically what happens in the evening, is the boats come in and they land the fish themselves. They weigh it on to electronic scales and it's sorted by species, weight, size, and so on. All of that's kept as a record, and the fish is stored in the harbour fridge, in boxes overnight. Bear in mind too that this is all day-boat quality fish and the boats usually come in on the high water, which can be any time between four and midnight, depending on the tides. At 6.30 the following morning the auctioneer starts the electronic auction system, sits on this thing – it looks like an electronic selling board driven by an electric bicycle, it's actually called a Moby Clock. After the auction Looe Fish Selling prints out all the boat settlements, the daily sales sheets for the skippers, and also the buyers who have bought the fish on the market that day. Once Looe Fish Selling settles the boats, in other words it pays the boats for the fish that's been landed, and also collects the money for the fish sold from all the buyers like Steve, because he buys on the market too, as an independent buyer. There are other wholesale traders down there, some of them have units here in Looe, some of them don't; there are also one or two restaurants who come and buy themselves. There are a number of wholesale buyers who drive down to take the fish away to their own factories elsewhere.

As well as the Looe boats that use the market here, we also have boats from Polperro and Mevagissey. We ourselves, on the other side, as Bluesail, also buy fish in from the markets in Plymouth and Brixham, and also regularly import fish from France. Sometimes it's not necessarily different species, sometimes it's volume, we need more than we can find locally, and we can buy it in at competitive prices, so that's the way it is for us sometimes, particularly with some of our customers who have quite a rigid structure to how much fish they want and what they want. We try our best to make sure that they buy through us rather than through other suppliers. Most of our sales go on to other wholesalers, but we do supply some restaurants locally and further away as well. We can get fish into France the following day if we're exporting it, it goes to Boulogne, and goes off from there to places all over France.

> *Fishermen recognize that you have to have a level of control over stock exploitation, but they wouldn't do it through quotas.*

I've been involved since the business began. I've always worked in the office, and I've become more and more involved over the last four or five years, I would say, and now I run the Bluesail office completely. It can be very fraught in the mornings with a lot going on, but the afternoons are more peaceful, and I often have time to look at all the swans and cygnets that live on the river directly in front of

The Moby Clock, or electronic auction system at the fish market in Looe.

my office window. I probably enjoy one of the best views out of any office window anywhere in Cornwall.

There's a lot more traceability and accountability in the industry now, and demands on temperature control, things like that. The harbour is well off for ice supplies here, and the boats take ice or use tanks of iced water at sea to guarantee the fish is kept at a certain low constant temperature. And when Steve has his men downstairs filleting the mackerel, for instance, they've got like a sink and there's ice in it as well, you can imagine how cold it is, but that's to keep the temperature just so.

Today's fishing industry is so important to Looe, it brings it life, otherwise what would we be? We'd just be a tourist town. We're quite unique, as a village, having this vibrant fishing industry. It feels different from other fishing villages, because although some of them have a small number of boats it's the auction here that makes Looe different.

Steve Farrar: What changes have I seen? There are significantly less boats, and significantly less fish. The fish is significantly more expensive, even allowing for inflation. It is a premium product. I got an eight-and-a-half-kilo turbot today that cost

Steve Farrar checks prices during the fish auction in Looe.

me £125 to buy. Actually … where's the calculator, I'll tell you exactly what it is. OK, £131.58 pence to buy, and it will get more expensive before it gets to the end user, because there's restaurants in this country who pay a lot of money for fish. That doesn't mean that we get it, because we don't. We'll probably make about £15 on that fish, having laid out £135. Of that £135 how much goes to the boat? Nearly all of that – about £127 after paying its dues.

I wish we had more help from the politicians, but present-day politicians are constrained by past agreements, particularly the agreement that was brought about by Edward Heath entering into Europe. He sacrificed a number of things, one of which was sovereignty over our waters out to 50 miles, in our case that was the mid-line down the Channel between here and the French coast. The biggest load of nonsense ever dreamt up was the philosophy of 'equal access to a common resource' that was applied to all European seas. I'll say that in public and I don't care who's listening. You don't have 'equal access' to olive groves or orange tree orchards, do you? It was represented as a high-minded deal, but in reality it was a way in which other European Union countries at that time legitimized grabbing huge chunks of fish stocks that had previously been British. The Heath government sacrificed the British fishing industry because they had fouled up British accession to the European Union beforehand.

Nowadays the problems that affect the industry are twofold really. One is the rising relative cost of running a boat, largely through rises in fuel prices. There is also a squeeze that is universally applied to fishermen by the quota stock management system, that is the way certain species of fish are controlled by quotas. Fishermen don't generally have a great argument with the system itself, because they recognize that you have to have a level of control over stock exploitation somehow, but fishermen wouldn't do it through quotas.

What you're up against is trying to make sure that the fish remains a sustainable resource for the benefit of everybody, and that's what fishermen want, what everybody wants, but you need to take the progressive evolution of technology into account. It means you're always permanently having to address how you control fishing effort, and these issues are very complex. What's now happening, interestingly, is that fishermen's efforts, and also what the fish merchants can do, is now so tightly controlled that it is difficult to get round any of the rules and regulations. Some people try to break the rules and they are taking a very great deal of risk. The fines are massive. It doesn't happen here because there's no need for it, but you do see cases occasionally in the *Fishing News*.

If you start with fundamentals in the North Sea, or anywhere else, you don't have to be terribly intelligent to realize that if you over exploit the feed that's at the base of the food chain, you are depriving other higher food-chain animals of that feed. Now either fishing boats from Denmark and Norway will go and catch lots and lots and lots and lots of sand eels and fish by the millions of tonnes a year to make fish meal, or they'll be better controlled. They are starting to be controlled, there's much more restriction than there ever was, a little late I suspect. The effect that brings an emotional response is that people see numbers of sea birds diminishing dramatically, puffins and skuas and the rest of it. That's point one, and that I think is one of the most significant. But for the fishermen, the destruction of feed fish means simply that there is less to support the more valuable species such as cod and haddock, and all the other important fish stocks.

The second point is that the science and knowledge of fishery resources is proclaimed to be accurate by the scientists. And it is the scientists' recommendations to ministers that eventually end up in policy, right, mostly. In the last few years it is true to say that fishermen's representatives have also had an input on policy decisions. But primarily, fisheries management is a science-based concept. It's based on science that may or may not be accurate. Now I'm a scientist, so I'm reluctant to immediately say they're not accurate. But I think there's significant doubt in fishermen's minds as to whether or not the science is accurate enough. You have scientists making recommendations to ministers, who then have to go and sit in the Council of Europe with every other country's ministers. You then get the fishing and fisheries resources being subject to political pressures and trade-offs, for other deals. And eventually the poor fishermen out there get the result of all that. And while those decisions are made, fishermen's representatives such as the NFFO try to lobby the Minister, and sometimes successfully do so. Eventually, it ends up with a consensus view that such-and-such a quota can be applicable this year to Dover sole management. You can't really argue with the fact that management works. Whether it works fairly for our fishermen or not is a debatable arena I don't want to go in because I'm a fish merchant, not a fishermen's representative – I could spend my whole life arguing politics if I'd got involved in it – whether it works fairly or not, fishermen feel that it doesn't. They've felt it hasn't done ever since the accession to Europe. On the other hand, having said all of that, you've got to allow that Europe is the single most significant market for the fish caught in the South West.

I think the perceptions of an industry on its knees and not doing well emanate from the fact that the Scottish industry is under severe pressure, because they are much more dependent on cod and haddock up in the north-east of Scotland than we are, and in many respects they've got fewer fishing opportunities to pursue. Having said that, there are very successful boats and businesses in Scotland as well, but a large number of boats have been driven out of business, and merchants as well, and I think that's a great shame. They are much more adversely affected by us belonging to the European Community, in terms of where they can fish and how much quota they've got, than perhaps we are in Looe. Having said that, Newlyn's more adversely affected than we are. Brixham's more adversely affected than we are. We don't have in Looe a lot of Dover sole, which are severely quota-restricted, we don't have a massive amount of monkfish, we don't have a massive amount of cod or hake. We're uniquely favoured and blessed with the fact that in Looe the main species, the vast majority of the catching opportunities for fishermen here, are lemon sole, squid, cuttlefish, scallops, and are non-quota species. So we are somewhat less subject to the sort of perniciousness of the quota system that economically affects other fishermen. We are less affected than other ports regionally and also, particularly, other ports nationally.

I think the fishermen of Looe hopefully will have a valid and sustainable future, a well-managed fishing business. The talent that is applied to catching the fish is well matched by the talent that is applied to selling it. I'm not referring to me, I'm referring to the overall picture of 15 major merchants buying and selling fish all over western Europe and the UK, who buy on our market every day.

Our Cornish fishermen believe in well-managed and sustainable fishing, and our most important customers are more and more committed to only buying fish from such well-managed sources, and in the long run that's got to be best for everyone, we think.

Display at Pengelly's fishmongers in Looe.

5 It's not Conservation, it's Political Madness

'You had this battleground of log-books and quotas and are you going to go over it? You've got to throw fish away, and it was getting to be a nightmare. And then they were bringing in rules about tracking the boat. Whichever area you were going to fish in you had to phone in to the Ministry and say, "I'm fishing in this area, I'll be there for so many days," and if you moved out of an area you'd have to phone in. Quite often with wrecking you'd cover 60–70–80 miles in a trip, because we were looking for 11 wrecks a day. And if we were looking for 11 good ones there might be an area of 40 wrecks there might only be 11 good ones, and they'd be scattered around, so we'd be changing areas within hours.'

It is often assumed that concerns about overfishing and stock management are a recent innovation. However, as early as the fourteenth century there were anxieties about the effects of medieval forms of trawling; about using fish as animal feed, and about the tiny mesh sizes used by competing fishermen – never, of course, by Cornish fishermen! In 1376 Parliament was petitioned for a ban on small mesh sizes in trawl nets, while 250 years later Charles I was asked to take steps against 'the great destruction made of fish by a net or engine now called the Trawle'. In the eighteenth century fishermen who ignored laws on minimum landing sizes and small mesh sizes were heavily fined – all familiar issues today.

Between 1890 and 1910 a number of sea fisheries committees were set up around Britain's coast to manage and enforce regulations in local fisheries. The CSFC was one of the first, established in 1890, and the newest is the Isles of Scilly SFC, set up in the 1960s. Although its area of regulation is limited to just six miles offshore, the Committee's role is primarily to conserve fish stocks, taking a broad overview of all issues affecting the industry. Fishing's other regulators are Defra, which enforces UK and EU policy, and the Environment Agency.

Right: The three-man rib (rigid inflatable boat), *Lyonesse,* speeds away from the stern slipway of the *St Piran,* the CSFC protection vessel, to make an inspection in Carbis Bay.

The *St Piran* at work.
Right, from top: Skipper Shane Liddicoat watching for fishing vessels off Porthcurno; Fisheries Officer Zac Haining secures the *Lyonesse* after safely docking in the *St Piran*. *Lyonesse* in action. *Below:* An ICES map showing the sea areas around England and Wales.

Within a few years of Britain joining the EEC there was clear evidence of the impact on fish stocks of the rapid growth in the number of boats fishing in the North and Celtic Seas, the English and Bristol Channels. This was not surprising as other EEC member states' fishing fleets were cashing in on what had previously been unavailable to them. In 1977 the North Sea herring fishery was closed, and even before the 1970s mackerel boom ended, a 3.5 tonne quota for every man fishing for mackerel off the Cornish coast was introduced in November 1978.

When the CFP became law in 1983, fishing quotas, initially for what were described as pressure stocks such as North Sea cod and sole, were introduced as part of an attempt by EEC politicians and scientists to tackle what was already perceived to be a serious overfishing problem in some areas. The quotas dictate how much of some species, such as cod and plaice, can be caught in each of the specific sea areas. So cod quota for Area VIIe (the western end of the English Channel) may be larger than for a similar-sized boat fishing for cod in the North Sea (Area IVb), simply because the cod stocks in the North Sea are under far more pressure and in a worse state than cod stocks in the seas around Cornwall.

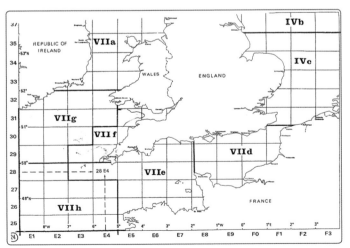

Each successive year since 1983 the legislative burden has been moved up to another level, mostly by Brussels bureaucrats but with occasional intervention from first MAFF and latterly its successor, Defra. (Note that fishing no longer appears in the title – the Department for Food and Rural Affairs – which indicates how highly the present Labour government regards the British fishing industry.)

By 1993 every commercial fishing boat, of any size, had to be licensed, regardless of whether it was fishing for quota stocks or non-quota fish, so the licensing regime has become another restriction on fishing effort. Licences are strictly limited, so new vessels can only be licensed if an existing boat of a similar, or greater capacity, gives up its licence, which in most cases means the boat is either scrapped or decommissioned.

'Licences have become much more restrictive over the last 20 years. Once upon a time a Category A licence enabled you to fish in any type of fishery; now licences are restricted to certain types of fishing. If you're a beam trawler you're beam trawling; if you're a netter you're netting; if you're a trawler you're trawling. So there's a lot less leeway than there was 20 years ago.' (Former fisherman)

During the 1990s the Government proposed to introduce another measure to control effort by limiting the number of days at sea for each vessel. Another new rule required vessels to operate from and land their catch regularly in nominated UK ports, and to inform Defra when they were due to land. This became a skippers-versus-politicians

battleground of more reporting, more log-book information, and more form filling. It also culminated in a series of fishermen's protests against some of these proposed regulations that led to the occupation of the MAFF office in Plymouth, a blockade of Plymouth Sound, and demonstrations in the centre of Plymouth where tonnes of fish were dumped to illustrate the nonsense of discards caused by the quota system.

Since the early 2000s Defra has used satellite tracking to follow all the over-10 m fishing boats. For these skippers it is mandatory to log all movements across the various sea areas, and to inform Defra when they are changing from, say, Area VIIe to Area VIIh. While at sea, any boat bigger than 15 m long has to carry a Vessel Monitoring System, which can track exactly where it is at any time. The costs to the taxpayer of monitoring this enforcement are huge. Quota and licences have also been tightened up to apply to specific sea areas – for example, there are individual quotas for catching plaice in Areas VIIde, VIIfg and VIIhjk.

The inshore, under-10 m boats are not immune from the plethora of regulations either. These also have to be licensed to catch fish for shellfish, and are also subject to quota restrictions, for the relevant species, in the same way as larger boats. Shell fishermen have to make monthly returns showing the numbers of lobsters or crabs caught; where they were caught and landed, and the numbers put back. Quotas for under-10 m boats are managed by Defra. Rather than allocate quota on a monthly basis, as the CFPO does for the larger boats, once the under-10 m quota is exhausted, Defra closes that particular fishery.

A new regulation, introduced in 2005, requires the first seller and buyer to register the sale, whether selling direct from a boat to the public, a pub or restaurant, to the Looe or Newlyn fish auctions, or to wholesalers or fish merchants. This gives a more accurate measurement of catches, but the subsequent paperwork attached to this has undermined what would once have been a lucrative business, particularly direct to the public or the local catering sector, for many of the smaller boats.

For a Cornish fisherman to go fishing in 2006, he needs not only a boat and the relevant fishing gear but a licence and, in many cases, quota (see panel). He also needs four certificates before he can set to sea: safety awareness (health and safety), sea survival, fire fighting, and first aid. All vessels are inspected by the Maritime and Coastguard Agency, and anything that is not correct will lead to an immediate ban on sailing until it is corrected. Fishermen also have to answer to the Marine Fisheries Agency and Defra, and the CSFC.

In 1993 the CSFC's remit was extended to six miles from the shore, ostensibly to protect UK waters and the small fleet of low-powered inshore boats. Despite the battery of EU and UK laws and local by-laws many fishermen feel this particular measure has not worked. There are continuing problems with historic rights for French and Belgian ships that can fish up to the six-mile limit, and increasing dismay over large scallop dredgers (usually foreign ships towing greater numbers of dredges than are permitted under UK laws) that can fish between the six- and 12-mile limits, even though beam trawlers are banned from fishing these grounds.

There seems to be general agreement that the key to the future of successful inshore fishing is to restrict access to the six- to 12-mile waters to local boats only. Many would share the view of David Muirhead, Chairman of the CSFC and himself a shell fisherman:

Quota fish

Fish subject to annual quotas in areas mostly fished by Cornish vessels:

- Cod
- Haddock
- Whiting
- Pollack

- Saithe (Coley)
- Ling
- Hake

- Monkfish
- Megrim sole
- Nephrops
- Herring

- Mackerel
- Horse mackerel (Scad)

Plaice (separate quotas for ICES management areas VIId, VIIe, VIIf, VIIg, VIIh, VIIj, VIIk)
Dover sole (separate quotas for ICES management areas VIId, VIIe, VIIf, VIIg, VIIh, VIIj, VIIk)

(Lemon sole, skates and rays not subject to quota in area VII, but are in other ICES management areas.)

Above: Brian Burton, Coastguard

'*Every nation state in the world needs an exclusive 12-mile zone for artisan fishermen for local, inshore boats. The best way for the UK is exclusive UK fishing in the 12-mile zone and strictly controlled towards smaller boats as a conservation measure, to keep out the large beam trawlers and scallopers.*'

It was also in 1993 that the Government allocated millions of pounds for decommissioning grants, targeted at bigger ships rather than the inshore fleet. Cornwall may have escaped the dramatic fleet reductions seen in Scotland and the North Sea ports, but this had other effects in the South West. The first was to put more pressure on inshore fishing, as some of the skippers whose boats were de-commissioned switched to inshore fishing in smaller boats instead. The second was the lack of incentive to invest, unlike in other EU member states, leaving Cornwall and the South West with a rapidly ageing fishing fleet. In January 1995 the funds for decommissioning were increased to £53 million, and the following year there were savage cuts in quotas to try to stem the EU-wide depletion of fish stocks.

This decision was typical of the political fudge, as the Chief Fisheries Officer, Eddy Derriman, wrote about the annual fishing negotiations in December 1995:

'*Particularly badly hit is the pelagic sector resulting in a loss of 90,000 tonnes. The predictable ritual process, witnessed at the end of every year when Fisheries Ministers argue amongst themselves as to what levels of TACs are to be set, was again seen this year. All too frequently in the past Scientists' recommendations for modest cuts in quotas were ignored. The loser at the end of the day is the fish stocks, and this has a knock-on effect to the fishermen. Nobody seems to be happy with the present system, with fishermen requiring more fish, scientists recommending less fish, and environmentalists proposing ever more radical means to control fishing.*'

It was, as fish merchant Robin Turner describes it, a painful process of exorcism: 'It started to be strategically exorcised from the middle '90s on and when we hit the year 2000, the size 15 boot was on top of the industry and well in a position to squash an awful lot of players.'

It is little wonder that British fishermen felt aggrieved at having to stay tied up in port watching foreign boats fishing just outside the six-mile limit. To rub salt into the industry's communal wounds, the Spanish government was supporting significant investment in its fishing fleet, while Britain's politicians were paying fishermen with years of experience and expertise to leave the industry.

Decommissioning is also seen by many as a poor panacea, for while it pays off a vessel's owner, it does not create new employment for, or compensate, the crew or the employees in other, onshore businesses that depended on each individual ship's fishing capability. In many cases, the settlement was often only enough to repay debts; rarely did the grants provide any form of recompense for removing the livelihood and way of life of several families. The psychological damage usually goes unseen, for both individuals and entire communities. Fortunately, Cornwall has escaped some of these negative effects, unlike many North Sea and Scottish fishing ports. Nevertheless, between 1995 and 2001 about 75 Cornish vessels were decommissioned, cutting the trawler and netting fleet by about 30 per cent. Since the mid-1990s there has also been an underlying rationale of self-decommissioning, where two boats might be scrapped and replaced by one. This has perhaps helped to ease pressure on some fish stocks, and in this case it is the Cornish fleet's relatively small scale that has been its salvation.

One of the results of introducing quotas and heavily regulating fishing was that for a number of years fishermen were driven into what was perceived as a significant amount of illegal fishing, landing 'black' fish, particularly in ports further north and in Scotland where the fishing was limited to a few species. However, the Cornish fleet and other South West boats were not totally blameless in the past. 'It's not conservation, it's political madness' is how many fishermen and their representatives summed up the catastrophe of discards and black fishing caused by the quota system.

In 1989 a 5 per cent by-catch rule was introduced which reinforced one of the most contentious, and emotional aspects of fish quotas, that of by-catch or discard, which forces fishermen to throw away perfectly good, marketable fish because they have caught too many. The rule allowed fishermen to retain only 5 per cent of any by-catch of stocks for which they did not have quota. So, for example, a trawler targeting squid and lemon sole that also caught haddock could keep only 5 per cent of the haddock caught, regardless of its size or market value. Here were fishermen going to sea, being forced by the distortions of quota to throw away perfectly good, healthy fish, because it exceeded either their quota or their by-catch allowance. It is not surprising that many of them were determined to find a market for this high-value catch rather than throw it back overboard. Since then the by-catch rules have become even more complex.

Paul Trebilcock, Chief Executive of the CFPO, explains the moral dilemma:

'It's always been an issue that fishermen are exactly that, it's in their blood to go and catch fish. They're not out there for anything else, they want to catch fish to land for people to eat, they don't want to chuck

it back and waste it. And when quotas are out of line with what's there and they are seeing this come over the rail, chucking it back, some of them can't morally justify it.'

This has to be set in the context that some fishing methods, particularly beam trawling and trawling, catch more than one species of fish, whereas others such as crabbing with pots and handlining for mackerel, are much more species-specific. This means that when a trawler hauls in its net, along with sole, megrim sole and monkfish there may also be the occasional crab, and other round white fish, such as cod and haddock, pollack, ling and red mullet. A boat may have quota to land x kilos or tonnes of cod a month and a similar, but possibly higher quota, for sole. Once the cod quota is exhausted, any cod caught while fishing for other species must be thrown back over the side, usually dead.

One beam trawler skipper summed up his lack of control of the problem succinctly: 'We went to fish out in Ushant because we had caught our sole quota for the month and needed to catch monkfish. But all we kept finding was sole, really big ones. All we could do was eat some and throw the rest back, but this was not an area where you would expect to find any sole.'

Tales abound of the massive amounts of fish unnecessarily discarded, and clearly no fisherman is happy with what he sees as an indefensible and immoral practice. Without any prompting, almost everyone I spoke to while researching this book took the view that it had been made impossible to market black fish, and that very little, if any, is now landed in Cornwall. 'Boats aren't being built off the back of it down here, that's for sure' was one comment I often heard, giving an idea of the former scale of the problem.

The UK fishing fleet as a whole has suffered from what most fishermen regard as an overzealous interpretation of the regulations in order to manage the CFP, which comes down to Britain's habit of 'gold plating' every European directive. Other countries, such as Spain and France, take a more *laissez-faire* attitude to regulating and managing their fishing fleets, in order to avoid serious socio-economic impacts in their fishing and coastal communities. There often seems to be a considerable variation between each EU member state's interpretation of the rules and management of their annual quotas. Spain is often cited as an example of a country that has encouraged its fishing fleet to expand, using EU funds to do so. In Britain, however, little of the EU funding for modernization and decommissioning has been available to UK fishermen because of a lack of willingness by the Treasury to provide the necessary matched funding.

Left: Fish that is undersized, above the quantitiy permitted by the boat's quota, or not of a species that the boat is licensed to catch, is known as by-catch, and inadvertently makes up an unwelcome proportion of the haul. It is pushed back out to sea through a side hatch where it is devoured by waiting seagulls.

Eddy Derriman
Chief Sea Fisheries Officer for Cornwall

Eddy Derriman: I'm employed by Cornwall Sea Fisheries Committee. We're a very old fisheries management organization, been going since 1890. There are 12 Sea Fisheries Committees around the coast of England and Wales, but none around Scotland. Originally the Committee managed the three-mile limit, which is the old territorial sea, and that has in the last decade been put out to six miles offshore. There is now a review going on as to whether we should go out to 12 miles, which is the new territorial limit. When the Committees were first set up they were really concerned mainly with shellfish, very little white fish, but they did also keep an eye on that, but we've got a far wider remit than that now. Shellfish is still our central role.

Originally there was one Fishery officer, he used to patrol round the coast of Cornwall on a push-bike or catch trains. There was one in Mevagissey, for instance, for several years, Mr Williams, and he would catch a train down to Penzance and spend some time down here, or he would go on small, inshore Royal Naval mine sweepers, and that lasted until the '40s, '50s, I think. The service has built up since then as the fishing industry has increased dramatically, in recent years. It's quite interesting to note that in the early part of the last century a lot of his work was collecting statistics, and at one time there was something like 40,000 people in Cornwall working in the fishing trade, the majority of those ashore – because in the days of the pilchard cellars or the pilchard palaces, the women and kids would all be working when the fish came in. Of course, now it's very small against that. However, the impact on the environment is now greater than it was then, even though there were more vessels then.

The Committee itself is made up of 26 people – 13 are county councillors, 12 are appointed by Defra, and they are people that are familiar with the needs of the fishing fraternity, so there's anglers, there's environmentalists, there's fishermen, there's merchants, fishermen's wives, and one member is appointed by the Environment Agency, that's a hangover from the days of the old river boards. We meet four times a year in County Hall, and it's quite a powerful organization in that it can make and enforce law. So it makes by-laws, which have to be confirmed by the Minister, and they meet and discuss issues within their district and adjoining districts, and anything to do with the fishing industry, the fishery, the environment and anything else like that.

On a day-to-day role the service has ten staff altogether: there's myself, I have two senior officers – one who's head of enforcement, another one who's a research officer; I have a master of the patrol vessel – the patrol vessel's 21 metres, five-year-old vessel, £2 million's worth; there are two engineers aboard, and she's crewed by Fishery officers, of which I have three. And I have one admin staff, so that's the team.

Fishery officers regularly patrol either by patrol boat or ashore, using a Land Rover, and then they board and inspect vessels on an *ad-hoc* basis, or on a targeted basis if they think there's a particular problem. Generally we board between 700 and 800 vessels a year.

They are all British vessels because they are inside the six-mile limit. There's an argument, and this is one of the things the Government is struggling with at the moment, that we should be able to board foreign vessels as well. If we go to the 12-mile limit then we will be expected to, because the French and the Belgians come into six miles, and in preparation for that I've trained one of my officers in French. We also have an interpreter on the books if we needed one. I speak Spanish, most of the lads speak a bit of French, so between us we'd do OK from that perspective.

> *I am not there for the industry, not there for the anglers, I'm not there for the environmentalists, I'm there for no human, I'm there for the fish, that's what my job's about. Generally we board between 700 and 800 vessels a year.*

That's one side, enforcement, so they check the landings, they check the nets, there's also rules and regulations for them to check for compliance. But we enforce with common sense. If we feel there's intent, or if we know there's intent in some wrongdoing, then we will come down hard and we will prosecute. And this year we've had about five or six prosecutions so far, we've got a court case next week. Generally 99 per cent of people are absolutely fine. Very, very rarely do we take the same person to court more than once.

Then on the research side we have Sam, who's my senior research officer, and Colin, who's also got a research background. They're doing a shellfish survey at the moment – three-year programme where they go aboard certain shellfish boats and they sample the catches. So they measure them, sex them, check them for disease, whether they're cripples, got eggs on, all the conditions and what have you, so we start to build up a picture of the stock in our waters. It has never been done in Cornwall before. When Government does any research, it's much more broad-brush basis, but we need to have a better understanding. Although we can sample the catches coming in, all that tells us is what's been caught. It doesn't tell us what under-sizes are going back – because with shellfish of course it goes back live. So we don't have any understanding at this time of what's coming on in future years. With this work we're already starting to build up a knowledge base, which is very, very interesting. The other thing we do, by the way, is take water temperatures at sea, where these pots are, to see whether there's any correlation between temperatures and catches and movements of shellfish.

We could be just an enforcement agency where, 'There's the rules, go out and enforce them.' That's not what we're about. It's far more about management, it's about encouragement for enhancing fisheries, developing fisheries, it's working with the industry, it's working with environmentalists, and other stakeholders. I suppose I'm biased, but I think it's the best job you can have. You can be enemy to everybody and friend to everybody, depending on the way you handle it. I think it's an important duty.

I was a fisherman. I've fished all over the world, starting at 15. I left home, went to college in Lowestoft for three months, and I went to sea, the day after Boxing Day, 1964, and was terribly ill, first trip. We only did four days, it was meant to be a 12-day trip, but we had all sorts of problems, and in the time I was away at sea, I'd lost two stone in weight. My mother, who never wanted me to go to sea, said, 'You'll never be going back to sea then,' and I said, 'Yeah, course I will, I haven't really seen much,' and I was never really sick after that. But then I fished all round the world, in the Falkland Islands, Africa, North Atlantic, North Sea, Norwegian deeps, all over.

Fishery officers on patrol regularly board and inspect vessels.

Yes, it gives me an understanding of the industry world-wide, I speak their language. We hold fishermen's meetings every two or three years, and on a couple of occasions fishermen have said, 'You know what I'm talking about, you've done it.' And because they realize that, they can put it perhaps in a way that a layman wouldn't understand. The other side is that if one of them decides to pull the wool over my eyes, that will only work for a very short period before I call a halt to it.

You've got three Fisheries enforcement agencies in England and Wales. You've got Defra, that go out to 200 miles, or the median line in the Channel; you have Sea Fisheries Committees inside six miles, and you have the Environment Agency, again in the six miles, but generally in the rivers and fresh water. It's inside six miles for salmon and sea trout, and migratory species. So we have the EU legislation, you have the national legislation, we come underneath, and ours is more restrictive than all the others. So in the six-mile limit, for instance, no vessel over 18.28 m overall length can trawl, unless it has historic rights. Similarly, shellfish boats if they're over 16.46 m are not allowed in unless they've got historic rights. The reason for those silly sizes is because pre-decimal they were in feet – 60 ft and 54 ft. So immediately that reduces the potential pressure on an area because it excludes the larger vessels. It's not because we are anti-large, it's because any large vessel coming in and towing a vast amount of heavy gear can devastate an inshore area. Most inshore areas are juvenile grounds, they have a lot of juvenile fish, and we encourage where possible methods that are sustainable, traditional fishing methods – pots, nets – although nets on their own can cause a certain amount of contention.

The industry, naturally, like any other industry, evolves. And one of the things that's changed dramatically in recent years is technical advances, commonly known as technical creep. You can never see today that certain things happen, but if you look back over five years you can see a dramatic increase. The amount of gear they work is more, so now fishermen on average are working three times the gear they were a decade ago. The amount of fish they are catching is very, very similar, so they are not catching three times the amount of fish. Some are catching a bit more, most are catching more or less the same. Now that starts to ring alarm bells. We are not at crisis level at the moment – this is where Sam's data is going to help us in the next three or four years – we think, just from gut feeling more than anything else, that probably we're at something called maximum sustainable yield. We haven't seen the decline as such yet, in fact there's an increase last year in lobster, but that's a natural variation. But when the declines come, they drop off quite dramatically and we never want to get to that stage.

So we restrict the size of the vessel, we restrict the power of the vessel, we restrict the type of gear they can use… . One of the things we can't do is restrict the numbers of vessels in the district. So what has happened? The numbers of small boats coming into the inshore fisheries increased … I'm not sure how many permits there'll be this year, but it'll be around 400–450. The EU and the Government had the decommissioning scheme, but that was for over-10 m vessels, so they're offshore, nothing's done for inshore. So what happens? A lot of the owners of offshore boats had a nice pay-out, and rather than give up fishing they go out and buy a small boat, so the inshore sector now is under far more pressure than previously. I think it's sustainable if we can keep on top of it. But then people keep dreaming up new ways of fishing, and always more efficient.

The same thing's happening offshore as well, but perhaps at a faster rate, so because it's a faster rate, governments have done something about it. The inshore sector, because it's very resilient, has resisted a lot of the more extreme pressures, but if we're not careful they are going to build up until there's a real big problem. But the saving grace, in a way, because it's in sight of people ashore, at the moment there's a lot of interest from environmentalists that in a way I welcome but in others I don't. I welcome the attention because I think it needs to be highlighted in positions of power, I don't welcome some of the interference that goes on by some sectors that should know better.

Groups like environmentalists and sea anglers are listened to much more now, definitely. I don't blame the anglers, I think they're flawed because they won't listen to the counter arguments. They think I'm on the side of the commercial fishermen. I'm not, at the end of the day I'm on the side of the fish, and trying to get that across to people is so difficult. I am not there for the industry, not there for the anglers, I'm not there for the environmentalists, I'm there for no human, I'm there for the fish, that's what my job's about. The argument of course, when you think about it, simplified version, is that if you have a healthy fishery then the fish industry will be healthy, the anglers will be, the environmentalists will be happy, it's all about balance.

All I'm saying is we need to be aware that one day, if we don't do something we're going to reach a situation where the pressure will be such that everything will fall over. I hope it's not in my lifetime, what I hope is in my lifetime the political will should be there to give powers to manage effectively. And one way to manage effectively is to have restrictive licensing, resource-based management.

What frustrates me a lot, and I spend a lot of my time trying to convince other people otherwise, is because everything looks healthy – stocks are healthy, could be healthier but they are healthy – now's the time to really put into place belt and braces measures to make sure that when cyclical changes occur that will have an adverse impact, that you'll be able to ride out the storm without people going bust, without too many pressures, without the need to break the law. So let's put something into place to make sure that when stocks reduce, which they will – there's always a natural, cyclical variation – that there won't be that need, there won't be that pressure to constantly eat away at the biomass. It's far more complicated than that, but I don't know how else to put it across to people. And the industry needs to be buying into that, they are already seeing the benefit of thinking that way. In a way the pressure is off, and now's the time to do something to get ready for the next lot of pressure coming in. It may not be for ten years, it may be next year, you don't know when it's going to happen, but it will at some time.

Superintendent David Whitehead
Port Missioner, The Royal National Mission to Deep Sea Fishermen, Newlyn

David Whitehead: I am the Port Missioner, which means I am appointed to the port at Newlyn and to the region of Cornwall by the Fishermen's Mission – the full title is the Royal National Mission to Deep Sea Fishermen. So I am appointed to look after the practical and spiritual welfare needs of fishermen, their families and the industry, and that is also regardless of race or creed. I am a lay person, really, but if you didn't feel called to the work, if it was just another job, you'd never do it. The hours can be very unsociable. Some of the things that you put up with can be really quite unsociable, but it's all part of being able to serve the fishermen.

You're living in the community with these people, living their life with them and that's what it is. I had a chappie came in to see me just now, very basic thing, just needs a lift to the hospital next week, to get an appointment. Just finding it financially difficult to keep going up to the hospital, and is asking for a bit of help with that, so that's not a problem. Very simple, practical thing.

How long have I worked for the Fishermen's Mission? Six and a half years. Funnily enough I started as a trainee, right here in Newlyn. But I'm not a Cornish boy, not at all. I was born and brought up in Bolton, Lancashire, son of a retail family, retail business, but I never really followed that line. I became a committed Christian in the June of 1997 and joined the Mission two years later, it was through that sense of calling. I just found my life being shoved in the direction of the Fishermen's Mission – for example, I would be reading my Bible, or I would be listening to something on the radio, or seeing something on television, any time I heard the word fish, fishermen, fishing, the words sort of jumped out at me in a way that nothing else does. I had a chat with my vicar about it and he said, 'David, I think God's calling you.' And two years later, almost to the day, I came here to start with the Fishermen's Mission. But you join the Fishermen's Mission on the understanding that you can be moved to any port at any time.

Before I joined, I had no direct experience of fishing. I tried it once with a rod and line by some little reservoir; however, I did have 5,000 miles of seagoing experience at least, in offshore sailing, I was very much into offshore sailing. I was also a member of the Royal Naval Reserve for two years, so despite coming from a landlubber family I've always been into boats.

How would I sum up the Mission's work? Christianity with its sleeves rolled up? Doing the Gospel? In practical terms, it is Christian faith worked out in practice, at least that's what we try to do, which is certainly not perfect, and I think anybody that claims to be perfect is obviously not!

Yes it does have a key role in a port like Newlyn. Our work as well as being practical help for the fishermen and their families, it is pastoral work. There's a lot of times when all I do is sit and listen. We are not noted for, shall we say, preaching. Although we have the open-air Remembrance Sunday Service and obvious things like that, and the blessing of the fleet service along with the Fish Festival, but you won't see me Bible in hand, standing trying to preach a sermon in the middle of a fish market, because that wouldn't go down too well. That's not the way to do it. We do a lot of visitation. We visit widows, young and old alike, we visit retired fishermen, poorly fishermen, all that along with running this centre with its canteen and bedrooms. The bedrooms are for visiting fishermen, and also for emergency cases as well. We've had a number of fishermen who've had to stay here overnight, and perhaps they've been in hospital, perhaps airlifted in and they've been treated in hospital and they'll come and stay with us before we can get them transported home. Some of them quite often are French guys, Spanish guys. We're certainly on call 24/7.

I worked in Shetland for three years before coming back to Newlyn, and while we were there, there was a 45 per cent cut in some of the fish quota, particularly the key fish. That meant that several boats had to be decommissioned. That is perfectly good boats, some of which were barely a few years old, being sent to a scrap heap

We're dealing with the quiet things in people's private lives ...

and being torn to pieces. The impact on skippers and crew are two-fold. It's like a bereavement, and it doesn't help them financially in the long run. Their livelihoods have been taken away from them, unless they can find another job to go to it really doesn't help them. What is happening is, the reason for decommissioning, is trying to reduce what they call the fishing effort. But I remember watching a programme on television of a fisherman from the north of Scotland, and his boat had to go over to Denmark. I think it was to be scrapped, and it was such a horrible, horrible experience for him. And the other side of it is that quite often the finances of the boat, the first place that any money is going to go to is the bank, to pay off any dues for the boat. So actually there's not really much left for the fisherman to have.

There's a lot of people in that sort of circumstance. That TV programme was just picking on one particular boat, it had to do that. And it's had a dire effect in Scottish ports. The difficulties I'm seeing here at the moment have been from very high fuel prices and also reduced fishing effort, quotas and things like that, especially for big boats, which make it difficult for them to make ends meet and to be able to carry out their work legally. There's an awful lot of pressure on them, and bureaucratic pressure that just doesn't add up with true fishing life.

You can see why people try and bend the rules. I wouldn't condone it, but it would certainly be a big test of my faith if I was a fishing skipper trying to make ends meet, pay my crew, pay my mortgage, feed my family, and still do so without breaking the law. Blokes have been coming to me and said, 'I'm really struggling, I'm struggling to make ends meet, this is the problem I've got, can you help me with it at all?' We do what we can to help.

One of our difficulties is raising awareness of what we do. Take the Lifeboats, for example. Very visible, and you know great photographs of Lifeboats with lots of spray, stories of heroic rescues, and that's absolutely valid, and they do tremendous work. But who cares for the fisherman when he comes ashore? Who deals with them after the Lifeboat or the Coastguard have done their job? We do. We're dealing with the quiet things in people's private lives, things that really are confidential. Confidentiality is very important in our job, we're dealing with some very personal issues that people wouldn't want known publicly.

What keeps them fishing? Survival. I can't think of anything other than survival. There's certainly a sense of dignity I think. People need to be able to work because their sense of dignity comes from that, of working, and doing what you can to feed your family. And it's a way of life.

I think it's often been said that you can take a fisherman out of the

Retired fisherman Douglas Gilbert talks to David Whitehead at the Mission in Newlyn.

sea, but you can't take the sea out of a fisherman. And there is something, I've found myself, after 5,000 miles of offshore sailing and some other boats as well, there's something addictive about the sea. There's a love-hate relationship, this is only speaking for myself personally, but I wouldn't be surprised if thinking that's how it is, is for others too.

I think when people go to sea, the families that are left behind, they know the risks, but they don't talk about it. They know that when their man goes to sea he may not come back. There's always that risk. It's not something that they like to think about, and it's probably pretty much put to the back of their mind. Furthermore, where

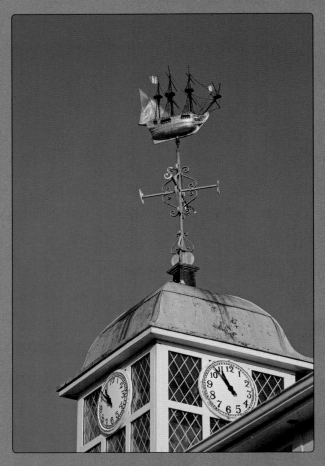

The Fishermen's Mission is a focal point in the heart of Newlyn.

people have been lost at sea in the past, when somebody else is lost at sea it brings it back again. The whole community feels it. It brings back the pain, time and time again. There are other difficulties as well. If somebody's lost at sea and there are no witnesses to the incident – for example, a boat that's just gone off the radar, all hands lost … it can be up to seven years before a death certificate can be issued. Just think of how important that document is in terms of the practical aspects of a person's life.

When you think each of those people is somebody's father, son, grandfather, husband, boyfriend, all those things in effect, it's just devastating. I lost my father when I was 19 years old. He died of a heart attack. The effect that had on my life was profound, as you can imagine. At least he was there for me to say goodbye to. I can still go to his grave, least I can if I am up in Bolton. But the effect on a community where that can't happen is just dire. Our Mission centre has a memorial room where people can come in and remember lost loved ones who have no known grave.

I want the industry to survive. I want the industry to flourish, because people need food on their tables. These people need an industry with which to earn their living. But I'm also interested, and care passionately, about the spiritual state of people. People can be very wealthy but have no peace, spiritually. And yet there are other people who have nothing, but what they have got is a living relationship with a living God, they're full of peace and they, by virtue of that, they are among the richest people in the world. I have a special testimony of how God has worked in my life and has improved my life, He's changed my life markedly, for the better, and I have peace in my life. If I was to die tomorrow I'm not scared about where I'm going, because I believe the promises of Jesus. In that I consider myself very, very rich, and therefore it's my privilege to serve other people for the God I believe in.

Right: Newlyn's busy harbour.

6 The Real Dilemma: Safeguarding the Future

It is dusk as *Pride of Cornwall* slips out of the harbour. She steams along the curve of Mount's Bay, but it is not long before skipper Stefan Glinski has spotted a shoal of sardines. He is less than a couple of miles offshore and the lights of Penzance and Newlyn are still clearly visible. The ring net is shot and the shoal captured. Carefully he brings the net into the boat where he and his crew brail the fish into tanks of iced water, which rapidly cools their temperature and ensures that they stay in the best possible condition. Later they will be packed in boxes with ice before being landed. The whole process has taken only a few hours. The catch has been good enough to meet the demands of Stefan's customers, and he is back in Newlyn just after midnight.

This is the modern version of fishing for pilchards, or sardines. It is fast, efficient and the fish are plentiful. But it is also a highly skilled process. Sardines are flighty and difficult to catch. Sonar and echo sounders may help to find a shoal, but then other factors come into play – the weather, tide, darkness, the mood of the fish – which is why these fishermen are highly skilled hunter-gatherers, as Stefan Glinski describes:

> 'It's impossible to quantify so a lot of it's touchy feely, sensing, instinct of a hunter really on this particular job. It's not, "Oh there's the shoal, I go round it, I catch it." It doesn't work like that. It's always a challenge, you're stalking, you're hunting and you get a feel for it in the end but that takes several years for it to come naturally.'

A man who has invested more than £150,000 in this new boat and new gear is clearly optimistic about the future. After a lifetime of fishing on inshore and

Right: Sardines caught by Stefan Glinski on board his purpose-built boat, *Pride of Cornwall.*
Pages 106–7: The 220 m ring net on the sea in Mount's Bay, at dusk.

deep-sea boats, trawling, netting, fishing on wrecks and handlining, he has found a way of supplying a specific market, rather than relying on the uncertainties of selling into the daily fish auction. This is highly sustainable fishing for a single species with no quota restrictions, no by-catch, a minimal environmental impact, and low overheads.

Other Cornish fishermen have recognized that if they want to continue fishing they need the flexibility to switch to what are known as non-pressure stocks – fish that are abundant in South West waters such as John Dory, squid, lemon sole, red mullet or line-caught sea bass and mackerel, and which have no quota restrictions – and to be able to work various fisheries at different times of year, demonstrating that they are committed to the concepts of sustainability and conservation. Many of the under-10 m and inshore boats are able to work specific types of gear, such as handlines, gill nets or crab and lobster pots. In many cases this virtually eliminates the problems of by-catch – that is fish that is either restricted by quota and cannot be sold, or fish for which there is no market. In the main these diverse fishing methods are among the most sustainable: they require much less fuel and make little impact on the marine environment, and by targeting a mix of different species over the course of the year, overall pressure on fish stocks is lessened. For these fishermen the benefits are fewer hours at sea and the ability to go home each night. Others, fishing further out at sea, are finding ways to target specific types of fish, but still come up against the problem that trawlers and beam trawlers, to some extent, are working in a mixed fishery and are likely to land upwards of 20 different fish types each time they haul in their nets.

There is a wide variety of views about the health and level of fish stocks, some more positive than others. One beam trawler skipper told me that he had 'been doing the same job over the same ground for the last 20 years and the fishing has improved,' though others say that some stocks are not as good as they once were. It is difficult and unwise to make generalizations, given the diversity of species and number of fish populations around the Cornish coast. Stocks 100 miles apart may be radically different, some doing well, some not. Fishermen understand the variations and make their fishing decisions accordingly.

Despite the difficulties of the last few years, the whole industry understands only too well the need to conserve stocks and protect them for their future. Paul Trebilcock, of the CFPO, believes that scare stories about collapsing fish stocks and overfishing are too often quoted out of context:

'The science for the North Sea is terrible and everybody catches cod, and then the headlines the public read, "Last fish has been caught". "Fish extinct". "Greedy fishermen", and it's totally different here. The whole North Sea and the west of Scotland rely on four or five species, nothing else. Down here it's 20 species. The North Sea are all trawlers, we are netters, potters, trawlers, beam trawlers, it's the diverse fleet, diverse species, versus the fairly mono fleet.'

During the two decades that they have been dominated by the constraints of the quota system and the CFP, Cornish fishermen have taken other voluntary measures to conserve stocks, driven by their need to create a sustainable future for both the industry and fish stocks. Minimum landing sizes, bigger mesh sizes, closed areas and restrictions on some types of fishing gear, all have a part to play.

One of the earliest conservation measures was the South West Mackerel Box, set up in 1981 in an area eight miles offshore, all around the coastline from Start Point in South Devon to Hartland Point on the Devon and Cornwall border on the north coast. It was extended again to almost 26,000 square miles in 1989. This exclusion area was drawn up to protect juvenile mackerel and to counter the after-effects of the 1970s mackerel boom. The net effect is that large boats targeting mackerel are excluded from fishing inside the box, where mackerel can only be caught by handline fishermen. Although at 1,750 tonnes the annual mackerel quota for the entire South West handline fishery is quite low – about as much as one industrial trawler could catch in one night – this conservation measure seems to have worked, and mackerel stocks appear to have recovered.

Another area that has recently gained protection is the Trevose Head Box. This area of 3,600 square miles, centred around Trevose Head on the north Cornwall

Left: Stefan Glinski on board *Pride of Cornwall*. After the shoal is trapped in the ring net, the sardines are transferred to tanks of iced water using a small net called a brail.

The National Lobster Hatchery, Padstow

The idea of starting a lobster hatchery was first discussed by the CSFC before the Second World War, understanding the need to boost lobster (*Homarus gammarus*) stocks off the Cornish coast. Some work had been done by the Norwegians, showing that eggs could be hatched and grown on to a juvenile stage before returning to the sea. The idea was revived in the 1990s, and took almost ten years to come to fruition, with the hatchery opening in 2000. The first five years were dogged by a number of teething problems, but it is now thriving as a conservation and research centre. In 2005 more than 16,000 tiny juvenile lobsters were put into the sea at a number of locations around the Cornish coast.

Eddy Derriman, of the CSFC, has personally been one of the driving forces behind the hatchery's success: 'In all we've put in 40–50,000 baby lobsters, gradually that's going to start making a difference. We hope that in 2006 between 35,000 and 40,000 will be going out at selected sites around Cornwall.'

Situated in Padstow, overlooking the Camel estuary, the hatchery encourages fishermen to bring in berried hens (female lobsters carrying up to 20,000 eggs). After the eggs have hatched and the larvae swum away from the female, the lobster is returned to the sea. The larvae are fed on plankton in special rearing tanks, until they have grown to about 0.5 in long. As they begin to look like miniature adult lobsters they are carefully moved into individual cells. Lobsters are extremely aggressive and carnivorous, and would attack each other if reared in groups, which is why it is not possible to farm lobsters using conventional aquaculture methods. Instead, the hatchery concentrates on restocking by rearing the juveniles until they are big enough to be released back into the wild. The survival rate of eggs laid in the wild is low, thought to be less than 0.1 per cent compared with a 40 per cent survival rate for eggs raised by the hatchery. By the time the juveniles are returned to the sea, usually at about three or four months old and when water temperatures are warm enough, they are able to fend for themselves.

The hatchery has installed a new sea-water life-support system using modern recirculation techniques, which should increase the number of juveniles raised, and is trialling new stacking housing systems that will expand its rearing capacity. Other work includes using variable water temperatures to control when the berried lobsters hatch their eggs.

Dominic Boothroyd became hatchery manager at the end of 2005 and sees its role as being a centre for sustainable fisheries. 'This is a very positive way of doing something to improve shellfish stocks,' he says. 'The hatchery will be able to make a significant contribution to managing stocks more effectively and ensuring their long-term sustainability.'

The National Lobster Hatchery differs from other lobster hatcheries at Anglesey Zoo and in Shetland in that it is multifunctional, combining its scientific role with education, and providing a visitor centre.

coast, is one of Europe's richest spawning grounds for cod, plaice and sole. From 2006, under a new, voluntary agreement between British, Irish, French and Belgian fishermen, in February and March it is closed to all boats so that the fish can spawn undisturbed.

For five years between 1997 and 2002 there was a similar, but much smaller, no-take zone off St Agnes, where shell fishermen agreed not to fish for lobster as part of a bigger lobster conservation programme.

One of the most successful local by-laws introduced by the CSFC has been to increase the minimum landing sizes (MLS) for lobsters and crabs. The Cornish MLS for lobsters was introduced in 1994, and is measured from the rear of the lobster's eye socket to the edge of its body shell. At 87 mm it was 2 mm greater than the national minimum size, and two years later was increased to 90 mm. For the rest of the UK and Europe, the minimum size remains 87 mm. For crabs the statutory minimum sizes are 150 mm for female (hen) crabs and 160 mm for male (cock) crabs, measured across the broadest part of the back.

In 1999 the CSFC introduced V-notching in the tails of female (hen) lobsters. Under this scheme, fishermen V-notch the tails of lobsters carrying eggs (berries) and return them to the sea to breed. This has been mandatory in Cornwall since 2001, and was extended across the UK the following year. Alternatively, berried lobsters are taken to the National Lobster Hatchery in Padstow (see panel, page 110). It is estimated that it takes a female lobster several moults to lose the V-notch in her tail, equating to several successful breeding seasons.

Left: Freshly caught lobsters. *Below:* Dominic Boothroyd, Manager of the National Lobster Hatchery, Padstow. *Bottom: A* berried female (hen) lobster, showing V-notched tail. Her eggs will be stripped from her and reared at the National Lobster Hatchery.

The industry did not stop with the introduction of its own MLS for shellfish. In addition there are MLSs for almost all fish species, usually related to their spawning ability, some fish species being slower to reach maturity than others. In 2000, responding to pressure from Cornish fishermen, the CSFC reintroduced local by-laws with MLS for 13 species that had been dropped by the EU. These included hake, red and black sea bream, megrim and lemon sole, brill and turbot.

During 2005/6 Defra introduced a consultation on increasing the MLS of sea bass from 38 cm to 45 cm. For fishermen this encapsulated the debate about the monstrous injustices of the CFP and the UK government's habit of 'gold plating' the rules. Whatever agreement is reached, they argued, it would be meaningless unless applied universally to all EU member states. Beyond the 12-mile territorial limit, they could be fined for catching anything smaller than 45 cm, while any other nationality, fishing alongside them, would be within the law catching smaller fish.

Probably one of the most contentious issues between fishermen and environmentalists is cetacean by-catch. Most fishermen say that this is an age-old problem, and that many of the environmentalists' claims are without any justification. The environmentalists see it as a highly emotive issue, dominated by what has become the controversial method of pair trawling for sea bass, where two trawlers fish with the trawl net slung between them. Although this is illegal for English boats, at the

Top: Taking samples of the enriched feed solution from one of the breeding tanks at the National Lobster Hatchery. *Above:* A plastic tea strainer is the best implement for scooping up minute baby lobsters from their breeding tank full of protein-enriched solution.

time of writing the law had not been applied to other EU fishing fleets, and pair trawling continued outside Britain's 12-mile territorial limit. Privately, fishermen and officials say that there are other factors to consider, including a possibility that changing migration patterns of both cetaceans and their feedstocks have brought more dolphins and porpoises into local waters. What is often overlooked is that fishermen hate to see dead cetaceans just as much as the environmentalists and members of the public. Cornish fishermen have introduced a voluntary code of practice for inshore netters working with fixed nets and for trawlers, based on the principle of not shooting their nets if a pod or school of dolphins or porpoises is sighted. Trials were also being carried out to see if acoustic pingers could deter these mammals from swimming into nets.

Another experiment is using what are known as benthic panels in trawl nets. These are designed to allow bottom-dwelling fish and creatures (benthics) such as starfish and sea urchins to escape before the net is hauled in. Results so far suggest that this cuts benthic discards by up to 80 per cent, and improves efficiency for trawler crews. The quality of the fish is better; work on deck is reduced, and discards cut to, in some cases, single-figure percentages of the overall catch.

Cornish fishermen are also taking part in a hake recovery programme that restricts gill-net mesh sizes to 120 mm, the size already used by Cornish netters working this fishery. Started in 2003 because the spawning biomass of hake (the scientists' measure of the health of any fish stock by assessing its ability to reproduce) had reached dangerously low levels, this measure limits the amount of fishing effort targeted at hake, and protects juvenile hake which had previously been caught by the smaller-meshed nets used by Spanish fishermen.

Despite a lack of political will to provide the real investment needed for recovery programmes to be effective, the Cornish fishing industry seems determined to help itself out of what only a few years ago appeared to be a desperate situation. The fact that political decisions in Brussels and the scientists' messages bore little resemblance to what fishermen knew from their experience at sea, led to the creation of the FSP. Scientists from CEFAS are funded by the Government to go to sea on Cornish boats to assess fish stock levels. Since the FSP's inception in 2003 there has been much closer co-operation between scientists and fishermen. Up until that point political decisions for stock management strategies were based on scientific advice that, in the fishermen's view, was fundamentally flawed, and which the scientists often knew to be out of date by the time their research findings were translated into policy. This new partnership is already bringing considerable benefits, building relationships based on trust between the two sides for perhaps the first time in fishing history.

Not all the results have been in fishing's favour. While there is no argument that cod stocks have been decimated all around the UK, they are probably in a better state in Cornish waters than anywhere else. Nevertheless, there have been cuts in Cornish quotas for cod and sole in some areas. However, the scientists have confirmed that stocks of monkfish are healthier than had previously been thought, leading to an unprecedented quota increase for three successive years.

Fishermen and fisheries scientists also seem to agree that fishing follows cyclical patterns, without any logical explanation for why a particular species can be abundant one year, but virtually vanishes three years later. Add changing environmental conditions, rising water temperatures and other factors, and it is little wonder that fish disappear or appear in waters where they are previously unknown.

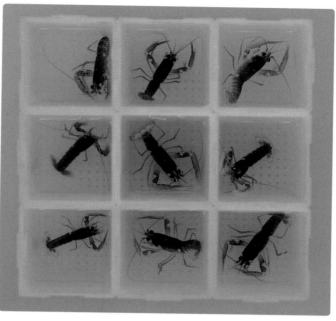

Above: Inch-long baby lobsters reared at the National Lobster Hatchery, already spoiling for a fight and almost ready for release at sea.

Where does that leave the overall picture of Cornish fish stocks? There is no definitive answer, but plenty of anecdotal evidence to suggest that in Cornish waters there is no danger of an imminent North Sea-style collapse in any one fish species, perhaps because action has been taken in time to move towards long-term sustainable levels of all species. Perhaps it is helped by the abundance of different fish and shellfish, the spread of fishing effort and the industry's ability to switch fishing methods and species according to season. Advice from the International Council for the Exploration of the Sea (ICES) suggests that in the absence of any detailed analysis of the state of all the fish stocks, a cautious approach is the best option. There also seems to be general agreement with Eddy Derriman, the Chief Sea Fisheries Officer, who takes the view that while stocks may be in a reasonable state, this is the time to take further action to ensure long-term sustainability.

Wherever I went I found a willingness among fishermen to embrace conservation measures, and an understanding that a secure future for their communities and their livelihoods depends on responsible fishing in the present. This doesn't ignore the threats, but shows that Cornish fishermen are taking many positive steps to safeguard the future, both for the fish and for themselves.

Elizabeth Stevenson
Partner, W. Stevenson & Sons, Newlyn

*W. Stevenson & Sons own one of Britain's biggest privately owned fishing
fleets. The company also auctions fish, is a fish merchant and vessel agent,
and owns two fishmongers' shops.*

Elizabeth Stevenson: In the fishing industry, I'm Elizabeth Stevenson, and I'm a partner in W. Stevenson & Sons. I'm not a chairman, I'm not a manager, I'm nothing else,
I'm a partner in a private partnership. It just so happens that somewhere along the
line I drew the short straw and took on the PR side of things, or certainly I'm the face
or the person that the press and TV come to. There's my father and my two sisters,
and then there's my uncle and his three children, and we are all partners.

I was born and educated locally, and had absolutely no idea what I wanted to do
– mistake number one! I came down here when I was 14, in August 1971, as a summer-
time job and a Saturday morning job. And when I left school in July '73, I started work
here the next day on a full-time basis. In September of that year, when my friends all
went back to do their A levels, I panicked and went up to the school, deciding I had to
do something instead of working here, and was given all the list of things I could do
in the Sixth form, and I didn't like any of them. So came back down here again two
hours later, where I have remained.

When I first came, I was sitting at the big desk out there where I still am, beside
my grandfather, and I was just literally a general dogsbody, adding things up, writing
things, copying things, writing out fish lists for trips of fishermen that landed, because
we only had carbon paper then, and there weren't computers. Well there probably
were big-frame things, but not things that you would have in a business like ourselves, and that was it. And there I remained and the job evolved from there.

The representational role began when my uncle asked me to go to a meeting in
Plymouth, and I went to that meeting, but it turned out I'd already been co-opted on to
this committee that was with the South West PO [South West Producers' Organisation].
Then there was the cod ban in, I can't remember when, and I did an interview on BBC
Radio 2, the Jimmy Young Show, except it was with Angela Rippon because he was on
holiday. And that was the beginning of the TV-papers-radio role. Of course I went on to
sit on other committees, training committees, the Cornish PO, all sorts of committees.
I then did a six-year stint with the Sea Fish Industry Authority, I was a government ap-
pointee on their board, and then I got involved with the NFFO, and eventually became
chairman of that, which I currently am. That's for two years, and my time is nearly up.

And of course, in between I've attended hosts of meetings with either the Minister,
or Defra officials, either in London or wherever they happen to be, which is a good
thing because going away meant that I spoke to and met a huge number of people
from other ports and other areas, which enabled me to see the bigger picture. And
wherever I go, whether it's in this country or abroad, I always seem to head for the
harbour, and it gives you a better insight as to what's happening within the industry
rather than just seeing your own port.

A lot of it is very similar, but some of the problems are very, very different because obviously the fishing in the North Sea is very different. I certainly enjoy meeting the people from other areas and other ports. I suppose in the modern world that's networking isn't it?

I did go a couple of times to Brussels for the [annual EU fishing quota] negotiations as an observer, but I've just done two years as NFFO chair, I don't know whether you are the head of the negotiating team, but you are seen to be. So you come back totally shattered. This year [2005] I left home at seven o'clock on the Monday morning, and I got back at seven o'clock on the Thursday evening. When they say, 'Well, we don't know what time it is going to finish tonight, we're going to go through the night,' you think, 'Now shall I stay up or shall I go to bed?' At about half past eleven this year I thought I was going to go to bed. And at two o'clock you get the phone call, 'Foyer 15 minutes,' and this is usually for the final announcement. You carefully lay your clothes out the night before almost in the order you've taken them off, so you make sure you go out fully clothed! Don't take any make-up or anything off so you can go out almost as you are.

> *It's one thing obeying rules and regulations, it's another thing when those rules and regulations take a quarter of your pay cheque and rip it up.*

One of the things I am proudest of is getting scientists to go out on the fishing boats, yes that was brilliant. I think it must have been 2003. We were throwing back huge quantities of monkfish because the quota was insufficient for the amount of monkfish we were catching. The scientists were saying the stock was in trouble, and the scientific evidence appeared to show that. Yet our men were saying it wasn't right. I'd been away to a meeting, and the following day I'd met one of our skippers down here who told me how much he'd thrown away, which was enough to send you into the total depths of despair, financially as well as mentally. I at the time had been speaking with the Fisheries Secretary, and we'd been getting on reasonably well, enough to be on first-name terms, and on the whole he tended to listen if I said something, and I listened, didn't always agree. I remember saying to my husband I had a damn good mind to phone up the Fisheries Secretary, and he said, 'Well, why don't you then?' So I sat down and phoned him up, and he just said, 'Well, OK, both can't be right, somebody is wrong.' And very shortly after that we had a couple of scientists down here, and I think they were put at our disposal to go out and prove that the fishermen were wrong. We hurriedly with the PO [Cornish Fish Producers' Organisation], put together a very quick, *ad hoc* project, and these two scientists were just looking to see if the men were right. And it appeared from the trip that these scientists were on that the men were right. It sort of took off from there. One minute it

was, 'Ah but they're the wrong age,' 'But what age are they meant to be?' 'Well, we'll have to look at that.' Then it was the wrong size and various other things, and then a slightly more credible project was put together with the scientists on board, and they went out and, hey presto, they aged the monkfish, and they were the right age; lots of different ages of monkfish spread over a wide area. We had an interim quota increase that year, albeit late, it was something like November. And then we had an increase at the December council, and then we had one in 2004 and we've had one again in 2005 for this year. So I think that really was the start of the Fisheries Science Partnership, and they now do it on all sorts of species in all sorts of areas, not just down here.
I think that was a boost to the scientists, because they didn't get on terribly well with the fishermen; there was a lot of suspicion, 'Bloody scientists what do they know?', and I'm sure the scientists said, 'Bloody fishermen, what do they know?'. The men were on board the boats, our men spoke to the scientists, they could see what they were doing, and they could see the reasons why they were doing it. I think it was very good for all concerned.

Newlyn harbour, home of W. Stevenson & Sons' fishing fleet.

And there were one or two photographs, and the BBC got hold of it, and the Countryfile programme was good, and we didn't go over the top with it, it was just right, because sometimes when you do a media campaign it runs away from you. What we didn't want to have on the media was the idea that we were polluting the seas with all the fish that were going back, because then we'd have the Greens after us. Because of course years ago there was the problem with the mackerel boats when they were dumping huge quantities of mackerel, and they were actually damaging the sea-bed, it was making it so grim that things weren't growing there. So we didn't want them to think that we were throwing back millions of tonnes of fish and polluting everything, but we wanted them to know that it was actually causing a huge problem.

There was this problem with discards, because a while back discards didn't always mean over-quota fish. Of course you had the things that go back because there is no market for them – the starfish, the dead men's fingers, sea urchins and things like that; then you have the fish that is undersize, then you would have the over-quota stuff. So years ago discards weren't over-quota stuff, because there wasn't any quota to have. So 'discards' is not quite the right word to use for some of the things that are thrown back. They are not marketable, but the fish that is over quota certainly is marketable, and it is discarded purely because there is no quota for it.

Back in 2002, 2003, there were a lot of people who had had enough. It's one thing obeying rules and regulations, it's another thing when those rules and regulations take a quarter of your pay cheque and rip it up. It's one thing if you haven't earned it in the first place, but when you've actually caught it, and then had to throw it back, in the same way as if you got paid £100 in a wage packet then throw a £20 note and a £5 note in the bin when you've already had it given to you. It was very difficult for them, they found it hell. It was physically hard to throw it back over, it was financially hard, and it was mentally hard as well.

There were no licences when I started working, I was here before quotas. When quotas were introduced for a lot of species, we weren't taking the full amount. What Defra are very good at doing, they introduce something and then they turn the screw afterwards. What you thought was bad wasn't anything like as bad as it later becomes. It was a bit like the days at sea thing that they tried to introduce some years ago. I remember being given something like 220, 240 days. Well now they are introducing days at sea and people are on 16 days a month, so that's a lot less than when we were complaining. When we had licensing introduced, as far as I can remember, you were just a licensed vessel, and you could fish anywhere you liked, when you wanted, for whatever you wanted, you could land it where you wanted and when you wanted.

Now you can't fish in half the places you were allowed to fish when your licence was issued. It's a bit like giving you a driving licence to drive a motorbike, a car, a bus, you name it, and then every year them knocking one off. When at first you could drive any vehicle all over the UK now you can only drive a car in Cornwall.

We restrict our fleet to fishing in Area VII: we go up to off Lundy up the Bristol Channel, and across west to the Irish side and then down sort of south as far out as the 10-degree line towards the Bay of Biscay area, although we don't go into the Bay of Biscay area, down and then across to the French sector and up the English Channel. It is quite a big area, but quite a few of our men have their own little patches that they prefer.

There are one or two partnerships and firms on the east coast, one person I know quite well who has a similar thing to us, a family with several boats and an auction and an agency, but not on the scale of ours. I think we're pretty unique now in our size and our scale, from catching through to retail. We own more beam trawlers than anything else and currently we are working I think it's 16 beamers, one netter and one trawler. So we really are a beamer firm.

I remember in the early 1960s being in my grandfather's window, upstairs, watching with great excitement because I'd been told these two or three vessels were coming. And they came into the harbour as absolute wrecks, I'd never seen anything like it in my life, they'd been laid up for a long time and we had to do them up. They'd got all rusty and awful, but they were very good boats and we've still got some of them. When I started work I started going away with my father when I was in my very late teens to buy boats from Holland with him.

I didn't go to sea fishing, I regret that because I'd like to. I've been to sea several times on trial trips, but I've never actually been out on a proper fishing trip, one day I will do it, but I haven't done it yet.

I'm hoping that the industry is going to go from strength to strength, and that we will have a fleet here that will be able to use the quotas effectively and use the facilities that the harbour is providing, and that Newlyn will go from strength to strength. I have to be positive in order to carry through the restructuring that we have started to undertake, but sometimes it's difficult to see the light at the end of the tunnel. Sometimes you have your bad days.

Newlyn has so much potential, but it is not easy being a member of a big family that is trying to run something, there's a lot of people to please, a lot of people have different views, it's not the easiest of tasks. It's much easier if you own something on your own, all you've got to make is your own decision, and it's only your fault and only you to blame. If you do it wrong you're not responsible to anybody else. Before Christmas I couldn't see a way out of the problems our family business was facing, and I couldn't see the future. It looked as if the only way was to shut down and that would have been horrendous.

Rob Forster, Jon Ashworth
and Oliver Wade
CEFAS Fisheries Science Partnership, Newlyn

Rob Forster (left): Our official job title is Catch Sampling Officer, but this is to be changed to Industry Liaison Officer to emphasize our role of trying to provide a line of communication between the industry and fisheries managers. We mainly make trips on commercial fishing vessels to observe fishing behaviour and to record the composition of catches. The data is used to assess total catch mortality, and it's hoped that it could be used for stock assessment purposes in the future.

There are 12 of us covering England and Wales – three in Newlyn (shortly to be four), and the others in Weymouth (now Exeter), Lowestoft, Scarborough and Whitehaven. We are responsible for recording what fishermen see, and this includes trying to record and quantify, as far as possible, how much fish is thrown away, so we can get a true idea of the abundance of fish on the grounds.

Over the last three years our priority has been to get to sea on commercial vessels. We also work on the market, sampling the landings of fin-fish, such as Dover sole, plaice, lemon sole, megrim, cod and haddock, and rays, and we visit shellfish merchants to cover crabs and lobsters. The priority species down here for the beam trawlers are Dover sole, megrim sole and monkfish, but the South West fishery is so mixed that every species is important.

We each spend about 100 days a year at sea, but this will be reduced slightly so we can get involved with FSP surveys. The FSP uses government money to look into fish stock or fisheries management issues of particular concern to the industry. It's a partnership between the industry and Fisheries scientists. The industry provides the vessel and the fishing gear, CEFAS organizes the survey method, records the data, and reports back to the industry. The rest of our time is spent entering and checking data, and contacting skippers and owners to arrange trips.

Are they open to that? I think they are, yeah. To begin with they were very closed and very nervous, I think because there had been bad experiences with some other projects where information had been used out of context, and they were understandably anxious not to repeat that. Many fishermen, though, probably accepted that information needed to be more accurate and representative if fishing is to be regulated in a rational manner. Not all skippers want to take part in the sampling programme, but that is their choice. Bit by bit, I think fishermen realize that we behave discretely, and we're not there to enforce regulations. We are there with their good will to try and describe something that they aren't really able to. That was the reason I joined the team, it's certainly not for the money or for the comfort.

On the market we take length and weight measurements and otoliths for a number of species. Otoliths are ear stones that we extract through the gills so as not to damage the fish for market. The age of the fish can be determined from the annual ring pattern in the otolith, and thus the growth rate. We also look at the reproductive condition of each fish to determine what portion of the stock are spawning, and the capacity of the stock to replenish itself. All this information is used in the stock assessments. These form the scientific basis of recommendations for total allowable catches and fishing effort, which is done through ICES and Europe. We're funded 50 per cent by Europe and 50 per cent by Defra, but it's channelled through CEFAS.

We do trips on most types of fishing vessel. Our sampling effort is divided between the different gears according to fishing effort. Apart from potters, long-liners and scallop dredgers. Although these fishing methods are important in the South West, discards from pots and dredges are returned to the sea alive. One big omission from the programme is the under-10 m fleet, the inshore boats, but I think there are plans to include them as well, if they'll take us.

Oliver Wade: Until that time, there's a big hole in the data of how much fish is being caught.

Rob: Scalloping is of huge importance to the industry in the South West. Many vessels switch from beam trawling or otter trawling to scalloping as part of a normal seasonal pattern, but we've noticed in the last year that more seem to be making the switch, and have remained scalloping for longer. This can all change depending on prices, the weather, days at sea restrictions or quota restrictions, and catch rates.

" Quotas are not the best management tools. In reality they don't actually conserve fish because they are limits on landings not on the amount of fish that is caught. "

Jon Ashworth: One of the industry's biggest difficulties is understanding why quotas for some stocks are set so low when catch rates clearly suggest higher stock levels. But the scientific community, quite rightly, is reluctant to make any far-reaching concessions on quota when there may be serious concerns about the age structure of given stocks and, in the case of Dover sole in the English Channel, where the reliability of landings data has been undermined by black landings and misreporting by some vessels.

Rob: Data on the quantities of fish landed on the markets do not accurately reflect the abundance of fish on the grounds. If a boat has reached its quota for sole, say, it will carry on fishing, keeping the monkfish, megrim sole, and so on but heave all the sole back over the side. In the same way, a boat may avoid grounds where sole is known to be plentiful to conserve quota for later in the year. The discard sampling programme is designed to monitor these effects.

Jon: Maybe 75, possibly 90, per cent of the vessels we sample would fish in the same manner irrespective of whether we were on board or not. The fishing practices of some vessels do change somewhat, but it's a very grey area and hard to quantify. If our presence does alter fishing behaviour on 10–25 per cent of the vessels we sample, and some of those are the larger, more powerful boats, our understanding of catches on a regional basis could still be way off the mark.

Rob: Misreported and unreported catches are still a problem in some ports, but enforcement efforts have increased lately. Although one or two boats may benefit, the rest of the industry is made to pay because fishing mortality is higher than that determined by official statistics. So how can stock assessments ever be accurate? ICES knows that fish is 'blacked', and tries to account for this in its assessments, but I don't know the inner workings of this.

Left to right: Oliver Wade, Rob Forster, and Jon Ashworth.

Jon: The data used for fisheries management doesn't just come from the fishing industry. Each EU fishing country has a responsibility to supply data to ICES, or certainly to ACFM [Advisory Committee on Fisheries Management], from professionally conducted surveys aboard Fisheries research vessels. These surveys don't mimic commercial fishing. They don't only cover grounds where there is known to be fish – they consist of timed tows using the same fishing gear on each survey, at the same predetermined positions at the same time of year over many years. This way, you get a good idea of upward and downward trends.

Rob: For the last couple of years the FSP has done surveys for sole and monkfish using beam trawlers from Newlyn and Brixham. The additional information from those resulted in increased quota for monkfish one year. But quotas are not the best management tools. Although they may be sensible on paper, in reality they don't actually conserve fish because they are limits on landings, not on the amount of fish that is caught.

Jon: Quota is a very good method of managing a single species fishery, assuming there are no associated discarding practices, for example a mackerel fishery or a pilchard fishery where only one species of fish is being caught.

Rob: But with mackerel you've got a number of shoals. Very often you don't know what the size composition is. They could take 200 tonnes of fish in one haul, but if the fish are too small they've got to release the whole lot dead. So even for a single species fishery it's not straightforward.

Oliver: I've just done a trip on a pelagic boat, pair trawling for mackerel and pilchard. They use multi-beam sonar, a sophisticated type of echo sounder that locates shoals of fish. It can also tell you what kind of fish you're targeting to a degree. Market preferences and quota restrictions meant that the whole catch was slipped [discarded] on several occasions. There was no point using up quota on fish that had little value, or wasting valuable time sorting through the catch.

Rob: Some fishermen realize the value in recording what is thrown back, it gives a truer picture of abundance. I don't think they really feel it is going to be an embarrassment to them if we are recording stuff and that it's being wasteful. It's staggering the amount of fish we see thrown away, good marketable fish.

Jon: If they are throwing away pressure stock species that has a value to them, they are throwing it away because it is over quota. They want it recorded, most definitely. If, on the other hand, they were blacking it [selling on the black market], or misreporting it, then there are other implications.

Rob: A number of fishermen have suggested that if boats were allowed to fish where they wanted and land what they wanted for a year, you'd get all the information you'd need. It sounds a good idea but I can't see that ever being allowed.

Jon: Fishing's a boom-and-bust industry. I don't think beaming effort has changed radically over the last few years. We have seen some older beamers leave the fleet to be replaced by newer vessels, and there are obvious improvements to efficiency, but on the whole the effort on the ground remains the same. Some of the stocks would seem to be able to sustain that. I'm not suggesting for a minute that any of the stocks are not heavily exploited, but since working in this job I've become aware of how closely dependent fishing is on recruitment. In a heavily exploited stock, the bigger, better breeders become rare. Don't get me wrong, there are still Dover soles out there that are 25, 35 years old, but they're nowhere near as common as they were. If fish are being caught as soon as they are large enough to be caught, but before they can breed successfully, you have a problem. And if the majority of the South West's demersal fish stocks suffered several years of poor recruitment, then the fishing industry would probably experience a serious decline.

Rob: Ideally, you want several year classes contributing to the fishery so you can keep going during periods of lower recruitment. If the fishery becomes dependent on the arrival of a single strong year class it becomes almost impossible to predict, because it's determined mainly by young fish being able to find the right food and avoiding predation, rather than the size of the spawning stock and the number of eggs released. The survival of young fish in the sea can't be managed, which is one reason why there has to be a precautionary margin in setting quotas and fishing effort. As for the future, it's one thing to manage a fishing fleet, it's another to manage the environment, and I think there's growing concern that climate change is affecting our fish stocks, and no-one really knows how to account for it in fisheries management.

Jon: It's a change that the fishing industry's yet to get to grips with. For years and years people have blindly towed around any amount of different gear, catching fish, but with no idea of what the long-term effects would be. That is beginning to change, but I fear the change won't be fast enough to keep the environmentalists happy.

Rob: Down here, there seem to be fewer and fewer larger vessels. Some owners have been steadily buying old boats for their quota, transferring them across, and they seem to be the ones that will survive. And there's also clear evidence that there's a particular size of boat, probably smaller, around 15 m, which can use a variety of gears, probably towed gear, to target a much greater variety of species. The cost of fuel will probably be the main deciding factor. One of the other things is the way fish is marketed, and how much of the retail price actually reaches the fisherman. I think supermarkets are probably the

Removing the otolith – a small ear-bone that enables scientists to determine the age of the specimen.

worst thing for the industry. Attempts to bring the consumer closer to the point of first sale, which help people to see where the fish they buy comes from and how it's caught should be supported. The important thing is that fishing remains a reasonably profitable livelihood so that the South West has a diverse economy. Otherwise, we'll be plagued with yet more theme parks and heritage centres which are irrelevant to the majority of the local population.

Oliver: Most supermarkets aren't even sourcing most of their fish from the UK. A lot of it's from aquaculture, it really makes me angry. I think fishing will continue, it's such a dynamic situation, I don't think it will be the same as it is now but I think there's always going to be fishing going on.

Jon: I think the Cornish fishing industry is vibrant and has a future, and the next four or five years are going to be crucial, but as long as there's fish to be caught, there will be people to catch it. Fishermen are not hunters any more, they're resource managers. If they were allowed to use the technology and fish freely you could still class them as hunters, but they are now managers of the resource they have available, and that's a product of quota, enforcement and the mountain of bureaucracy that is slowly gathering on top of all of these issues.

7 Fish Markets: The Twenty-first Century

The Newlyn fish market is buzzing with activity, even though it is barely light on a chilly December morning. Bright red plastic boxes of fish are stacked and ordered the length and breadth of the market building. Forklift trucks drive in and out of the market on to the quayside, bringing more boxes. At one end a gang of men is sorting and grading megrim sole, weighing each box, re-icing and returning it to the correct group of boxes. Further up the market others are weighing individual fish and repacking them, while the Fisheries scientists are dodging between the men, fish boxes, buyers and auctioneers, measuring fish and taking samples.

At the top of the market are the boxes of fish landed by the netters and small, inshore fishing boats. The catch includes hake, dogfish, shark, ling, pollack, haddock, red mullet, sea bass, cod, turbot, ray, cod, plaice and megrim sole. It has been a sizeable catch, but the abundance of fish for sale means that prices may not be so good. In the middle are several boxes containing cuttlefish – an important export but barely sold in Britain. At the other end are the hauls of the beam trawlers and the bigger boats. Here there are considerably more boxes lined up in each boat's distinct area: the catch also includes conger eel, ray, Dover sole, turbot, plaice, megrim and lemon soles, and sacks of scallops.

The auctioneer moves down the first row of boxes, followed by the group of buyers, a motley group of men, and one woman, all dressed for the chilly conditions: a mixture of woolly hats, white coats, fleece jackets, jeans and wellies – anything to stop the penetrating cold and damp affecting body and soul. The fish need to be kept cool, humans don't. He steps over to a box of conger eel. 'Now what am I bid, where shall we start? £1?,' he asks. One buyer discretely calls 80, then the bidding moves off, '90, £1 ...', barely a nod or acknowledgement and the deal is suddenly done at £1.35 – a better price than anticipated.

Herein lies one of the prime difficulties for the overwhelming majority of Cornwall's fishermen – the fact that in many cases they are price-takers and not

Right: Early morning at Newlyn Fish Market.

price-setters. Selling through the auction exposes them to market conditions, with no ability to negotiate prices. A glut of fish inevitably pushes prices down. In some cases a shortage of fish, at a difficult time of year or when the weather is bad, means a good price. On other days, when the catch and the quality are good, prices do not match what is on the market floor. Disappointing for the fishermen, better for the wholesalers, fish merchants and their agents.

At Newlyn it is an early start. First on the market, probably at around 4 a.m., are the graders and sorters, whose job it is to sort each boat's catch and line it up for the sale. Boats can be arriving all night, depending on the tides, and even as we walk around the market that dark, cold, winter morning, other netters are landing their catch. By the time we have finished many of the trawlers and netters have refuelled, topped up their ice stores, and moved off to sea again. This is the harsh reality of what happens when a boat returns from a fishing trip. The netters, dependent on neap tides, have only two weeks of each month to earn their living. So in the winter, if the weather and tides are right and the fish plentiful, it will be a swift turn around between landing, selling and setting out to sea again.

On the other side of the market the road is lined with vans and lorries of various sizes. The big, refrigerated, intercontinental lorries will be taking more

Below: Early-morning landing in Newlyn.
Right: The market at Looe is a more intimate environment than Newlyn, with fewer buyers, all of whom know each other well.

than 70 per cent of the fish straight across the Channel to French, Spanish, Belgian and other high-value western European markets, or supplying the big buyers from up country. Then there are the smaller vehicles of the local merchants and wholesalers – Wing of St Mawes, Fal Fish, Matthew Stevens, major processors and merchants with a range of top-notch customers including some of Britain's best chefs – and the smaller, independent fishmongers.

In Looe, on the south-east Cornish coast, the new market operates differently, using an electronic auction, known as the Moby Clock. Here the fishermen are reluctant to be the first back in on the tide, as the first catch landed is usually sold first, often setting the price for the rest of the day. Here too, when tides dictate a late-night or early-morning landing, the fish is held in cold stores, so the auction floor is clean and empty before the day's business begins. Looe is a much more intimate market, with less sense of urgency, feeling like a club holding a daily meeting rather than one of the country's top fish markets selling £2.3 million of fish a year. To join this club you have to meet certain criteria – a love of fish, the ability to get up early and start work in cold, damp conditions all year round, and being able to simultaneously bid electronically (while appearing supremely disinterested in the lot on offer) and talk on the phone.

Access to either market is a privilege. It is not easy to navigate your way around the wet, slippery floors between the boxes of fish and piles of ice, dodging the

forklift trucks moving rapidly in and out, loading the waiting vehicles. But it is here that you can see how the Cornish fishing industry has been taking steps to boost its reputation for catching some of the best quality fresh fish and shellfish in Britain.

A walk around the market with Robert George, the Quality Adviser for Seafood Cornwall, gives an opportunity to see how fishermen are responding to consumers' growing demands for traceability, freshness, quality, and simply a better product. So more fish is held in slush ice as soon as it is caught; the fish are scored for the way they are washed, gutted and presented, and the boxes are then lined and covered with perforated plastic sheeting, which helps protect the fish from ice burns and improves their overall appearance and presentation. Fish meeting the Seafood Cornwall standards are graded accordingly, helping to give them a price and marketing advantage. After a while your eye becomes tuned into what to look for: megrim sole with an almost glossy finish; perfect red mullet with not a scale missing; fresh cod or haddock with bright pink gills showing; fish without any damage from where it might have been caught in the nets or incautiously removed. Here only the best will do, and the best command the top prices.

Responding to the growing controversy over sustainable fish stocks, UK fishermen are signing up to the Seafish Responsible Fishing Vessel Scheme. Skippers can show that they have caught the fish responsibly, with minimal environmental impact, and that the crew meets given standards for how the fish is caught, handled and stored on board. Two Cornish vessels, Stefan Glinski's *Pride of Cornwall* and the Lakeman family's *Resolute*, took part in an early pilot scheme, and were among the first to be accredited. This brings another marketing advantage, particularly given the supermarkets' new concerns (egged on by some environment groups and non-governmental organizations, or NGOs, which might be accused of having a vested interest) about buying fish from ecologically sustainable sources.

If the fish auctions in Newlyn and Looe are the territory of the wet-fish merchants and the processors, the shellfish sector operates quite separately. Although seen as a relatively niche market, in 2004 shellfish represented more than 30 per cent of the catch landed in Cornwall, worth almost £5 million. Virtually all Cornish shellfish boats supply direct to specialist merchants such as Hawkins Shellfish in Hayle, or W. Harvey & Sons in Newlyn, Cornwall's largest shellfish processor and wholesaler. This family-run business, set up in 1955, not only exports crab, lobster, spider crabs and crawfish, but also processes an increasing amount of the shellfish catch. The Harvey family have their own boats, and also buy from shell fishermen all across the South West. Working in the latest modern, high-tech processing facilities, the business, like others in Cornwall, still insists on the traditional method of hand picking crabs, believing the end product is infinitely superior. Reflecting changing markets and consumer trends, exports are now increasingly sold cooked

Left: A king's ransom in live crawfish in the tanks of shellfish merchants W. Harvey & Sons at Sandy Point, Newlyn.

or processed, instead of being sent abroad alive in vivier tanks filled with temperature-controlled sea water. Few holiday-makers enjoying a plate of *fruits de mer* in France, Spain, Belgium and many other European tourist destinations will know that they are eating shellfish that has been landed and processed in Cornwall.

Newlyn's fish market officially opened in 1908, but in other ports fish continued to be sold out of doors, usually on the slipway or quayside, until the middle of the twentieth century. Now virtually all the pelagic and demersal fish landed in Cornwall passes through either Newlyn or Looe, while most of the shellfish bypasses the markets and goes direct to specialist merchants and processors.

Above: Crabs are hand-picked at W. Harvey & Sons'new unit in the Coombe, Newlyn..
Right: Redevelopment of Newlyn harbour.
Top: After years of discussions, plans to redevelop the harbour were made public in 2006.
Bottom: New pontoons have been installed for the under-10 m boats.

Looe reinvested significantly in its market when it reopened in 1987. The second largest fish market in Cornwall, it has built a reputation for high-quality fish caught by day boats that are usually at sea for less than 24 hours, due to the tidal nature of Looe's harbour. After the fish market was rebuilt, processing units were also constructed in the harbour area to improve the industry's ability to add value to the fish before it leaves the port. The harbour commissioners have an ongoing improvement programme worth around £1 million. Much of the recent investment at both fish markets has been to comply with growing demands for traceability, and to meet the growing slew of new regulations, mostly coming from Europe.

Development and investment is taking place in other Cornish ports and harbours too. Around the county up to £2 million in European and UK government grants has been spent on projects to improve facilities to ensure the industry's future, ranging from ice-making machines and chilled storage, to better lighting, cranes and upgrading facilities on boats. While the most significant investments are in Newlyn and Looe, in ports from St Mary's on the Isles of Scilly to Mevagissey, Polperro and St Ives, smaller-scale developments all suggest an industry trying to move forward with the times and confident about the future, rather than one that is in terminal decline. Even in tiny, remote coves such as Penberth Cove in the far west of Cornwall, an ice-making machine and scales have been installed to improve fish quality. (See 'Ice' panel, page 134.)

In 2005 the Newlyn Fish Industry Forum embarked on a £2 million programme to upgrade the harbour's facilities. Set up in 2002, the Forum recognized the need to find ways to reinvest in the harbour and surrounding facilities in a way that would fit with local community demands, would support and develop the local economy, and would ensure the future of Cornwall's most important fishing port. This included building new pontoons for the small, under-10 m inshore and cove boats, and installing new cold rooms on the fish market so that fish could be landed overnight and kept in optimum conditions. The previous year the market was the first in England to install tracking and grading machinery, which guarantees buyers that they are purchasing a consistent size and grade of fish that is fully traceable. The next stage of the redevelopment plan is to redesign and modernize the fish market; further development in the harbour area will include new processing and retail units, giving processors and merchants direct access to the market. However, there is the small matter of raising the £9 million needed to pay for this.

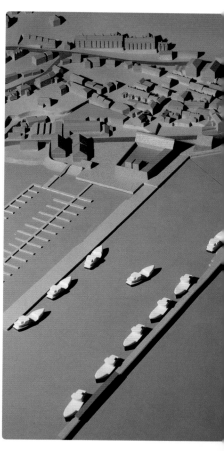

The Newlyn Harbour Commissioners, one of the major partners in the Forum, recognized that without investment for the future, the industry would continue to decline and Newlyn would lose its historic position as England's premier fish market. In 2004 fish and shellfish worth more than £21.4 million were sold through Cornish ports, with Newlyn taking the lion's share, at £15.8 million. This figure does not include fish landed

Ice

Ice has been another key, but often overlooked factor in the development of Cornish fishing. Although ice, initially imported from Norway, was widely used from the mid-nineteenth century, probably the biggest single change in the contemporary Cornish fishing industry has been extending the availability of ice and chilled storage facilities. This has significantly altered fishing practices, helping to improve fish quality and prices.

The establishment of the Gulval ice works, near Penzance, in the 1870s supplemented the daily Norwegian shipments and enabled fishermen, particularly on the steam trawlers and bigger boats, to sail greater distances and stay at sea longer. By 1893 ice was also supplied by the Newlyn Ice & Trading Co., and R.R. Bath, a Devon fisherman who first imported Norwegian ice and later established the Newlyn ice works, now owned by W. Stevenson & Sons. Ice was also used to preserve fish sold in towns and villages further inland. More importantly, for fish sent to other markets first by boat and later by train, it was crucial for improving quality and freshness. From the last decades of the nineteenth century the combination of ice and rail access to the rest of England opened up markets for Cornish-landed fish, including fish caught by Brixham, Plymouth and foreign boats, and set off the industry's expansion up until the First World War.

Since the Second World War almost all the ice in Newlyn and West Cornwall has been provided by either W. Stevenson & Sons or the Cornish Ice Company, which was set up in the 1990s as a fishermen's co-operative to meet the growing demand for greater volumes of ice, particularly during the summer months. In recent years there has been a considerable upsurge in the volume needed, and investment in new county-wide facilities to meet this demand. Ports and harbours around the county, from Looe and St Ives to tiny coves and smaller harbours such as Sennen, Port Isaac and Polperro, have installed their own ice-making and chilled storage facilities. Day boats and small inshore boats also take ice or slush ice to sea with them, as trials have shown that rapidly cooling the fish as soon as it is caught significantly improves shelf life, appearance and keeping qualities. This drive for quality means that hundreds of tonnes of ice are used on board the trawlers and netters that spend longer periods at sea, and even more is used at the fish markets for packing and repacking fish.

by foreign vessels (a further £1.1 million), or fish caught by Cornish boats and sold in foreign ports. Small beer, perhaps, compared with the £513 million total landed by all UK fishing vessels that year, but still making a significant contribution to the Cornish economy, while the social and cultural importance of fishing are vital, yet impossible to measure. Research shows that across the county at least 4,000 jobs rely on the Cornish seafood industry. Every boat lost to Cornish fishing is a marker of the slow decline since the mid-1990s that needs to be arrested. Newlyn may be in a prime position to access some of the richest fishing grounds in the English Channel, the Western Approaches and the Celtic Sea, but without the best on-shore facilities more fishing vessels will choose to land their fish in France or Spain. For Newlyn to thrive it needs to expand and modernize, and onshore businesses will thrive with it. Economic arguments suggest that for every man fishing there are at least four jobs onshore – in processing, merchanting, transport, support facilities such as fuel and chandlery, and so on. At least 750 jobs in Newlyn rely on

a healthy fishing industry and boats landing fish to sell through the town's fish auction six days a week.

Although much of that seafood is exported, an increasing amount is first processed in Cornwall. Since the mid-1980s there has been considerable investment by wholesalers, processors and merchants, creating jobs and wealth by adding more value to more of the fish and shellfish before it leaves the county. Processing fish has changed beyond recognition from the days when salting, smoking or drying fish were the only ways of preserving it. Fish processing in the twenty-first century means cleaning, filleting and preparing fresh fish, often into ready-to-use, conveniently sized portions, or even premium products such as fish cakes, cooked and dressed shellfish, or marinated fish ready to be barbecued, making cooking seafood as easy as possible for the cash-rich, time-poor cook to use. Other companies have built up a lucrative trade supplying the catering sector with fish that is filleted, scaled and ready to be cooked – a cost-effective and labour-saving option for hotels, pubs and restaurants.

Further up the county are companies such as Ocean Fish and Fal Fish, processing for and supplying the supermarkets. The multiples are still the major outlet on the domestic market for fresh fish, responsible for about 87 per cent of UK seafood sales. Fal Fish is probably the largest single fish-processing business in Cornwall, processing around 60 tonnes of fish and shellfish a week. This innovative and award-winning business is constantly looking for new ways of adding value and making fish more accessible and attractive to a range of customers. It also seeks to improve sustainability and traceability: waste fish is sold on to be processed into fish-meal, and new ways are sought to raise the profile of less popular fish from non-pressure stocks.

Top: Alec Stevens filling boxes with ice from the ice store in the fish room of the trawler *Crystal Sea*.
Above: Ice is as important as fuel and food, helping to improve the quality of catches.

Robert George
Former skipper,
Quality Adviser, Seafood Cornwall

Robert George: I fished all my life. I had quite a big boat with eight crew, and we actually produced a very high-quality fish, but I could do that because I had a lot of men and that was the whole point, catching quite a lot of fish and handling them well. So I had, or my crew had, a reputation for actually producing this sort of quality, so I was invited along to Seafood Cornwall, as a sort of adviser because I'd sold the boat and retired. Obviously for the fish that are caught, you are trying to make as much money as possible, that's really the idea. You've got a limited resource, so let's make Cornwall get the most out of it.

So you start from the fishing side and say, 'At least when it reaches the quay it must be in as good a condition as it possibly can be.' And then you look at the market the same way, and then the merchants and so on. The [Seafood Cornwall] committee in their wisdom thought that that was the best way to look at it – to actually start with the fishermen, rather than start anywhere else. You see there's Seafood Cornwall and there's Seafood Scotland and Seafood Northern Ireland, and Seafood Northern Ireland is just merchants, there are no fishermen in it at all. Seafood Scotland is sort of where we are. Anyway, that's how I came into it really.

And what's been encouraging is how the fishermen, the skippers especially and mates of the boats, have really taken it on. I think if they'd advertised nationally and got someone quite well qualified with a degree or whatever, in fisheries or something, and they'd come in, I don't think you could have started the same.

Quality Adviser, I think they call me. What do I do? To start with, I said I wanted to have a look at Seafood Scotland, and see what they'd done. And then I had a chat with all the buyers and said, 'What are the problems generally with the product you are getting?' And then I looked at it, and I thought the two things that initially we should look at were mackerel, because they are a thing that the small boats depend on, and are a fish that deteriorate rapidly. You want a very fresh mackerel that is looked after very well, it's not the kind of thing you can really mistreat. So it was mackerel really with the small boats, and with the bigger boats, the biggest, it's all about the quotas.

Probably one of the biggest assets Cornwall has is the quota on megrim sole. The quota's built up over the years because there was a bigger fleet than there is now and they were catching more, so they've got a quota of megrims that they probably won't be able to catch, or just about, which means they can really go at it and all they need to do is make sure the quality is right.

As you know, the megrims are actually the softest of the flat fish, and looking at it from the point of view that it was a fantastic resource, and it was something that we ought to make sure that we could increase or get the maximum value for, if you actually got the quality of *that* right, you could forget the rest because they were bound to be OK. Dover sole and lemon sole and plaice are quite firm fish relative to megrim, so I've just assumed they'll follow suit. So what I've concentrated on with all the beam trawlers is getting them looking after the fish so that the megrims are coming out well. I haven't really looked at the rest at all.

There's a thing called the Torry score. It's Torry in Aberdeen – the research station for sea fish was there, the White Fish Authority I think it was then. And they developed all sorts of things at the Torry: after the War [1939–45], quite a lot of money was spent in trying to promote fish and developing fisheries, and they produced this score sheet that actually looks at fishes' eyes, gills, how well they're gutted, how well they're washed, how firm the flesh is, and it's done on a nought to five basic scale. So I looked at megrims to start with, and went out with a score sheet with the boats. And we did it for three or four months, and to say that a fish was in good condition we reckon that it had to reach a score of 85 per cent of the maximum, and if they reached a score of 85 per cent or better over a period of say about two or three months, then we would give them a book of labels that they could actually put with their fish and say, 'This fish reaches the required standard.' And I thought nobody's going to be really interested, but actually it has become quite a competition, it's quite good, and you know quite hard-bitten guys, I know 'em well, it's quite surprising and they come along and say, 'What's my score this week?'.

> ❝ *What's been encouraging is how the fishermen, the skippers especially and mates of the boats, have really taken it on. It has become quite a competition and they come along and say, 'What's my score this week?'* ❞

And then with the small boats we've looked at these insulated bins, so hopefully the small boats are going to use those for the mackerel.

Price benefit on megrim market? Very difficult to prove. The megrim market has improved so much this year, the general price has absolutely jumped this year, dramatically, so I *could* just go along and tell all the buyers it's because of Seafood Cornwall, but I don't honestly think we could claim that. I think it's only because the boats are working harder at it. I don't think you could pick one boat and say, 'His fish are always best, his always make the most money,' I think by most boats coming on board with it that the actual overall price has improved.

It's the same with the handline-caught bass. You couldn't always go on the market and say the ones with the tags are making it, but the publicity and whole idea has brought handline-caught bass right up. There's been other years that the handline boys have moaned that the ones caught in nets were making just as much money. Well there is quite a dramatic difference: one day during the last week the handline bass were £6.20 a kilo, and the net bass were £3.80. It's very encouraging, and I think it's a brilliant scheme.

I was brought up in Penberth; I started with a 14 ft boat and then a 16 ft boat. When I got married first I had a 16 ft boat, and then I had a crabber built that was 30 ft, and I worked from Newlyn. I sold that, and I had a 45 ft boat which I worked with nets catching monkfish and crawfish, mostly around the Scillies. I had that for quite a few years, then I bought a seine-netter, decided it was a good idea, which nearly bankrupted me! It was a fly seine, it's never really been done here at all, and I fancied it because I thought it sounded like a great idea. With a seine net you catch all the flat fish, all the fish on the bottom, demersal fish, the same as a trawl. I bought a 65 ft boat and had a go at it, with a certain amount of success. I had it three years, and then I went into this boat which was 27 m or whatever it was, 85 ft, a much bigger boat, a steel boat. And we struggled to make it pay for quite a while, but then we did eventually get it working. I was chasing hake really in the deep water south of Ireland, west of Ireland, it was basically in the 60- to 100-fathom line, eight-day trips from Galway down to the west of the Scillies.

Early-morning landing in Looe.

We had eight, no six years, then we went in the North Sea for six years fishing from Aberdeen, for November, December, January, February to March, out on the Bergen and round the Shetlands, which was silly, but it was a necessity. Sometimes it was dreadful, just dreadful. My crew hated it, but it was the time of year that if you could actually go and if you can cover those three, four, five months then you could actually make things pay rather than struggle along and not make it pay. So we'd leave here beginning of November, then we'd fish two or three trips and come home for Christmas. Then we'd do two long nine–ten day trips, back to back, and we'd just sort of land, go away next day, then come home for a week. We did that for six years, but we had an accident in Shetland, and we had one of the crew killed – that was that, we came home. We were in sheltering from bad weather and he got hit by a car, which is about as unlucky as you can get. I thought this is just not meant to be. But it was an interesting time.

One of the things that worries me is the Cornish beam-trawl fleet, because this megrim quota that we're talking about, which is a huge part of the Cornish catch, I don't think it could be caught without beam trawlers, which for Cornwall is quite a worry. I have great doubts that you will see beam trawlers here in a few years' time. The fuel cost is just ridiculous. The boat I had, you could draw a good comparison, because we weren't using much fuel, we were doing a ten-day trip for 3,000 gallons, which is a lot of fuel, but when you look at the beam trawlers there are several burning 1,000 gallons plus a day.

It's always been that fishermen have looked on the fishing that it will become unviable before it becomes a danger to the fish. Fishermen have always thought that, and it's always been that fisheries have come and gone. It's become uneconomical and they've moved on to something else. That's always been the way that fishing has progressed. But I'm not sure that it's quite the same any more, because in the fishing season you can change from one job to another quickly.

Future of stocks? I don't quite understand what's happening with the reduction in the fleet, because there was a drastic reduction in the fleet over the last 15 years, I'm sure a lot of the fish stocks are healthier than we're given … the fishermen think they are anyway. I can't see that you could keep reducing quotas; I think it's got to the stage where the actual catching ability of the fleet is probably control enough, so many boats have come out.

There is definitely a question of safety, no doubt about that. The boats that are left are working harder and harder. Boats have always worked hard, but in good times everyone makes a living and then as things get worse, the ones that are left are the ones that are efficient and work hard, that's the name of the game.

Megrim soles landed at Newlyn market.

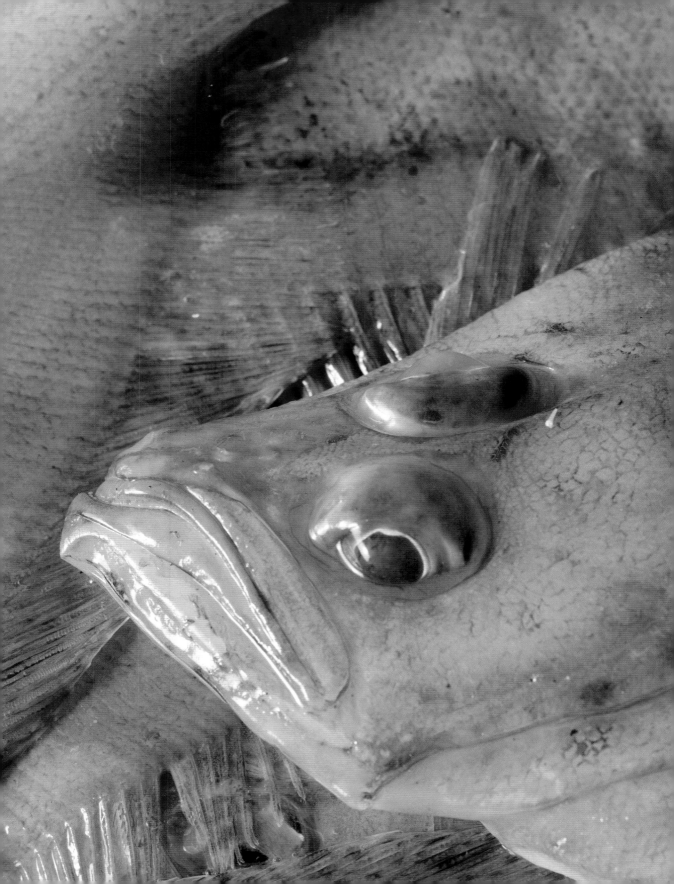

Mark Greet
Managing Director, Fal Fish, Redruth

Falmouth Fishselling Company Ltd. is Cornwall's largest fish processor.

Mark Greet: My father started the company in the late '70s with the Taits brothers from Fraserburgh, a very famous fishing family who are pelagic mackerel and herring fishermen. There was a very large fishery, based mainly in Falmouth and Plymouth from the late '70s through to the mid-'80s, where many of the Scottish pelagic trawlers and purse seiners came to this part of the world to target mackerel. My father came up with the concept of Falmouth Fish Selling and put it to the Taits brothers, to set up an independent, integrated, marketing and catching organization. The vast majority of the processing at that stage was through Klondike methods of freezing at sea, through factory ships. Fal Fish's role was really to negotiate, to organize the logistics, to get the freezing capacity here for the various fleets mainly from Romania, the former East Germany and various other parts of that Eastern bloc area. So that's really how Fal Fish organized it to make sure there was enough freezing capacity to take the catch, clearly because Cornwall at that time did not really have enough capacity shoreside.

So Fal Fish started off with those roots, then expanded from just having pelagic interests to general white fish as well, which was more of an all-year round activity, whereas pelagic fishing has slightly shorter seasons and off-seasons. So we developed first of all from Falmouth docks, with the local fishing boats, the St Mawes boats, Flushing and Falmouth boats fishing for us. Then we developed into Mevagissey, and then we actually put a processing unit at Newlyn in about 1980–81.

In my pre-college days I worked for Fal Fish for a couple of years. I worked at Falmouth and I also ran the depot at Mevagissey in about 1980, '81–'82. And then I went to college and went into the supermarkets as a buyer and as a product manager. I worked for the Co-op in Manchester in the food division, buying, and then I worked for Somerfield after that, and then I came back into the business in '95. The whole thing had changed considerably over those years. The white fish and locally caught fish-processing side had grown quite a bit, as had Fal Fish in general. In 1998 my father and I bought the company back from the Taits and specialized it as just a South West-owned company, rather than having the Scottish-side interests as well.

Since 1998 we've been an independently owned company, we've focused completely on locally caught fish, looking at as many diverse ways of entering into the fisheries as we could, shellfish as well as white fish and pelagic fish, and then trying to find the very best markets we possibly could for those species. We've focused on primary processing and secondary processing in terms of freezing products, and filleting and portioning products. And we've really focused on the supermarket area, traditional wholesalers and food services. We're about 60 per cent export and 40 per cent UK.

The thing that's really transformed our business is not only being reliant on fresh fish, we have diversified into scallops. We've developed markets for frozen scallops as well, so it's enabled us to take the whole catch from vessels, and keep the continuity of buying on windy days and nice days all around the year, which is what fishermen require. They require to be paid the correct price and to know that their processor is able to take the fish and not just say, 'Oh, sorry, I'm full up with that stuff this week, I can't take it,' but to keep working with the boats. You cannot do that by just operating the fresh market, you have to consider freezing for that. I know it's a fairly simple thing, and it's been adopted in Scotland for many years, but the South West has never really had the investment infrastructure to be able to do that, or if it had done it had died out on an old wave of companies, and it hasn't really been reintroduced until more recently.

The new facility we have here, we bought it in July 2003, now it's 2006 – what's that, two and a half years, time flies. This new facility is really well connected by road and to all the ports, and the fact is that we've got the kind of volumetrics that we have to keep consistently fed now, so that means we are 90 per cent South West in terms of sourcing, but we are increasingly sourcing from elsewhere as well, Europe and the UK. Diversity is the key to it, I think. We haven't just specialized in one area, we've tried to operate with about 40 plus species, which we are lucky with in this area; we have got the diversity of species, we haven't got the quota issues by and large that affect the North Sea. We also have all the raw material advantages in terms of quality and freshness, a smaller fleet, and a fleet that tends to fish much shorter trips – day-boat trips by and large.

There's a team of about 80 people within Fal Fish, and we all have different parts to play in the business. My day typically doesn't start as early as some of the sales team, but I start at about say 6 a.m., when I start to take telephone calls and be involved, and that's because of the start time of the various fish markets. Because of the various customers we've got, and dispatch times, this plant is a 24/7 operation, and fishing doesn't respect weekends or bank holidays. Why should it? It's about getting a natural resource. So, yes, the hours are notoriously long in fishing, and we keep hoping we can find ways to make more of a quality life for our staff, but the truth is that we have elastic days. Some days are very, very long – can be six in the morning or earlier – until seven or eight in the evening, unfortunately. But when there is not so much fish about we can have quieter days as well, so you hope there's some kind of balance to be struck.

> " *We really are the last part of England that has a fleet, in terms of bulk fleets, Brixham, Newlyn, Looe, Plymouth, those are the last bastions in England.* "

My time working away has proved to be a huge advantage. It wasn't the game plan I sort of engineered, but it's been fortuitous to work that way and to have that perspective. I'm not sure of the latest figures, but supermarkets must buy more than 80 per cent of retail fish. And, of course, the other very important area is food service. Luckily, regionality is becoming a more important thing in vogue now, so the Cornishness of a product, for example, becomes a good selling point; and Cornish lemon soles or Cornish scallops, line-caught bass, various things which are of a premium nature really do help to market the product and endear us to the consumer. People are worried about the provenance of foods now, that's where we really can score quite highly. Things like Cornish lemon sole or MSC [Marine Stewardship Council] mackerel, which is something we're supporters of and have been since its inception. People can understand that is a sustainably caught mackerel, and should be very fresh and full of quality.

Processed scallops, packed and ready for export at Fal Fish.

The public are becoming increasingly conscious about where their seafood is sourced from, and by what method. Cornish seafood with its well-managed fisheries, abundant and diverse supplies has a real strength and future opportunity to explain this to our customers.

A main objective of Fal Fish is to promote this region's responsibly managed fisheries. Cornwall has a significant amount of line-caught species, non-quota species which are in abundance, and day boats and inshore trawlers predominate. The profile of the Cornish fleet is about smaller fishing vessels which make a low environmental impact.

The great thing is that you have got this wide range of fish available. You've got sardines and mackerel and other pelagic fish, other white fish which are very affordable, and then at the other end there are hake, monk and Dover sole, and then there are mid-range fish like sea bass and other fish. It depends what you fancy to eat, and it's got the health qualities and all the rest of it which make it a real treat.

There is a lot more information in the public domain about sustainability, and about various environmental issues, and I do think there is a skewed media portrayal of these things, and the doom and gloom thing; the fact is that they print an over-simplistic national picture, when the South West is quite a different area and has its own characteristics. We're in a very, very fortunate position. We can't say that everything is all rosy, but on the other hand there are a lot of pluses in this area. The key issues are the fact that you've got diversity; you have got good supplies; most of the species caught down here are not pressure stocks, and you have a fleet which, by and large, is low-impact in terms of environmental impacts. The only thing I'm concerned about is in certain sectors it would be nice to see some new renewal of fleet. There are new builds happening at the moment: there are two in Falmouth, for example, on the scallop side, and you're seeing some really nice new netters in Padstow, and also at Newlyn – the *Silver Dawn* and various boats. But it would be nice to see more of that, it just gives that new life-blood coming in.

We really are the last part of the world in England that has a fleet. If you look at it, Lowestoft doesn't any more. There are some little fleets around the ports, Newhaven and various other areas, but in terms of bulk fleets, Brixham, Newlyn, Looe, Plymouth, those are the last bastions in England, aren't they?

I think that everything comes right when there's a profitable industry. People are drawn in if the rewards are there and the crews can earn the money. The profitability of the industry can be there, and it is there in good measure in many sectors around the South West. I think it's got quite a bright future, and I think this point about the younger generation, they will be drawn in, there will be people coming into it as always, who are attracted to fishing and the sea. Fishing has been a little bit in the doldrums in the '90s, and although people have still made good livings out of it, the portrayal of it externally has been a turn-off for younger people.

I am confident and optimistic about the future, but not unrealistically so. I think there are various unknowns, but in general terms, having been away from the industry and in 1979–80 hearing fishermen say, 'Oh, there's not much fish out there,' probably people are still saying that, 30 years later. You're bound to have that kind of message coming through occasionally. The industry is terrible for gossip, it's terrible for rumours, and sometimes they circulate around and everybody takes a gloomy message out of it. But generally speaking we're pretty confident as a business, and you've got to be, I think. We're not here for the short term, we're here for the long term.

The business works because it's in Cornwall. It also only works because of the confidence and trading relationships we have with the fishing fleet, individual owners, crews and skippers. Apart from the buying skills of the staff on all the fish markets; apart from all the hard work by the team to get the job done at a very high quality, it's really having a very strong amount of trust and confidence with the fishing fleet.

Fal Fish processes tonnes of scallops and white fish each week.

8 More Than Just Fish and Chips

'There are warnings of gales in Humber, Thames, Dover, Wight, Port-land, Plymouth, Biscay, Fitzroy, Sole, Lundy, Fastnet, Irish Sea, Shannon, Faeroes and southeast Iceland … . Plymouth, Biscay, Fitzroy, Sole southwest veering west 6 to gale 8, occasionally severe gale 9, but 4 or 5 in south Biscay and south Fitzroy. Rain then showers. Moderate or poor becoming good…'

The shipping forecast is the life-blood of any fisherman's day, the most important information on which key decisions will be made. With a forecast like this, which was for Friday 19 May 2006, you can be certain that the harbours in Looe, Mevagissey, Polperro, Falmouth, Porthleven, Newlyn, St Ives, Newquay and Padstow will be full of boats. Any larger vessels still at sea after several days of poor weather will be running for home or the nearest shelter, as soon as possible. This is a reminder of why fishing is the most dangerous peacetime occupation in the world, driven by so many factors over which fishermen have little or no control. Yet despite the vagaries of weather, tides and political imperatives; despite the relentless downsizing of the industry over recent years, there are many signs that perhaps the Cornish fishing industry has turned a corner. While fishermen say that there has always been the ability to make money in good times, the remaining businesses are those that are smart enough to understand how to get through the bad times and turn events to their advantage. At sea and onshore, there is a real willingness to look beyond the simple economics of supply and demand, and to respond to consumer demands. This means raising the image and profile of Cornish seafood, making it easy to find, guaranteeing its quality, freshness and provenance, and making it convenient and easy to cook. By responding in this way, Cornish fish businesses at all levels are setting a benchmark that others can follow.

Right: Mystique II, one of the newest catamarans built to catch mackerel using handlines. Running three lines, and with four crew members, this trip landed 73 boxes of fish – a season's best.

From the top: Gurnard, spider crab and monkfish. *Right:* We prefer fish and chips.

Despite the fact that we are an island race, surrounded by the sea, and that in Cornwall the sense of the sea is what gives the county its unique identity, the British are among the lowest consumers of fish in Europe. According to the EU, we each eat a measly average of 20 kg of fish per year. In the league table of member states before the Eastern European countries joined, Britain languished fourth from the bottom, hardly figuring compared with the Spanish, at 44.4 kg per head, and the Portuguese who were way ahead at 61 kg per person per year. The irony of this is that much of the fish they eat is fish exported from Cornwall. Next time you eat calamares or paella in either of these countries, this will probably not be locally caught or landed but Cornish squid or seafood, although there is never any acknowledgement of its real provenance.

So how do the British prefer to eat their fish? As fish and chips (see panel, page 151). According to Seafish, more fish is eaten out of the home in fish and chip shops than in pubs, hotels and restaurants. Britain's 11,500 fish and chip shops sold more than 250 million portions of fish and chips in 2005. Here is the ultimate irony. In an age when a growing number of consumers are concerned about the quality and origins of what they eat, when Britain still has a relative abundance of this last truly wild source of food, the first fish choice of millions uses imported, often frozen, cod or haddock. Meanwhile the majority of the diverse range of high-quality seafood caught by Cornish boats is exported to a far more discerning consumer base.

Thanks to the influence of Rick Stein, the growing band of television chefs and a seemingly endless procession of new food programmes and magazines, more opportunities for foreign travel and new trends such as sushi and sashimi bars, the British are becoming more adventurous in their seafood tastes. The range of fish and shellfish on sale in Cornish fish markets and fishmongers tells an interesting tale. Monkfish, now a high-value catch, was once almost a discard, then used for the ubiquitous, battered 'scampi' that was one of the high spots of 1970s cuisine or, by the less scrupulous, as a substitute for lobster tail meat. Its change of fortune probably owes a lot to its meaty texture and lack of bones. Gurnard, which was once used for bait, now commands premium prices. Spider crab, which is eaten with enthusiasm in Mediterranean countries, is virtually overlooked in this country, apart from by its handful of dedicated fans who relish its sweet white meat and intense flavour.

At the top end of the fine-dining spectrum, Rick Stein has raised the profile of Cornish fish to the highest culinary levels, and has worked hard to persuade his well-heeled clients to explore the less popular fish caught in Cornish waters. Stein's influence on consumer attitudes, and the rise of specialist fish restaurants in the last decade are universally acknowledged. Nowhere is this clearer than in Cornwall where more and more chefs are recognizing the quality of the seafood that is landed just yards away from their kitchens. Even in non-specialist restaurants, the high proportion of fish dishes featuring on specials menus and as dishes of the day, shows how attitudes to fish are changing. This is helped by fishermen such as Chris Bean, who have realized that by developing a speciality niche market, selling top-quality fish direct to local chefs on the same day that it is landed, they can give chefs and their customers some of the best seafood they will ever experience.

Despite our enthusiasm for seafood when someone else is cooking it, for too many consumers fish still falls into the 'difficult' food category, being apparently time-consuming and difficult to prepare – all that gutting, scaling, filleting and skinning. It is hard to get excited about something on a fish counter that smells less than fragrant and looks stale. Let us debunk these myths immediately. The freshest fish should smell of nothing but the sea, and if it looks tired and dull, don't buy it. Fish is perceived as bony, and therefore difficult to eat – a view that has been encouraged by decades of fish fingers and chunks of reconstituted fish masquerading as fish ready-meals, and by the deskilling of cooking by the supermarkets. Jack Turner, father of Newlyn fish merchant Robin Turner, understands the effect of changing consumer attitudes, particularly on what was once one of the mainstays of Cornish fishing, the herring:

Fish and chips

The first British fish and chip shops appeared in the 1850s, selling fried cod or flat fish with bread or baked potatoes. It took another 20 years for chips to migrate across the English Channel from France, setting the trend of a complete meal that was an instant hit with the working-class poor in London and northern industrial towns. It was the start of the British love affair with fish and chips, and a significant increase in the amount of fish eaten in Britain. It is debatable whether this became as popular in Cornwall at the time, given that from the 1860s most of the fish was transported out of the county by rail, depriving Cornish working people of a relatively cheap food. Fish and chips relied on white fish such as cod, haddock or huss, whereas the Cornish fishery still concentrated on mackerel, pilchards and herring. Perhaps more important, Cornwall already had its own complete meal in the Cornish pasty.

As a result of the crisis facing British cod stocks, particularly in the North Sea, many Cornish fish and chip shop owners are offering a wider variety of fish species in an attempt to wean consumers off cod and on to other equally tasty, but more affordable non-pressure stocks, such as pollack, ling or coley. Jewell's in Newlyn, just yards from the fish market, offers anything from lemon sole to John Dory, pollack or whiting. In Padstow, Rick Stein's fish and chip shop sells battered monkfish tails, ray and haddock, or griddled fish such as tuna or mackerel, according to seasonal availability. Further north, customers in Yorkshire and Humberside prefer haddock, while everywhere else cod remains supreme. Given the state of North Sea cod stocks, it is not surprising that most of the battered and deep-fried cod and haddock eaten this way are imported from countries such as Iceland or Norway, but it seems perverse, given the range of other suitable white fish with similar firm flesh and texture that is caught around the British coastline.

'Purely and simply people don't want to buy fish with bones in, and herrings are very, very bony, and they don't know how to eat them. They don't eat kippers any more, you'll get the odd person they'll have the one kipper once a year, well we used to sell hundreds of boxes, now I don't sell one box of smoked in one week. ... It's the supermarkets basically, presenting stuff that's easy to cook, easy to deal with and it's robbed the fishing industry of its heart.'

Jack Turner's observations on the convenience element of fish are a true reflection of what our time-poor, cash-rich society wants its fish to be. However, if the Cornish kipper has fallen out of fashion, other smoked fish have become popular as one of the easiest ways to eat fish without any effort. It was the 1970s mackerel boom that kick-started the vogue for smoked mackerel, followed by the development of a number of artisan fish smokers looking for other fish to smoke. Cornwall has a well-developed, specialist smoked fish industry that sells a large range of products, most using only locally landed fish and traditional cures, often extending beyond fish to meat, poultry, game, and even cheese. Fish merchants and wholesalers still have their own smokers, and smoke fish to order or as and when needed.

The best way to buy fresh seafood is from Britain's diminishing band of dedicated, independent fishmongers. Cornish fish counters can be dazzling displays of a wide range of the freshest fish and shellfish. Fishmongers play a vital role in encouraging us to eat more seafood, providing a specialist and personal service, always happy to prepare fish to their customers' exact specifications. Knowing when, where and often by whom their products were caught, this is the best guarantee of the fish's provenance. Guilt-free fish. The result is that their customers can take home a piece of the freshest Cornish fish, landed within the last 24 hours, which requires short, swift cooking, perfect to meet the modern criteria of a nutritious meal that can be ready to eat within less than 20 minutes, and is packed with health benefits (see panel). The best, which include John Strike's Quayside Fish in Porthleven, Fowey Fish, Trelawney Fish in Newlyn, and Pengelly's in Looe, not only sell fish from their own or local boats, but also offer a service that includes filleting, boning and vacuum packing, recipes and any additional ingredients you might need.

While Cornwall is blessed with a higher number of fishmongers per capita than many parts of the country, distance from the market or a good fishmonger should be no barrier to the rest of us getting the best quality fish and shellfish. A number of dedicated online services, such as Martin's Seafresh or Cornish Fish Direct, together with fish merchants, fishmongers and wholesalers, have spotted the steady growth in mail-order and online sales, providing the ultimate solution to getting Cornish seafood delivered overnight to your door.

More and more businesses are selling clearly branded Cornish fish and shellfish, with the most enterprising fish merchants, processors and retailers consistently finding new ways of making fresh fish even simpler to use. These include relative newcomers such as Jefferson's Seafoods in Looe, who make top-quality products – fish cakes, fish salads, and ready-to-cook or ready-to-eat fish fillets. Peter Grosvenor, the man behind this enlightened business, has also recognized the need to capture the next generation of seafood-eaters, so offers fish ready-meals

Health benefits

One of the strongest arguments in favour of eating more fish is the acknowledged health benefits of both oily fish, such as herring, sardines and mackerel, and white fish, both round and flat fish. Oily fish are acknowledged as a rich source of omega 3 oils, which bring a large number of specific health benefits. These polyunsaturated oils contain essential fatty acids, and are much more beneficial than the harder, saturated fats and oils found in meat. All kinds of fish are low in fat, and provide a good source of protein, vitamins and minerals, particularly vitamins A, B12 and D, iron, iodine and selenium. Regular consumption of oily fish is recommended for its health-giving properties, and the Food Standards Agency recommends eating at least two portions of fish a week, one of which should be from the oil-rich species.

Left, from top: John Strike's new premises in Porthleven – John is considered one of the best fishmongers in Cornwall. The harbour in Porthleven.
Above: Tony Howes of Newlyn Fish Co. delivers fish to outlying farms and homes in West Cornwall.

for children. Unlike the mass-produced version, his fish nuggets shun the concept of using reformed fish from fish off-cuts, and use fresh fish fillets landed that morning a few yards away in Looe's fish market. His target market is metropolitan customers disillusioned with the supermarket offering, and upmarket shops such as Fresh & Wild.

The same is happening with shellfish. The innovative business Scilly Shellfish, for example, has recognized that its customers are willing to pay a fair price for crab and lobsters caught by Mark Pender in the clear waters around the Scillies, then cooked and prepared before being despatched by overnight carrier. W. Harvey & Sons in Newlyn sells a growing range of pre-packed shellfish products that require little more than opening and serving, ranging from packs of prepared crabmeat to freshly cooked and dressed spider crabs, crabs and lobsters.

In the past perhaps fresh fish and shellfish's most important quality – wild and not interfered with by man – has indirectly been one of the greatest obstacles to marketing Cornish seafood, because of its lack of identity in terms of a single producer, or in this case a boat, skipper and crew. The well-informed consumer increasingly wants to know where that fish has come from, and how it was caught. A growing number of fishermen have spotted the opportunities offered by selling quality, fresh fish, which is traceable, and clearly branded Cornish. Handline-caught mackerel, sea bass and pollack are three prime examples of what can be achieved. Consumers feel comfortable with knowing exactly what they are buying, that it comes from sustainable stocks, fished in a manner that has minimal environmental impact, and that their purchase is supporting remote coastal communities in the far South West. All good plus points, all good perceived values that they are willing to pay for.

In 2001 members of the South West Handline Fishermen's Association (SWHFA) were among the first UK fisheries to gain accreditation for the MSC handline mackerel scheme. Mackerel carrying the MSC mark is guaranteed to have been caught in South West waters, inside the South West Mackerel Box, using this unique, traditional fishing method. More recently, the SWHFA has introduced tagging schemes for line-caught sea bass and pollack, clearly identifying these fish as line-caught in Cornish waters. Visitors to the SWHFA's website (www.linecaught.org.uk) can match the tag numbers with the fisherman and his boat.

Dave Bond, chairman of the SWHFA, is certain that these have all contributed to 'a definite improvement' in prices for these fish. He is another shining example of a fisherman who is confident about his future, and has recognized that the way forward is driven by the concept of sustainability. He recently invested more than £150,000 in a new catamaran, *Mystique II*, which he uses for a mix of netting and handline fishing, or taking out parties of anglers, according to the time of year. The benefits of his new boat are that it provides an efficient and more sustainable way of fishing:

> 'The netters in the channel can catch 200 stone of pollack, whereas we're catching 100 stone. They're leaving at four in the morning, they're steaming all over the ocean, burning god knows how much diesel, and getting in at midnight. Whereas we're going out at six in the morning and we're back in by one, and we've still done a day's work, not as much as them but it's still a day's work.'

A handful of fishermen have developed alternative new markets for themselves. Cornish sardines are a classic example, where the small number of dedicated boats sell direct to merchants, and the fish are clearly identified as Cornish in major retail outlets such as Waitrose and Marks & Spencer. The boats catch to order, knowing what the market needs and matching supply with demand. A growing number

Above: Dave Bond and his crew rapidly landing line-caught mackerel on board *Mystique II.*

of new partnerships between wholesalers and retailers are extending the range of other fish and seafood products branded to distinguish them as Cornish.

The marketing drive for quality fish and seafood has been led by Seafood Cornwall, which has become a regular presence at consumer and industry events, while also working with fishermen, fish merchants, processors and retailers. Seafood Cornwall's mission statement encompasses all fish and seafood-related companies and organizations in Cornwall and the Isles of Scilly, and talks of 'improving competitive performance, increasing sales and improving margins' and, above all else, focuses on one word – quality. As we have seen in earlier chapters, this includes working with vessel-owners to improve the standards and quality of the catch, and continuing right through the supply chain with the markets, processors and merchants. Then there are consumer campaigns to raise awareness of the diversity, abundance and quality of fish found off the Cornish coast, and to create a national and international presence for quality seafood from Cornwall.

David Stevens junior, skipper of the *Crystal Sea*, recognizes the benefits Seafood Cornwall has already brought:

'It has helped us as fishermen to understand the market better and why prices go down and the need for marketing. It makes us more efficient, we can change our practices but understand much better why we need to do this. We're landing every two or three days, and we fish to a particular market. The beam trawlers have vastly improved their quality so we've had to up our game as well.'

Seafood Cornwall also works with larger processors, recognizing the range of markets for the right Cornish product, marketed correctly, which brings us to the supermarkets, the dominant players in the retail market. The multiple retailers account for 87 per cent of sales of seafood each year, and although many have introduced wet fish counters, most of the fish they sell is either pre-prepared or frozen, and much of that is imported. While it is admirable that these corporate businesses are starting to take the issues of overfishing and over-exploited fish stocks seriously, their solutions raise other issues. Too often the supermarkets are influenced by green lobby groups, which leads to a situation in which the retailers unjustifiably de-list ray, and recommend that their customers buy imported hoki from New Zealand instead of monkfish from Newlyn. That monkfish will have been caught within quota limits, and will have provided income for not just the boat and crew involved but also the auctioneers, fish market operatives, fish merchants, processors and transport companies before arriving on the supermarket fish counter. The hoki, apart from being in danger of becoming an over-exploited species, raises other issues of food miles, sustainability, and the long-term impact of the supermarkets' buying and transport policies.

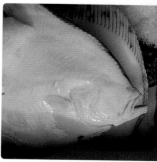

The four most consumed fish in Britain are salmon, cod, haddock and prawns. The UK exports £881 million of fish and processed fish a year, and imports seafood worth £1.47 billion. Surely there is scope for more locally caught and landed fish to be sold by the supermarkets, particularly now that these companies have acknowledged the need to improve their corporate environmental image?

From the top: John Dory, turbot and lobster.

One of the benefits of the range of fish and shellfish landed in Cornwall is that there are species at all prices to suit all pockets. Pelagic fish such as sardines and mackerel are still relatively inexpensive, and crab is probably the cheapest shellfish; there are mid-range priced fish such as John Dory and sea bass, while the most expensive, luxury items include cod, turbot and lobster. All consumers and purchasers of fish need to understand that with less abundant stocks worldwide, and some species in short supply, seafood is becoming more of a luxury product. For fishermen, high prices are there for the taking, and a growing number of consumers are increasingly willing to pay for good quality – for the freshest, best fish.

Jackie Provost and
Angela Harrison
Pengelly's fishmongers, Looe

Jackie Provost and Angela Harrison are the fifth generation running Pengelly's fishmongers in the South East Cornwall port of Looe. They are two of only a handful of women licensed to buy fish at auction in the UK.

Angie Harrison: My great-great-grandfather's family were fish sellers and fruit sellers. He was called Moore and used to send out two of his sons, one to do the Millbrook-Torpoint area with a horse and cart, and the other one used to do Liskeard and all that area, Menheniot way. I think my great-grandfather came back probably the worse for wear because he'd sell all his fish but he'd spend the money on refreshments. And apparently the story goes the horse used to bring him back.

Anyway from there our grandad, he used to go fishing on the *Our Boys* and *Our Daddy* – which, incidentally, were our other grandfather's family's boats, the Pengelly family. So both grandparents went fishing.

Then there came a time when my Grandad Moore thought maybe this was not the life for him, and he decided he was going to start selling fish out of Looe. So he went out into the street with our cart, and the first day he had such a queue they said, 'Mr Moore you can't stay here, there's no way you're causing chaos in the street.' So they moved him to another place.

Jackie Provost: It was under the arch, and the same thing happened again. Then the only lady on the harbour commissioners, Esmée Couch who was a councillor at the time, she put a word in for him and said, 'Right Mr Moore, we'll try and get you a place under the market.' That was in the early 1960s.

Angie: So he started there on the quay with the cart – a very handsome man in his day, so they say – but he would actually go to Plymouth market, and he'd take some of the fishing boats' fish up to Plymouth to put on the market for them. My uncle used to do a round, but he got to the time when he thought, 'This is not very warm work I'm going to stay into Looe,' and he's still working for Tim Alsop [Looe fish merchant]. Then Mum used to go and help Grandad out because he was so busy. He'd say, 'Look, Ruth, you'll have to come down and give me a hand.' Then when Grandad wanted to retire her brothers didn't want to take it over, so Mum and Dad took it over in 1974–75... .

At the time my Dad, he didn't really go fishing, but he worked as a foreman on the harbour. So he had his two weeks' holiday pay, which was about £20, which was not a lot – you have to remember there were five children – and he said, 'Right, we'll give it a go.' He got his fish from Plymouth, and he would also buy direct off the boats as well. My Mum said they didn't even have a till, and they were selling so much fish she didn't know where to put the money. Even now she'd say they'd never seen so much money. We didn't have very much did we? They worked really, really hard, and they were the ones that really got a name for themselves and got it going.

Jackie: We've moved twice. From the old market we moved into a caravan for 18 months, which was actually quite cosy. From there into another one, and from that one we gradually moved up again, and we've been here about 18 years now.

Angie: When we opened the shop in Liskeard in '97 I did hairdressing as well, so I did part-time in the fish shop and part-time hairdressing, and Mum and Jackie said, 'If you don't come in with us we're not going to be able to open it.'

Jackie: That's the time we changed the name to Pengelly's, our dad's name. I think my grandad might have been disappointed, but it was because we opened another shop, and we needed to put another name on it. The older customers that used to know us, they still say Moores. We've got photos so that they know that we were actually Moores before, and we've still got some of Grandad's customers.

Angie: Mum still helps a couple of days. The only sad thing about it, about five years ago my dad wasn't very well and he said he couldn't do it any more, so it was a case of we had to go on the market. I can remember I went home and I cried to my husband and I said, 'I don't know what I'm going to do.' And he said, 'What would Grandad say to you?', and I said, 'He'd say, "Come on girl, pull yourself together, get down there, you two can do it".' That really helped me. At the back of my mind, all the time I thought he was there looking out for us.

Jackie: I used to go down with you and give you that little bit of support, because if I was on my own I would feel the same as how you felt. Us together, it was a little bit of moral support. I did it one week when you were away on holiday, and I was put right in at the deep end, and it is a lot of concentration. But I'm glad I had a go and I realize what you have to do.

Angie: You learn actually … you can't show that you are concentrating too much, because you don't actually want them to know what you want. That's the worst of it. If I know that there's something we're desperate for I'll press the button, and I'll just start looking away, thinking otherwise they'll know it's me. And then they do things like turn your bidding machine off. I do like that system of bidding, dropping and then going up, I think the fishermen do very well out of that

> *The market is fantastic. We're so lucky, we don't appreciate what we've got here really. I want small trawlers, little boats – they're the best boats – small nets. You can see the fishermen that take pride in what they're doing.*

system. They were saying about the Dutch auction, the dropping clock, I don't know whether it would be quite as good for the fishermen.

Jackie: When the other buyers get to know what you like they'll push you right up on it, they just see how far you'll go. At some of the auctions, the buyers don't even go in and have a look. They have it all on computers and they bid for what they think is hopefully the best quality. You don't always know if it is the best of quality unless you look at it.

Angie: That more than anything for us is most important, to be able to see it and feel it and to turn it over. Our zapper [for electronic bidding] is filthy, absolutely full of fish scales. It's the only one because we are obviously handling it. It's funny really.

Secret consultation between Jackie Provost (left) and Angie Harrison during Looe's early morning fish market ensures they achieve the best prices for their shops and customers.

The only thing with fish is that quality doesn't come cheap. And people come and say, 'It's so expensive,' but the thing for us is we put ourselves on the line because we pay a lot of money for it. Sometimes you feel that people think they are being ripped off, but you can't explain it to people.

Jackie: Some people still think fish should be cheap. A lot of elderly people do, they look back years ago and this is where they compare it, whereas it's just so different now. How they caught it, how long it takes to come in, the line-caught, how long they're trawling, how quickly they gut things, that's really important.

Angie: You can see the fishermen that take pride in what they're doing. You can see the ones that it's a passion, and you can see the ones that maybe it's just a job.

Jackie: We want people to have the best fish. Best quality. Unless it's really fresh they don't really understand that flavour. I say, 'Try ours and then judge it. If you don't like it you're obviously not a fish person.' I think people are more aware of where it comes from nowadays, whereas you really know the people that go to supermarkets, they don't understand the quality of fish – they're not the ones that come in regularly and buy it. Also, the size of the fish is so different from years ago – hake in particular and cod and haddock. You definitely see the decline in the size now. But the variety of what we sell is really good.

Angie: In five years it's changed, without a doubt. No way would they ever have caught cod and haddock off Looe when my grandparents, and when my mum first started, that's why they'd go to Plymouth for that. I think the market is fantastic. We're so lucky, we don't appreciate what we've got here really. I don't want to see big beamers in here. I want small trawlers, little boats – they're the best boats – small nets, fish that hasn't drowned, just much better quality.

Jackie: Customers want to know if it's local, that's the main thing, is it fresh, they always say, and then how to cook it. Have you got a recipe they'll ask?

Angie: I'm a walking recipe book. If I haven't done it I definitely know how to do it, and I tell them, and they say, 'Angela, that was fantastic.' I told a lady once who wanted salmon for like an *en croute*, but we didn't have any left. So I said, 'I know what you can do, have some puff pastry, slice some potatoes and some leeks, pepper and salt and some smoked haddock. Parcel it up', as I was thinking about Rick Stein's pasties. She came back and she said, 'Oh, it was absolutely fantastic.' You've got to think and adapt, be versatile with everything.

Jackie: I go round to different places, and wherever I go if there's a fish shop I go and have a look, and I can honestly say I've not ever seen anybody that's as good as what we've got here on the counter. They're completely different.

Angie: It takes time to build up a reputation. You have to source things carefully, even our crab meat, and we tried so many smoked mackerel from different local ones when the smokehouse at Charlestown closed. People know that we won't have it if it's not good enough. It takes a long time to get your customers, and just ten minutes and they're gone.

Jackie: Fish is the only natural thing to eat nowadays. It's the last thing that we've managed not to pollute.

Angie: I know they're farming it, but that's fine for supermarkets, they're welcome to it, but we wouldn't go along that road. That would be us finished with. It's sustainable fishing, without a doubt, that is really important. We don't like female lobsters, we try and make a stand on things like that. I shame anybody buying them on the market.

Light-hearted banter, but the business during the auction is deadly serious.

Chris Bean
Fisherman, Helford

Chris Bean: I've been lucky, I've had a few good breaks in my life, which have been fortunate. Moshi Moshi [a Japanese restaurant in London] is the tip of the iceberg, but they've been good to us because they've recognized the fact that if we can produce fish of very, very high quality, sashimi-grade quality, to eat raw and we can get it to them the same day that it's caught, then in fact price is not the issue. It's a niche market. On the Moshi Moshi days, or other days when we've got to be in for a customer, we have to get up very early and we just go like hell for the six or seven hours we're out. And we have to be in here by 2.15, have everything weighed, packed and graded, and on to a courier by 4 o'clock up in Redruth, so that takes some doing. But the differential on the price, because of that niche marketing, makes it worth more than staying out till 6 o'clock and humping it down to Newlyn.

It does mean that we can't do certain types of fishing which take longer, but we've sort of got over that because we've tailored our fishing to our customers' needs. So we're catching red mullets, mackerel, scad and rock wrasse, and all sorts of under-utilized species, which if they're caught and landed very fresh, they're ideal for sashimi. On the days our sashimi markets are not available to us, we haul monkfish nets which take longer, just do more things, we've got sole nets as well, they take rather longer.

I was lucky enough to go into higher education, my parents wanted me to do that, so when I finished I earned some quick money in Canada, working in gold mines as a mining engineer. And then when I got enough money I came home and got myself a boat. So I started fishing when I was 22, full time. It was only a cheap, small boat, but I could see there was a future in it from the first year's fishing. Then I went into partnership with another local chap, and we had a brand new boat built called *Lady Hamilton*, which is the one I've got now. And after a year he moved on, he got another boat of his own, so I bought him out and I've kept my boat, kept it up, kept it maintained and done all sorts of different types of fishing. My boat is a small boat, about 28 ft, just an open boat doesn't even have scuppers you know. It cost me £5,000.

My daughter has been crewing for me for the last 18 months, and she's brilliant, best crew we've ever had. My son is a partner with me now, though we tend to rotate two on a boat and one off, so the boat can work 365 days of the year if the weather would allow us. As it is we probably work close to 300 days a year.

There's been a spin off since we started with Moshi Moshi, because other people have realized that this sort of quality fish which we are producing is not really generally obtainable. We have four or five boxes of ice on the boat and make a slurry, first thing in the morning, before we even start shooting or pulling the nets, and as soon as the fish comes in we cut a bar of the nets, so the fish don't get spoiled, so as not to take a scale off, and then it goes straight in the ice.

Catching choice fish for a few selective customers that really appreciate the quality, that's what makes me really happy. What we've managed to do for the first time, and

I've been trying to get this for all my life, is that the customer is told what we've got and they have to organize their menus to suit what we've got. And that is a real break-through. We've got several local restaurants who just put 'Catch of the Day' on their menu, and when I come in from sea I carry it down to wherever it's got to go and it's chalked up on the board. I get it there before the customers come, and somebody preps it and people are sitting down in the restaurant eating fish that was alive a few hours earlier. And that really works.

Well, we've got red-mullet nets which concentrate on the red mullet, and we get two by-catches that are quite valuable: one's horse mackerel, and these are highly prized in the sashimi market. My daughter-in-law is Japanese, and she's helped us on that. The other is tub gurnard which have also become important. These you can eat raw, lovely. We tend to take the belly section out which goes for bait, but all the rest of it has got lovely firm meat and it's ideal for sashimi with wasabi and soy sauce. But it's also a nice fish for cooking. I think it was well promoted by Rick Stein. You couldn't pick a fish up at Newlyn like that. We have had up to £5 a kilo for them at the market, but this week they've been making £2.20, pound a pound. In the early '70s I was working from Falmouth, because we were catching mackerel in such a bulk commodity that you needed to be near a quay to land it, but with this sort of new, specialist fishing you just need a van, and five or six boxes a day. It's easy.

> *Catching choice fish for a few selective customers that really appreciate the quality, that's what makes me really happy.*

The mackerel boom was a phenom-enon really. The scientists reckon it was the largest pelagic shoal that's ever been known on the planet, and it sat off the west coast of Cornwall from the Eddystone right the way down to the Scillies for two or three winters, or maybe more. Those years of the '70s really jump-started the fishing industry, because prior to the mackerel boom there was no fishing, hardly anything. The pilchard industry had gone flat, there was a building boom that followed the war years, in the '50s and early '60s, and every-body left the industry. And so there was only about two boats fishing in Falmouth Bay when I came in full time in 1971.

It was mayhem down here in the mid-'70s. There would have been 200 large vessels, Atlantic-size stern trawlers, Russians were here, Egyptians were here, every nation you could think of that had pelagic trawlers were here. They were fishing out-side of 12 miles because they were allowed to, and they were transhipping in Falmouth Bay. The big ones, the British ones, were fishing into three miles, fishing inside us, and sometimes you'd see a great stern trawler between us and the cliffs, going along. The problem with all those big boats was they killed the market, the handline fish was reduced to the same price as the prices gained by the big industrial boats. But we had

Red mullet, iced and ready to go to Moshi Moshi for sashimi.

enough bulk coming in, five bob a stone it was then, 25p a stone. What's that? Four pence a kilo. But it was enough to still earn five times as much as my old man who was a teacher, and I built my house on that and everything. A lot of people did, they got their boats together. The scientists say it would never have lasted, even if there was no fishing activity, because the shoal was so massive, like a dinosaur that just ran out of grass, and it would decay exponentially after it reached maturity.

I've always managed to keep my head above water, but it has been hard, but now fish is making proper money. The industry in Cornwall has got a good future, I think, if people concentrate on quality rather than bulk. I have seen certain stocks decline, but on the other hand, others seem to bounce back and you get very good years, when you don't expect them.

It's not been a very good year for monkfish, and you read in the papers what's happening out on the edge of the [Continental] shelf, the flagship boats leaving nets for endless days, and huge catches of monkfish, a lot of it being thrown away because the nets are in the water for too long. This is bound to affect the stock, it's poor management. I really don't know why they fuss about the sole, because we have good years and bad years and good parts of the year; you get a run of soles for a month and you think brilliant, what's all the fuss about? And then you find that you've got no quota. This has happened a couple of times, usually just before Christmas when you've got your sole nets out in all the bad weather and the price has climbed above £10 a kilo, and then you get a note through the post from Defra saying sorry it's stopped, under-10 m quota has been exhausted. But the beamers and the Frenchmen are allowed to carry on because they didn't fish in June or something, and kept something for the end of the year, this is rubbish. This is Mickey Mouse management.

Loading ice at Chris Bean's processing unit on the Lizard.

I think under-10 m boats should be taken out of the quota system altogether. Their catch should be monitored like we do now, but not quota, ridiculous. Because our range is so small, three hours is the most you are ever going to go from home, so you are talking about 20 miles from home base, whereas the over-10 m boats, usually on trips, if they run out of quota, they can move to another area, which they do.

Sustainably manage fish stocks? I think first of all you've got to look after the environment, like stopping the pollution coming down the rivers. I'm talking about the inshore waters, but it does affect the whole environment, because a lot of the nursery grounds are often very close inshore in the estuaries and the bays; turbot, sole, brill, plaice – all the young ones are in the shallow water. Now, if you're going to have a lot of pollutants coming down the rivers, slurry run off, sewage overflow, then you're going to deplete them. And we should definitely have a control of the predators in these areas. Now this is a sensitive issue. When we started fishing, you could shoot shags, as many as you'd mind to and get paid for it, to keep them down to a reasonable level, because they were quite rightly considered damaging to the nursery stock. Because every time you see a shag come up it's got a fish in its mouth, and now there are millions of shags. And the other thing is seals. I believe that the true way we're going to get over this seal problem is to push this inshore fishery management issue of seals hoovering up every bit of small fish they can find. We know that they predate on our monkfish in the nets, it's a big issue, but we're never going to win the conservation aspects of a few fishermen losing their monkfish. They're not being managed, they should be managed. They cull them in Scotland, they cull them in Northumberland; we should be able to cull them here, keep them down to about 20 per cent of the level they are now. Defra gave permission for 3,000 cormorants to be shot on the inland waters because they were affecting the reservoir fishing and anglers' coarse fishing. But it's okay to take out 2,000–3,000 cormorants, which actually are quite rare compared to shags, there must be a hundred shags for every one cormorant at least. So there you are, it's politics dictating these things rather than common sense.

The environmentalists have really influenced policy to the detriment of the industry, because they don't really have much to lose, do they? We can lose our shirts if we make any concessions, because we are going to lose our living, but these guys, most environmentalists, their income is secure; they're getting a salary every month. And whatever the environmentalists try to impose on us, whether it be closed areas or whatever, then it's going to hurt our income. So we have to resist it, but in a practical way. Make certain concessions where we think they are in order, but not as I've heard recently, one of the people from the Wildlife Trust they want to have Falmouth Bay a net-free area because there's cetaceans there, dolphins, porpoises, and therefore nets are a threat to them they say, so therefore all nets should be taken out and 'ghost nets' should be removed by divers.

First of all, they don't understand the situation, because there's always been dolphins, and there's always been fishermen, and there's always been nets. And 100 years ago there was probably a lot more nets around the coast, because all these coves had little boats and family boats, and they all worked trammels. Trammels are three-wall nets, and because they all worked trammels they would catch big fish and small fish alike, and they would catch cetaceans without a doubt. Stanhope Forbes, the Newlyn artist, if you look at his paintings where there's nets hung up over the walls and on the decks of punts and stuff like that, you'll see they're trammels. Historically, all the little coves around here, Durgan, Flushing, where there's no boats now, they all had little boats, working on really a subsistence living, a few fish for the family. I'm sure 100 years ago the inshore was really cluttered with nets, and they would row out or sail out. There's hardly any nets now, a few pots, and our red mullet nets which we leave in the water three hours, so I don't know what they are worried about.

The stock is good, you know, the resource is good, it's a huge variety of resources. They are having a very, very good season for the crab now (2005), best for years. Catch per unit effort of pot has been phenomenal. So there is nothing wrong with crab stock. Lobster's been the best year this year for 20 years as well. Everybody will tell you that. Now this must be a natural cycle, the lobster hatchery's doing a good job, but those lobsters haven't come on line yet. So it is to do with Eddy Derriman's policy on fishery management, and I have a lot of respect for Eddy Derriman. This V-notch programme, we know it must work because we've caught lobsters now with seven notches in them, big berried females that have been caught seven times and put back, so that means that lobster is having a real chance to reproduce.

You can't have hundreds and hundreds more small boats. The level now is ring-fenced, and that is correct. Luckily I'm in it. There's only so much to go around. Probably I think along the same lines as most inshore fishermen. I don't think I'm radical on any viewpoints really. It's common sense you know. Look after the waterways that come inshore, manage the seals and the shags, and stop people tearing up the substrait, and keep the numbers of fishermen no more than they are.

9 Net Gains

A photograph of Cadgwith in the late 1890s shows about 24 boats dragged up on to the shingle beach. Nets and sails are laid out to dry in the backyards of the cottages and in fields around the village. Today less than a dozen boats work from this, one of the last beach fisheries in England. During the winter months only half a dozen, the biggest no more than 25 ft long, will be moored on the beach, often pulled right up into the heart of the village during stormy conditions. In the summer, the numbers are swollen by smaller boats taking advantage of the better weather. Cadgwith is still a working fishing village, and has several pilchard cellars, reminders of the county's once thriving pilchard fishery. The Cadgwith fishermen are truly artisan inshore fishermen, most trying to work within the protection of the six-mile limit. Their fishing hours are determined by tides and daylight. Setting to sea and returning requires a winch and a tractor to get the boats on and off the beach. Instead of fishing for crab and lobster as their fathers and grandfathers did after the pilchard fishery died out, most of these fishermen now catch different species according to the season. They set gill nets for monkfish, turbot and ray, and use handlines for mackerel, sea bass and perhaps some pollack. Later in the year they put out pots for crab and other shellfish. They may be fewer in number, but thanks to better fishing gear, engines and improved efficiency these boats are probably catching far more than the previous generations in the photograph. Unlike in Victorian times, few of these fishermen live in this picturesque village tucked away on the eastern side of the Lizard. Most of the whitewashed, thatched cottages here are either second or holiday homes.

Does Cadgwith symbolize the future of the Cornish fishing industry? Is this the direction that many more of Cornwall's picturesque fishing ports and harbours are heading? As each decade passes and technology makes boats safer, and able to fish for longer in tougher conditions, and gear becomes more efficient and selective, will fewer fishermen be landing the same volume of sea fish?

Right: Cadgwith is one of the last working beach fisheries in Cornwall, approachable at most states of the tide with the aid of a tractor or winch. In stormy weather boats are pulled right up into the village street.

Below and right: Last match of the season at Cadgwith. About nine boats set out to catch the largest possible pollack in two hours. Professionals and amateurs take part in this friendly community event.

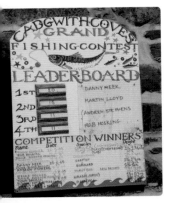

This book has tried to show that unlike the general portrayal of the state of Britain's fishing industry, the story in Cornwall and the Isles of Scilly is markedly different, both at sea and onshore. The industry has many positive points in its favour. It is learning to live with higher fuel prices and the effects of decommissioning, quota cuts, restricted days at sea and the general tightening up of regulations. If a balance is being achieved between effort and stocks, the industry should be well placed to face the future.

This balance between effort and stocks is the crucial issue, and while anecdotal evidence and general impressions tend to be positive, the expectations of fishermen, politicians and scientists differ. There is still a huge gap between what the increasingly influential environmental groups *think* is happening and what the Fisheries scientists and fishermen *know* to be true. Where fishermen, scientists and conservationists do agree is that the CFP has been a total and utter disaster, as much for fish stocks as for the fishing industry.

Cornish fish stocks are not in such a state of terminal decline as most journalists, anglers and the more confrontational lobby groups would have us believe; some are undoubtedly under pressure, but many others in the seas around the Cornish coast are abundant and thriving. The success of the FSP has started to overcome what was once seen as the major hurdle of persuading politicians that there are still plenty of fish in the Western Approaches and the Celtic Sea. Cornish fishermen are the first to admit that cod, while more abundant in Cornish waters than in the North Sea, is still a species to be concerned about. Even the scientists acknowledge that it is impossible to sum up the issues around fishing, the sea-bed and marine environment in simple terms. With so many factors at play they have no straightforward or easy solutions. They can make recommendations based on their observations, but they are measuring a constantly moving stock that has hundreds of square miles of sea-bed to roam over, and even the most sophisticated technology can provide only limited information when increasingly the impacts of global warming and other environmental changes must also be taken into account.

There is no doubt that globally many fish stocks are facing collapse – the UN's Food and Agriculture Organization believes that more than half the world's monitored fish stocks are fully exploited, and a further 25 per cent are over-exploited, depleted or recovering. The pressures of industrialized fishing by huge factory processing ships on a massive global scale unseen in the South West, are causing damage that is difficult to assess and, in many cases, has yet to be understood.

At a local level Cornish fishermen have responded to the crisis with a significant cultural shift, understanding the need for sustainably managed fisheries and the benefits of having an abundance of seafood that is not subject to the quota system. They are rethinking how and where they fish, and how their catch is marketed. Trips are shorter so that the fish can be landed that much fresher. More fish and shellfish, branded as Cornish, are being sold into quality, niche markets.

Although it is England's last fishing fleet of any size or description, the Cornish boats must be seen in their correct context. In 2001 the fishing fleet was estimated at 599 registered vessels: of these 71 per cent were under-10 m long, mostly inshore boats; more than half the larger vessels based in Newlyn were more than 35 years old, so this is clearly an ageing fleet. Similarly, the age profile of skippers, crews and fishermen is going up. The volumes of fish landed are showing a slight decline, although the monetary value remains more or less constant.

Beyond the South West, the rest of the British fishing industry faces a greater crisis, and is probably at the point where it is about to lose critical mass. Although in Cornwall and the Isles of Scilly real steps have been taken to avert that decline, the fact remains that those that have survived, the hard core, need to work every day possible to earn a living. Despite the positive things going for it, the industry faces serious problems of manpower, succession and future generations. New entrants to the industry are scarce, and many of the larger vessels are increasingly reliant on foreign, often Eastern European, crews in order to have sufficient men to go to sea safely. Recognizing this, two industry-led initiatives are taking steps to halt this decline: Invest in Fish South West (see panel, page 174) and the Duchy Fish Quota Company (DFQC). What all want to avoid is the massive decline that has left places like Peterhead, once one of the premier Scottish fishing ports, a shadow of its former self.

The DFQC was set up in 2001 in order to maintain sufficient fish quota within the county to help the next generation of Cornish fishermen to get started with their first boat. Despite the widely held view that the quota system has failed as a management tool for both fish stocks and fishing capacity, it remains the driving force that, in most cases, dictates who can catch what, where and when. When quotas were first allocated to vessels, based on their previous fishing track record

Invest in Fish South West

The dilemma of agreeing workable future fisheries management options, with conservationists seeming to want different things from fishermen, is one that Invest in Fish South West (IIFSW) has been set up to resolve. This ground-breaking project was started by WWF-UK, the NFFO and Marks & Spencer in response to the 2004 report *Choose or Lose*, commissioned by WWF-UK.

This South West pilot project unites a unique mix of stakeholders ranging from 'sea to plate', including not just environmentalists and fishermen but restaurateurs, supermarkets, processors, sea anglers and government statutory bodies such as the South West Regional Development Agency and English Nature. Their common aim is to find better ways to manage regional fisheries – ways that will sustain the fisheries, the communities and the marine environment. By working together these diverse groups could find options that would benefit everyone. After discussions around the UK, the South West was chosen as the place to start. Although based in Cornwall, home of the South West's biggest fishing fleet, the project covers the historic region of Wessex, and focuses on the waters most frequently fished by fishermen from Cornwall, Devon and Dorset.

While there is agreement that many, though not all fish stocks are in decline, there is still widespread disagreement on the best ways to manage them. One thing IIFSW is not is a mouthpiece for fishermen, or for any one of the sectors involved. Its approach is bottom up, working with fishermen and all other sectors that traditionally might find themselves on opposing sides of the debate, yet who share a common interest in the future of fish stocks, fishing communities and the marine environment. It may sound ambitious, but one of the shared goals is to find a way of devising strategies that will not only sustain but also maintain and manage all three elements better. Among the tools used by the project is a scientific model exploring trends and scenarios for the biology of the oceans, the fishing fleets, and jobs and the economy onshore.

This bio-economic model, that will test the social, environmental and economic implications of several options, has been developed by the Centre for the Economics and Management of Aquatic Resources (CEMARE) at the University of Portsmouth, and CEFAS.

Originally seen as an exercise to measure the cost benefit analysis of fishing in the South West, IIFSW evolved into a project hoping to show why it makes sense to support fisheries rather than regulate them out of existence. While each stakeholder started with clear individual aims, the group recognized that it would have a stronger negotiating position if its solutions represented a common consensus, albeit involving a degree of compromise. This way IIFSW hopes for a more effective response from governments, and less adversarial lobbying on fisheries in the region.

IIFSW will present its package of options in early 2007, and at the time of writing was consulting on options with stakeholder groups. It is hoped that the process and the scientific model, if not the proposed options, could be used in fishing communities in other EU member states facing similar problems. But the options for the South West will be specific to the region, driven by local experiences. This fits with the Government's and the EU's desire to devolve fisheries management to a regional level, through the Regional Advisory Committees set up in 2005.

If consensus is reached at the end of the project, what is agreed could include some tough recommendations. However, the results should be a wider and mutual understanding of the issues, while the recommendations should also contain incentives for all parties. This work is already leading to new ways of collaborating and communicating between groups that were once implacably opposed to one another. The logic is that by co-operating, all involved are striving for a better fishery, not necessarily fewer boats or fishermen, but a more productive future at all levels.

Contact details: www.investinfishsw.org.uk. info@investinfishsw.org.uk. Tel. 01736 333733.

in specific areas, the Government claimed that they would have no monetary value. However, as soon as the first boat stopped fishing and sold its quota, it became a tradable commodity. The DFQC's role is to raise sufficient cash through a range of activities, including bonds, merchandising and other-fund raising ventures, to invest in quota which is then leased to existing skippers and, more importantly, to new entrants. Given that they already face the cost of buying a boat and a licence to fish, the DFQC scheme is a cost-effective way of giving them a leg up into the industry. It was, as the DFQC's Chairman, Colin Warwick, explains, driven by a desire to put something back into the community. It is also, perhaps as importantly, a way of ensuring that fishing quota remains in Cornwall, as when a boat is decommissioned, its quota can be sold to the highest bidder. The DFQC estimates that since it was set up, quota worth more than £4 million has already been traded away from Cornwall. The company's ultimate goal is to retain £15 million of quota for Cornwall and the Isles of Scilly.

To see what the Cornish fishing industry is up against, you only have to look at what is happening in other EU member states that share the same fishing grounds. The Spanish and Irish have continued investing in their fleets, taking full advantage of soft loans and EU grants, to upgrade and modernize their vessels. Several Irish supercrabbers, capable of working 1,800 pots a day, are flooding the market with crabs. Yet in Cornwall crabbing has been traditionally the preserve of small boats, working only a limited number of pots. The limitations of the size of the boats, and dependence on good weather, made it a sustainable way of fishing that naturally managed its stocks.

One of the biggest difficulties for the Cornish, and other small-scale, mainly inshore fisheries is that the public automatically assumes that the relentlessly negative and misleading stories about overfishing put out by the press, and some environmentalists, are universally true. The development of the leisure diving industry has raised the issue of possible damage to the sea-bed by some fishing methods. But as more than one scientist pointed out, this may simply be a case of no change, it is just that it is now in the public domain. A little knowledge is a dangerous thing. The more one-sided stories about a complex industry like fishing that the public read or see on their televisions, the greater the danger of the misunderstandings. For example, most politicians, and others, assume that all fishing boats are trawlers. In fact in Cornwall there are fewer than 170 trawlers fishing out of a total of 599 registered boats. Few people realize that 75 per cent of the entire UK fishing fleet is made up of small, low-powered, inshore fishing boats.

There is a significant ethical debate to be had over the future of Cornwall's, and indeed the rest of the world's, fishing industry. On the one hand is the need to keep the industry alive, producing either a high-quality product for a quality

end-user, or limited quantities for the mass market. There is also the need for local communities to retain control and ownership of their artisan, inshore fisheries, rather than surrender management to remote bureaucrats or global corporations. This would go some way to addressing the socio-economic issues of jobs, both at sea and onshore, and the impact on surrounding businesses and local economies. It would help to maintain the sense that fishing is still the life-blood of many economically fragile coastal towns and villages. Without it they would lose much of the sense of community that binds them together. The oyster fishery on the River Fal encapsulates all these problems (see panel, pages 178–9). The need for fishing to survive is also intricately linked to the issues of heritage and history on which much of the Cornish tourist industry still feeds, although that is no justification for a 'let's preserve it in aspic mentality' that stifles future development.

Left and above: Dredging for oysters in the Fal estuary. Below: A plate of oysters.

On the other hand the world has a growing population, particularly in rapidly developing economies such as China and India, wanting to eat a more protein-heavy, Western-style diet, in which fish plays a major part. Add to that the Western view that food should be 'cheap', and it is hardly surprising that multi-national companies are prowling the world's seas looking for sources of cheap fish, putting

Oysters

Perhaps the most sustainable fishery in Cornwall is the Fal River oyster fishery (officially known as the Port of Truro Oyster Fishery), the last oyster fishery in Europe harvested under sail by Europe's last commercial sailing fleet. Here on the River Fal native oysters (*Oystera edulis*) have been harvested in more or less the same, highly sustainable, fashion, without the use of mechanical power, for more than 500 years.

Oysters are thought to have been found in Cornwall since the earliest trading with the Phoenicians, and were widely grown around the coast when the Romans occupied Britain. For hundreds of years they were seen as a food for the poor who would gather the plankton-feeding bivalves from the muddy banks of creeks and rivers at low tide. In 1298 they sold for 2d (less than 1p) a gallon, and were cheap in comparison with other fish.

By the time Sir Richard Carew published his *Survey of Cornwall* in 1602, oysters were being caught using dredges:

> 'a thick strong net fastened to three spills of iron, and drawn to the boat's stern, gathering whatsoever it meeteth lying in the bottom of the water, out of which, when it is taken up, they cull the oyster and cast away the residue, which they term gard, and serveth as a bed for the oysters to breed in.'

In Carew's time oysters were abundant around the Cornish shoreline, now they are found only in the Fal, Percuil, Helford, Fowey and Camel rivers. The Fal has the last wild oyster beds, in the other rivers both native and Pacific oysters are re-laid and farmed. The native oyster is slow maturing, taking up to five years to grow to a marketable size, and is thought to have a far superior flavour to the faster growing Pacific oysters (*Crassostrea gigas*, also known as rock oysters).

By the 1860s a combination of disease, pollution and probably overfishing had almost destroyed these native oyster beds. This was the point at which they became a highly desirable, luxury food. By-laws introduced by Truro Corporation in 1876 protected the Fal's beds from over-exploitation by limiting harvesting to non-mechanical means. This means relying on wind and tide in sail-powered working boats that tow the dredges across the beds in a fashion known as a drift. Many of these are historic vessels, such as Tim Vinnicombe's *Boy Willie*, a restored pilchard lugger driver that has been on and off the water for more than 150 years, and is used for fishing in the winter and racing in the summer. After each drift the working boats go about and start working the same narrow piece of the estuary again, adapting as the tide and wind patterns change during the day. Further up the river, in the less accessible, shallow creeks, single-handed, self-propelled, haul-tow punts use oars and a winch to harvest the oysters.

The dredges used by the gaff-cutter rigged working boats have changed little over the last 400 years: about 3 ft wide, the small nets with an iron bar top and bottom look like a small bag that is cast out over the stern, pulled across the river bed and hauled in over the side. They are hauled frequently as they quickly fill up with stones, mud and shells. Any oyster that is smaller than the statutory 2 5/8 inches in diameter is discarded and returned to the river bed to grow on. After they have been harvested the oysters are purified before being sold, mostly out of the county, either to smart, metropolitan restaurants or exported to Europe where they are highly sought after, even in France. Each autumn more than 10,000 oysters are consumed during the annual Falmouth Oyster Festival.

The number of licences issued by the Port of Truro Harbour Authority fluctuates each year – in 1980/81 it was 151, but in 2005/6 it was 38. A licence is issued for each dredge, and the sailing boats operate up to two dredges per man, with a crew of two. Haul-tow punts operate a single dredge. Fishing is strictly limited to 9 a.m. to 3 p.m. each weekday, and from 9 a.m. to 1 p.m. on Saturdays, from 1 October to 31 March. It is perhaps its inherent inefficiency and reliance on traditional methods that preserves this fishery, despite growing pressures for more river moorings for leisure craft, from antifouling paints (even though banned for small craft in 1987 it is thought that some still

arrives on tankers and ocean-going ships that shelter in the Carrick Roads), pollution, and invasive slipper limpets.

Although the number of oystermen fluctuates annually, most have other seasonal work during the rest of the year. In a good year the fishery still provides a reasonable living for the most experienced men who are prepared to put in the time and effort in all weathers as long as the season allows. A proactive partnership between the harbour authority and the Port of Truro Oyster Fishery Management Group is working to manage and improve the nursery beds for future stocks. Nevertheless, as in the rest of the Cornish fishing industry, there are concerns about succession, the lack of young people and skills coming into the industry, and that the continuity of several generations of oystermen families will be lost for ever if prospects and profits do not improve.

As with sea fishing, oyster dredging is a skill that cannot be learned by rote. It is learned through years of working the water, understanding which areas suit the oysters best, and that this is a highly unpredictable species that can be surprisingly difficult to harvest. Many say that signs of healthy spatfall (young oysters) can look promising, only to discover a couple of years later that adult oysters are hard to find, with no obvious explanation.

As with the rest of the Cornish fishing industry, this dilemma has social and economic implications too for the villages and support industries based around the creeks and tributaries of the River Fal. If the prospects for future oyster stocks are not good enough, this may be the last generation of oystermen working this unique, and highly sustainable, fishery on the River Fal.

more pressure on fish stocks, the marine environment and indigenous communities in less developed countries.

Consumers everywhere have a role to play too. The trend for better quality, traceable, local food, often organic or produced using traditional, non-intensive farming and production systems, includes fish and shellfish. Consumers are starting to turn against industrialized fishing in favour of more sustainable ways of catching seafood, often involving smaller boats that are not fuel-hungry and have little environmental impact on the sea-bed. But the influence of the supermarkets has been to make us see fish as a cheap food source, and while much of it is still good value, the future for Cornish seafood is undoubtedly as a quality product. If we want to know with confidence that we can continue eating the freshest Cornish crab sandwiches, handline-caught mackerel or sea bass, John Dory, squid or any of the other species found in the teeming waters off the Cornish coast, we need to accept that any fish comes with a price tag attached, and we should be prepared to pay it. We have four choices: a) fish from over-exploited stocks in distant seas that has been transported half way around the world; b) British-caught and -landed fish that has been shuttled around the country for several days; c) farmed fish which, in many circumstances, are produced unsustainably, requiring three times their body weight in food made from other fish; or d) fresh Cornish fish and shellfish. Every time that we buy indiscriminately, each of us individually is contributing to the decline of the county's indigenous fishing industry, draining another drop of the lifeblood from these vital, coastal communities.

I hope that I have given a true reflection of how the industry as a whole operates in Cornwall and the Isles of Scilly. It is too easy to take at face value the external condemnations and criticisms while Cornish fishermen, tasked with making a living in one of the most dangerous environments in the world, lack a unified voice to retaliate. For politicians at all levels, local, regional and national, fishing may not be a very high priority, but to Cornish ports and fishing villages, ensuring a sustainable, prosperous future for the fishing industry is paramount.

A final word, though, to fish merchant Robin Turner, explaining what I hope this book has shown, that the Cornish fishing industry is complex, hard work, and produces a wonderful end product, and it is something that no one should take for granted:

> *'Anybody who thinks we just go out, jump in a boat, throw a net over the side, come back in and go to the pub, think on! It ain't like that. We are dealing with the last wild, uninterfered with, natural, sustainable food resource on this planet. Every fish is special, it's the most precious thing, it's the jewel in the sea.'*

Left and above: The popular Newlyn Fish Festival takes place on August Bank Holiday Monday, and draws thousands of locals and holiday-makers.

Colin Warwick, MBE
Chairman, Duchy Fish Quota Company

The Duchy Fish Quota Company was set up to buy and lease fish quota, to help ensure a future for the next generation of fishermen.

Colin Warwick: From the Duchy Quota Company's point of view, it's been quite a frustrating three-year period, really, we've been held to ransom by the Government who keep on delaying their decision on whether we can use a loan offered by the County Council. We were faced with putting everything on ice, or we could try and start to raise funds by as many different methods as we could. So, we tried a calendar with Rick Stein, which was very glossy; then it was mooted the second year that we should go down the route of the Naked Fishermen, and it did prove very successful, gave a lot of laughter. But more than anything it raised the profile of the Company and what we are about, because it tickled the media's attention, and it had the desired effect. But there's only so many times you can repeat a winning formula, and we decided to break from it last year, and we did look at producing a calendar of fish recipes, and we went to Cornish chefs for the recipes in it, but it is from the fishing industry.

I started at sea when I was a young boy, and if you worked hard you'd get your own boat, there were no restrictions. It was just a case of if you were keen you would get on. But when the vessel licence was introduced, we said to the Government at the time that it would become something with a monetary value, they said, 'No, no, it won't.' A week later, the first licence was for sale. And then the same thing happened with the quota. So now to buy a boat of this size you would probably have to buy £150,000-worth of quota on top of the cost of the boat, and the licence, to make it viable.

So it's very difficult for the young to get established, and I suppose with the fellow directors of the Quota Company I thought maybe we can give something back to the community if we can hold the fishing quota. I know it's got to be paid for, so we'll have to lease it out. But if you project yourself to 2050, I won't be here, but say we own £2 million-worth of quota, and that quota's all paid for, we can feed that into the young boys to help them start in the industry. If you're just like my grandson, Jake, or the young Pascoe lads at Newlyn, who play in the harbour, they're born fishermen, and it's not their fault that they were born six years ago and all these draconian rules have been brought in.

So that was the burning passion we all shared, to put something back into the community, and it's self-generating really. If there's fish there'll be fishermen. Some people might say it's a pipe dream, but if you can't dream, well it's a pretty sad old world. We started with nothing, and every year we buy a little bit more quota. We've got another chunk of quota earmarked, it's going to cost us £150,000 to buy, it's peanuts maybe in some people's say, but then it's another £150,000-worth of business that might have disappeared for the Cornish fleet, and because of the Duchy Fish Quota Company it's still going to be there. So slowly, slowly over a period of years, we will get there.

We've got to make the best of what we've got. What we don't want is to lose any more boats; what we want is a sustainable fishery, and you know so much of this is misinformation bandied about by the various 'green' people, but it's never been in the fisherman's interests to catch the last of anything, because once we catch the last haddock, or the last mackerel, or the last monkfish, well it's gone for ever. We're not that stupid. We've got a very good lot of young skippers coming in, and that gives me the greatest encouragement. Young, keen men who look after their fish; who know how to promote it; who know that we can't plunder and not put anything back, so the balance is actually shifting.

I think there is a change in the industry. All right, there are some who still want to flaunt all the rules, but there's less and less. The industry as a whole, both in England and Wales and Scotland, is better now than it was a decade ago from that point of view. I think the fish stocks in the South West are in better condition than what the scientists first thought. Hence the sole quota's gone up and the monkfish quota's gone up, because there's more fish available. What we can't allow to happen is to get too greedy and say we'll double it again next year. An ideal situation would be to have quotas on a five-year management strategy, not every year going to the negotiations in Brussels so that we're all sitting a week before Christmas wondering whether we've got an industry left. That isn't the way to run a business. The Government wouldn't like it if they had to face a general election a week before Christmas. They just wouldn't do it, they would change the rules to give them a bit of stability. Why should the fishing industry be any different? We need that stability.

> *Fish is simply the last true wild food, and I'm wild about it. I want people to be wild about the taste, and the freshness, and the quality.*

I started fishing in a little village called Alnmouth in Northumberland, and I bought my first boat when I was 16, so it's a long time ago. I was fishing for crabs and lobsters. Like so many fishermen, we started with shellfish, and we worked our way up to white fish as a progression. A lot of the top white-fish skippers all started in the shellfish field; it's a funny thing because they used to say you'd go up the hill and then you'd come back down, because when you retired you probably had a little boat and a couple of lobster pots just to keep your hand in.

I've always fished in British waters, but became politically activated when we lost the distant-water fleet, and when we were left in the North Sea we formed the NFFO – 1976 I think it was formed. I was on the Seafish Industry board for nine years, and I was lucky enough to go out to Canada with the Seafish board, as a guest of the Canadian government, to have a look at their fisheries, and this was just after they put 30,000 fishermen on the dole. It was a quite extraordinary, crazy thing.

Me being me, I couldn't quite work it out. They took the soft option. Paid the companies out, put the men on the dole, and they turned them into alcoholics. I went to St Johns in Newfoundland, which was once the cod capital of the world – in your boyhood dreams you

Will young Jamma Phillips follow his father Danny and Uncle Tommy to sea for a lifetime's career as a fisherman?

read about the Grand Bank fisheries – and it was a ghost town. Shops boarded up, great big fisheries institute with the finest facilities for training fishermen, but not a fishing boat in the harbour. But then when you went to some of the small villages, where there were family-owned boats, lo and behold they were doing very well fishing for shrimp and crab, they'd diversified because they didn't want to go out of business. The companies took the option to go out of business, because they got a big payout, the men were expendable; but when you went and talked, you suddenly found they actually had a mackerel stock, a herring stock, and they weren't fishing it. I said, 'Well, in the UK there isn't a fish that we don't fish, right down to the whelks, we've found a market for everything. So why didn't you explore what you've got?' And they looked at me as if I was a green-eyed monster, but I was looking at it from a fisherman's point of view, from the UK where we utilise everything we've got. Now the UK fishing industry at its best only had six or seven thousand fishermen, so to put it into its context, Newfoundland had an enormous industry, and they put 30,000 fishermen on the dole. Just wiped them away; but they wiped the opportunity away at the same time, because once the infrastructure goes, you can't get it back.

How close is the British fishing industry coming to that? If you went to Peterhead ten years ago and you went to it now, you'd think it was a ghost town in comparison, but I would hope the cuts have gone as far as what they need to go. The trouble is that the coastal communities can only have so many art galleries and so many potteries, but a harbour is a harbour; and you can only have so many marinas, because basically yachts and pleasure boats are only floating caravans to a lot of people, they don't really go anywhere a lot of them. I'm not knocking them for having them, but it isn't the be-all and end-all to keep the coastal communities alive. We need working harbours to produce the finest food in the area.

I think we have turned a corner. Last year when we were working out of Newlyn we had a very good fishery, good quality fish, and there was a lot of fish on the ground that made good money on the market, but I don't think we were over-paid, but it was a good average. The highs and lows favour nobody; if we want to create a demand, we can't push the price up to create an élitist food. It has to stay within the grasp of what we are competing against, the meat products and that. Fish is simply the last true wild food, and I'm wild about it. I want people to be wild about the taste and the freshness and the quality. I think that fish is probably the best food in the world that can't be called organic.

This boat, *Valhalla*, is a 60 ft seiner trawler. We operate in the South West virtually all the time, but we alternate in the summer season, which might be from March until the end of July, out of Newlyn, and then we go back up to Brixham for the squid fishery and cuttle fishery, as do some of the other boats from Newlyn. My son is in charge now, I'm back to deckhand, and we have a crewman as well, but we might go four hands in the summer if we are seine-netting in the South West. We sold a boat that was built in Cornwall to get a bigger boat to prosecute the seine-net fishery, because it is environmentally friendly, economically friendly; because the fuel consumption is by half, and the quality is second to none, because the fish is only 20 minutes in the net, so actually all the fish you catch is still alive and it hasn't got a scale off. Quality is the name of the game, quality will sell fish better than anything else. Our objective is to land top-quality fish, and hopefully get the reward for it.

In the summer we try and land every third day if we can; obviously, if we have enough fish aboard we'll land every day. In the winter-time we land every day, because the squid they like to keep the quality up. The days of the ten-day trips isn't really what the market's looking for, because the market is looking for the ten days in the shop, not in the boat's hold. Again, it's a cultural shift, we are having to rejig the way we think, because you've got to look at it from the end user's point of view. The worst thing you can do as a consumer is to pay good money for some fish, and get the fish home and it's off. Because she, or he, won't go back to the fishmonger for a mighty long time, if ever. 'Never put in a box what you wouldn't take home to eat yourself' is our yardstick here. It's not a bad yardstick. If you don't want to take it home, why should you expect somebody to buy it?

Today's fishermen are concerned that the difficulties of the last decades are dissuading their children from taking up careers as sea fishermen.

Robin Turner

Fish merchant, Newlyn

Robin Turner is a fish merchant, auctioneer, retailer, boat agent, fish supplier and chandler in Newlyn.

Robin Turner: My business in general is dealing with fish. My phone is on 24/7 and I start work when necessary, and when I deem 'necessary' is when we have fish to land. I go to the market first thing in the morning, where you have to plan which boat comes first and how they moor up so that nobody is in the way. Then my staff lot up the fish before the market starts to trade. People have to know what fish is available, so my main aim is to get the information and the fish there in time for the sale to take place.

After that my staff then open up the retail shop in the Coombe. They get the wholesale side ready for action that day for other markets in Great Britain and across Europe. Sandrine, in my office, does the French, Spanish, Italian and Belgian sales, and I do with Steve the UK wholesale side, and Steve then does the retail sales as well. The rest of the staff are then picking fish up from the market, as we are buying from Stevenson's auction or our auction. The fish is taken up from the market, then graded, filleted, headed, sorted, packed and sold to anybody from Mrs Humphreys three doors up the street to people in Rome, on the Rimini coast of Italy, Madrid, France, Belgium and all over the United Kingdom.

Once we have achieved that and got everything working in some semblance of order, then we see what the boats are going to be doing for the next day, two days, three days; and we get as much information as we can during the course of an afternoon about their requirements, what the weather is doing, how they are fishing, so that when we come to supplying them with what they need in the way of fuels, oils, ropes, gear when they come in, we also have the staff planned to unload them first thing in the morning. So by the time the day ends, we know very well what we are going to be doing the following day, and also the day after that, and to a certain degree the day after that.

Information is what our industry survives on. The more information that you have about the quantities of fish that will be landed and what is marketable through the next two or three days, is so valuable, not only to the catcher, the merchant, the processor, the auctioneer and also, most importantly, to the end customer. The product itself is the most important part, it's the heart and soul of our industry. We have to put value to it, but not just value to say that it's a beautiful piece of fish, but monetary value to make the most of it.

We are agents for boats, so the boat owns the fish. I am employed as the auctioneer of fish, to make the most of their fish when they come to the market. We handle about 10 per cent of the market's throughput, about £2 million-worth a year. The other 90 per cent goes through Stevenson's auction, mostly because they've got the largest quantity of vessels landing to them and they also own 20 plus vessels. In comparison we are small potatoes, but we like to think that we are a challenging affair.

Our target is the smaller vessel and top-quality, inshore fish. It's good quality, and I would like to say that it is a guarantee of quality, that's the most important issue. It is not a case that we would have tonnes and tonnes and tonnes of x, y and z species of fish, but we have placed our faith in selling a top-quality product to good customers, at a premium price, to make it worthwhile people looking after their fish, catching it in a sensible, managed manner; landing it in such a manner, and being sold on the principles that fish is good to eat, it's good in your diet, and it's sustainable.

We've also placed our faith in experimentation, and when I say experimentation, that's on new fishing methods that could possibly save money and the environment by saving fuel, costs and consumption; by less gear loss, by also more selective gear and types of fishing management by bringing in at certain times what people want. And I'm also an advocate of shutting areas, so that fish have a chance to breed and reproduce properly.

There is nothing wrong with us being a predator on fish, because in the food chain, yes we are top. I don't see the point of interrupting it to feed other fish, i.e. in fish farming; that is totally, totally wrong, and the ethics of it do need questioning heavily, because people are still financing large businesses, to go and take huge amounts of sand eel and other small species of fish out of the sea, in millions of tonnes, to feed salmon, turbot, sturgeon and bass in farmed environments, which is basically devaluing the wild market, devaluing the ethics, the principles that we and the fishing industry have all survived by.

> " *The fish is sold to anybody from Mrs Humphreys three doors up the street to people in Rome, on the Rimini coast of Italy, Madrid, France, Belgium and all over the United Kingdom.* "

The food chain is the simplest way to describe the fishing industry. We're top. Right at the bottom there are tiny micro-organisms in the sea that other organisms feed upon, and so it grows, and the larger organisms feed on the smaller organisms, and blah blah blah until we get to all forms of fish, and to the huge mammals that live in the sea, and the food chain must continue. Man's interference with the food chain must be managed. If it isn't managed and it is not ethically right, it is categorically wrong, and must be stopped. It must be adjusted and brought into regimented discipline. If it doesn't we destroy it.

The natural cycles of food availability are as special as any vineyard wine. And when a John Dory appears here in April and May it is a special event. If it doesn't happen we all hold our hands up in horror, and we want to investigate why it hasn't happened. Precisely the same as the guy in the French vineyard, because his crop has failed one year, scratches his bonce and is left with a load of empty bottles and not a

Robin Turner with other buyers at the fish market in Newlyn.

lot of money in the bank. It happens. But we are as special as any wine, as any other food resource. We're not just fish. Every fish is special, it's the most precious thing, it's the jewel in the sea, it is different and it should be marketed on that principle, and we have to be cleverer about how we sell the gorgeous product that we have to work with. So little is being done. Because it is an immediate, perishable industry, it tends to accelerate the principle of get it out of the boat and get it gone on a lorry, and someone else will take care of it.

I own one little boat, I used to own two boats until the middle of last year, one was a little inshore trawler, but over the years I have helped people finance themselves into the industry. The fishing industry has not had the best press over the last ten, maybe 15 years. Banks and financiers react to that particular stigma and tend not to want to lend money to new entrants, and to be a boat-owner has been a way to help somebody in and then they buy the boat from me when they can afford to. So half way through last year, the last youngster that I brought into the industry bought his boat and is now fishing away merrily. I consider that to be a success story. I haven't earned a lot of money out of it, and he hasn't yet, but hopefully he will. The principle is not about cash, it is about regeneration in the industry, and how we keep the knowledge that has been hard earned and hard fought for under the natural conditions of a hostile environment.

Most mothers – and this is not a sexist comment even though it may sound like one – most mothers would not let their little Johnnies go into the fishing industry because it is bloody dangerous. Read a newspaper, another fishing vessel is lost. One was lost recently off Guernsey, a Frenchman, five lives. It is a horror story, and any responsible parent would look at it in that light. However, the sea is in a lot of people's blood, and no matter how hostile the challenge, when the sea and fishing are in your blood, I'm afraid it doesn't go away that easily. When I go inland, I enjoy it for a while, but where is the ozone, where is the smell of the salt, where is the sea? I want to always go back to the coast. It's that sort of drive that makes people want to go to sea on boats and ply their trade, so to regenerate the industry is a very, very important part that we in the industry all play.

The industry is regenerating itself and keeping its knowledge alive. Believe me that is the most important tool we have in the toolbox, and it is one that nobody who drives a Whitehall desk, or has an exterior view of the industry, sees.

This is not a simple industry, this is a very complicated industry. It has many, many facets. It has many, many skills mixed up in it, from the simpler skills of being able to look after and gut a fish properly, being able to catch one, being able to navigate a vessel, being able to speak more than one language, being able to understand political speak, thousands of pages of government legislation, to be able to perform well in the environments of tax – and when I say tax I mean multi-tax, hidden taxes, covert taxes, VAT taxes, non-VAT taxes, European tax systems, Great British tax systems. To operate in those particular environments of mesh sizes, gear sizes, where you can fish, where you can't fish. Tricky isn't it?

You don't just come in and say I am going to be part of the fishing industry; you might be a very small part of it, but to understand it, to get that drive, you have to live it. You don't go to bed at midnight and get up at four o'clock in the morning unless you're living it. It's a real thrill to see somebody who has been challenging the limits in a small boat, coming in pleased with themselves, done well; sometimes pleased with himself because he has done badly but has managed to get some gear back and has managed to get into port. That is a success story on its own. So you buy him a cup of tea, sit him down and have a chat about what went wrong and all the rest of it, and everybody has a glum moment. And then it's, 'What are you going to do next?', and the reply comes, 'Well I'm going to go back tomorrow.' Brilliant!

I have a huge optimism about the future, because I think that we can get out there and tell people what we do. Tell people about how interesting our business is, tell people about how fascinating every day is here. You want to be here every day when the sun rises and the sun sets, and I'll tell you how beautiful this place is. Every day is different, and we have a huge appreciation of what happens every day in the natural world, it's part of our lives. It is not sat in an office, it is not under artificial light, it is not disguised in any way shape or form by central heating; it is cold, it is wet, it does smell, let's not hide behind any of the falsehoods.

It has to be part of somebody else's lives apart from just ours. So we have to expose ourselves and our industry to the general public, and how we do that is a very interesting task, and is not necessarily that simple. Do the public want to come and look at the fishing industry? Nine times out of ten, they can't be bothered. However, when they are on holiday, why do people always home in on a fishing port and have to have a look at a piece of fish? There is a curiosity, and that is something that we need to exploit, because I think that is the trigger that would make people think, 'Ooh, I haven't got a clue what goes on behind that door, wouldn't it be lovely to find out?'

We have a huge amount of diversity to work with as far as fishing methods, fish species, the availability of different fish during different seasons are concerned, and we're on a migratory route for fish, so we have choices as well and that is a luxury, but it is a luxury we mustn't abuse. We are dealing with the last wild, uninterfered with, natural, sustainable food resource on this planet. It is a luxury that we must take very, very careful note of, and exploit carefully to make sure that everybody else who buys that product understands that it is a luxury. Anybody who thinks we just go out and jump in a boat, throw a net over the side and come in and go to the pub, think on. It ain't like that.

Dawn arrival in Newlyn harbour.

10 Enjoying the Harvest of the Seas

At the fishmonger's

You want to eat seafood, but are not sure what to look for. Let us assume that you have decided to buy from a good fishmonger. He or she will advise on what is the best that day, and also on alternatives, what's in season, perhaps who has caught it and when. Most importantly, he or she will also willingly take the pain out of the preparation by taking the heads off, cleaning and filleting. Many will recommend suitable recipes. The most important thing is to go with an open mind about what you want to buy. It is no good wanting sea bass in high summer, as the best season is from October to January. Then there is the question of availability. If there have been several days of bad weather, the choice of fresh seafood will be limited. Be guided by the fishmonger, be flexible, and remember that many fish can be substituted in recipes by other, similar fish – so, for instance, megrim sole or lemon sole could be used instead of brill. Pollack or gurnard are excellent substitutes for cod. In the recipes that follow, some use a mixture of fish that can be adapted to what is available (see pages 213 and 235). In others, the chefs suggest alternatives.

What to look for when buying fresh seafood

- The skin of fresh or whole fish should be bright and shiny, and undamaged.
- The scales should all be intact on fish such as sardines, red mullet or sea bass. Any loose scales means the fish is probably old.
- Bright and clear eyes. If they are sunken, dull or red the fish has been out of the sea for too long.
- Gills should be bright pink or red and look 'frilly'. If they are dark or going brown reject the fish.
- Fillets of white fish should be a translucent white colour – apart from hake.
- Fresh fish and shellfish should not smell of anything except the sea or seaweed. If it smells overwhelmingly fishy, sour or acidic, don't buy it.
- Smoked fish should appear glossy; the flesh should be moist, not dry, and should have a fresh, smoky aroma.
- Fresh-cooked crab and lobster should have no cracks in their shells, and should feel heavy for their size. Reject any that are light, because they will probably have watery flesh.
- Live crabs and lobsters should be kept cool and damp until they are to be cooked.

The chart on page 194 gives tips on what to look for when buying fish and seafood, and the one below is a guide to what is in season in Cornwall – when the fish and shellfish are in the best condition and at their most abundant. However, this is only an approximate guide. For instance, the handline mackerel season varies around the Cornish coast. Mackerel is caught by fishermen from Newlyn and St Ives during the spring and summer, then from October to the end of January by bigger boats working from Looe and other south-coast Cornish ports.

Fish seasonality

- **Brill:** May–September
- **Brown crab:** April–November
- ***Cod:** January–May
- **Conger eel:** September–January
- **Coley (Saithe):** September–January
- ***Crawfish:** June–September
- **Dogfish:** March, April
- **Dover sole:** caught all year, at its best February–April
- **Grey mullet:** March–May
- ***Haddock:** all year, but quantities variable
- ***Hake:** all year, at its best April–September
- **Herring:** October–January
- **Horse mackerel:** March
- **Huss:** all year
- **John Dory:** April–October/November
- **Lemon sole:** January–June
- **Ling:** January–April
- **Lobster:** April–November, at its best July–November
- **Mackerel, handline caught:** April–January
- **Megrim sole:** all year, at its best April–September
- **Monkfish:** all year
- **Mussels:** all year (farmed), at their best September–December

- **Oysters (native):** 1 October–31 March
- **Oysters (Pacific):** all year
- **Pilchards:** May–October, but some available all year
- **Plaice:** March–November
- **Pollack, preferably line-caught:** May–October for line-caught, but some (not always line-caught), available all year
- **Ray:** May–February
- **Red gurnard:** all year
- **Red mullet:** all year
- **Red bream:** June–February
- **Sardines:** May–October, but some available all year
- **Scallops:** July–November, but some available all year
- **Sea bass, handline caught:** October–January
- ***Sole:** March, April
- **Spider crab:** April–October
- **Squid:** November–March
- **Turbot:** April–July
- **Velvet crab:** March, April
- **Whiting:** January–Easter
- **Wrasse:** March, April

* indicates 'pressure stock' – a species where stock levels are vulnerable.

The following pages describe the types of fish landed in Cornwall and the Isles of Scilly, and the methods used for fishing them.

Fish types

In Cornwall and the Isles of Scilly, the fish and shellfish landed fall into four distinct types: *pelagic fish*, which are fish that swim relatively near the surface of the sea; *demersal fish*, which are found either on or near the sea-bed; *cephalopods*, such as cuttlefish and squid; and *shellfish*, which in this case include both crustaceans and bivalves. The demersal fish then fall into separate categories for *flat fish*, such as plaice and sole; *round fish*, such as cod and haddock, and *non-bony fish*, such as shark, ray and monkfish.

The panel below shows the 50 species landed in Cornwall and the Isles of Scilly, and the charts on pages 197–9 illustrate some of the most common ones. *Note that the drawings are not to scale.*

Fish in Cornish waters

The 50 different species landed in Cornwall and the Isles of Scilly are:

Pelagic fish

- Herring
- Mackerel
- Pilchard/Sardine
- Sprat

Demersal fish

Flat fish

- Brill
- Dover sole
- Lemon sole
- Megrim sole
- Plaice
- Witch
- Turbot

Round fish

- Black bream
- Cod
- Conger eel
- Grey gurnard
- Grey mullet

- Haddock
- Hake
- Horse mackerel (scad)
- Huss
- John Dory
- Ling
- Pollack
- Red bream
- Red gurnard
- Red mullet
- Saithe (coley)
- Sea bass
- Tub gurnard
- Whiting
- Wrasse

Non-bony fish

- Blonde ray
- Dogfish
- Monkfish
- Ray (skate)
- Shark

- Spur dog
- Tope

Cephalopods

- Cuttlefish
- Octopus
- Squid

Shellfish

- Brown (common) crab
- Spider crab
- Velvet crab
- Crawfish
- Lobster
- Langoustine (Norway or Dublin Bay prawn)
- Mussel
- Oysters (native and Pacific)
- Scallop

Note: Recent controversy has turned the spotlight on skate stocks, which in some areas are thought to be over-fished. In Cornwall almost all the fish landed and sold as skate are in fact ray. In Britain the two names have become interchangeable – no wonder consumers and chefs are confused. The species of ray landed in Cornwall include blonde rays, star rays, thornback rays and owl rays.

Pelagic fish

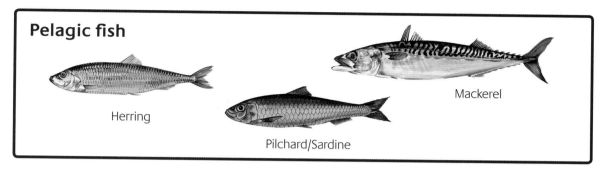

Herring

Pilchard/Sardine

Mackerel

Cephalopods

Squid

Octopus

Shellfish

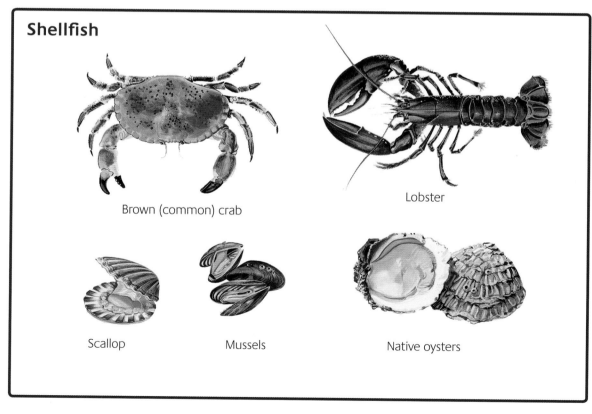

Brown (common) crab

Lobster

Scallop

Mussels

Native oysters

Demersal fish

Flat fish

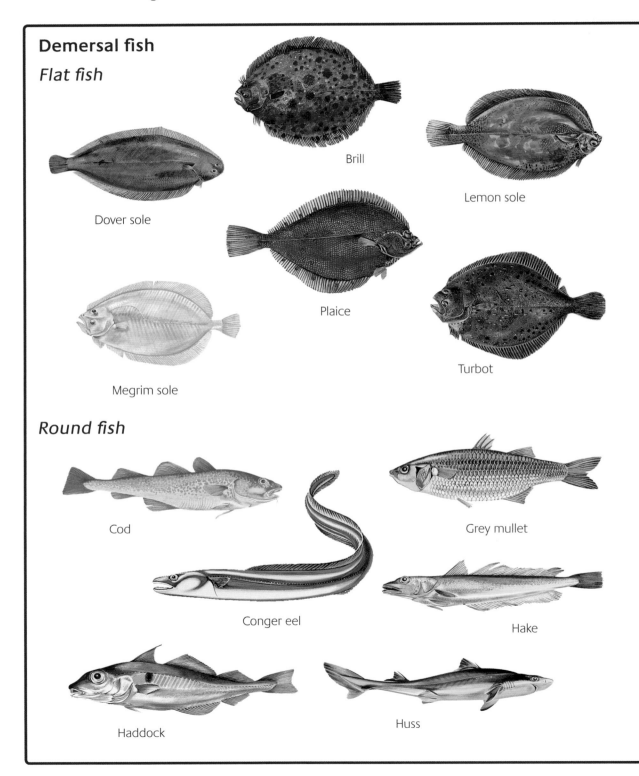

Brill

Dover sole

Lemon sole

Plaice

Turbot

Megrim sole

Round fish

Cod

Grey mullet

Conger eel

Hake

Haddock

Huss

Ling

Pollack

John Dory

Red mullet

Red gurnard

Saithe (Coley)

Sea bass

Whiting

Non-bony fish

Monkfish

Ray

Fishing methods

Trawling

A trawl is a stocking-shaped net which is pulled along the sea-bed. There are three types of trawler: beam trawlers, mid-water trawlers and bottom trawlers. A beam trawler has two nets – one on either side of the boat, suspended from a beam, with chains in front of the net to 'tickle up' the fish into the net. Mid-water and bottom trawlers tow the net behind the vessel's stern, either on the sea-bed or higher in the water. The nets are usually hauled in over the vessel's side. There are small inshore trawlers and larger trawlers that fish further out at sea. Most skippers trawl over soft, sandy ground to catch white fish such as cod, haddock or monkfish, and flat fish such as lemon sole or megrim sole, plaice and Dover sole.

Beam trawling and scalloping

For too long critics of the fishing industry have been very polarized in their views, arguing that big is bad – as in beam trawlers and scallopers – and small is beautiful, as in inshore boats and day-boat fishing. If only it were that simple.

For a start there are relatively few beam trawlers and trawlers in the Cornish fleet, and while many of them spend longer periods at sea, that does not necessarily mean they are damaging the sea-bed and removing every fish that gets in their way. It is true that beam trawling digs up the sand and agitates the ground in order to encourage the fish into the nets, but a good skipper understands which areas are suitable for trawling and which are not. In most wheelhouses the array of technology is impressive, with sonar, echo sounders and computerized 3D maps, all of which help to build up an exact picture of what the sea-bed looks like, which wrecks and rocks to avoid, and where the softer ground is best suited to trawling. Trawling over rocky ground is counter-productive. Any skipper will do his utmost to avoid sensitive areas or unsuitable grounds that might damage his trawl and cost him hours of fishing while he repairs his nets. Recent research has shown that 95 per cent of beam trawlers use 'wheels' on their beam shoes to reduce fuel costs, and these also reduce contact with the sea-bed. The maximum depth the trawl digs into the sea-bed is about 8 cm, but 3 cm is more typical, while the beam itself does not touch the ground. On a beam trawler towing two nets, each with a 4 metre-long beam, the average length of each net would be about 16 metres from the front to the cod end, which is where the fish gather. A far cry from the image perpetrated by their critics of nets the length of a football pitch or longer.

Small, inshore scallopers also have a place in the Cornish fishing industry mix, despite the controversy over this fishing method, which is coming in for intense criticism from the confrontational green groups. Cornish scallopers tend to fish local grounds, such as Falmouth Bay, selectively, and are usually small, inshore day boats, limited by a CSFC by-law to using no more than six dredges per side. It is bigger, mostly Dutch and Scottish boats, using between 17 and 20 dredges per side that take up far more scallops and cause more harm to the sea-bed. Smaller boats cannot afford to dredge anywhere other than soft, sandy areas, as the damage to their gear from working on rocky ground is too costly. Cornish scallopers try to rotate their fishing grounds to allow stocks to recover, but claim that this is often disrupted by foreign boats fishing in the same area.

Perhaps the critics should note the size and nationality of the boats they claim are causing the damage before making unqualified assertions.

Netting

Static nets are fixed on the sea-bed (as tangle nets), around wrecks, or at sea (as gill nets), and are left either for several hours or overnight. These would catch a variety of species including monkfish, pollack, ling, turbot, crawfish, spider crabs and hake, depending on location. Mesh sizes are controlled to avoid catching small and immature fish.

Potting

Crabs and lobsters are attracted into these pots, which are usually left out overnight and lifted every second day. The advantage of this method is that the shellfish are alive when caught and any undersized specimens are put back to grow on.

Handlining

Baited hooks on lines are dropped into the sea to lure the fish to take the bait. The number of hooks per line depends on the species being caught. Handlining is mostly for mackerel, sea bass and pollack, and tends to take only larger fish.

The following drawings are by Tony Knight of Brixham, reproduced with permission from the Living from the Sea Museum, Looe.

Beam trawling

Bottom trawling

Handlining

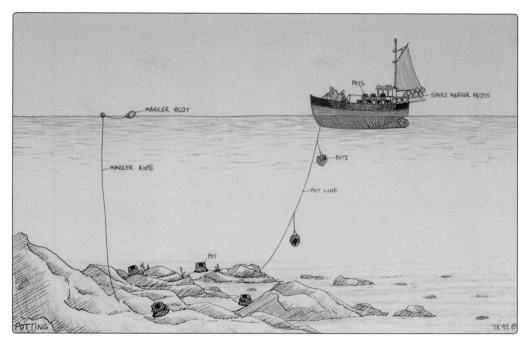

Potting

Netting

Ian Murray
Chef, and former fisherman, Cawsand

Ian Murray was a fisherman for more than 28 years before becoming a chef. He lives and works in South East Cornwall.

Ian Murray: I was born and bred in Cawsand, and I always messed about with boats. Various family, relations and friends had fishing boats, and as soon as I could walk practically I was in a fishing boat. I started fishing full time when I was 16, and I did it for about 12 months. At the time everybody wanted you to be having an apprenticeship and one thing and another, so I was persuaded to come ashore and learn an apprenticeship, which turned out to be a motor mechanic. And the day I got my indentures was the day I finished being a motor mechanic and went back fishing. I worked my way up from crew on various boats, crabbing, scalloping and trawling, and I crewed on big Brixham beam trawlers, and eventually I got my own boat – you know, skipper-owner and everything else, all the problems that went with that.

The first one was a 50 ft boat, I had a partnership in that, and eventually I had my own boat built in Holland, which was 40 ft, what they call a mini-beamer, and I had that one for eight, nine years. I sold that and then I went to work for a friend in Grimsby who had a long-lining business. Then I was long lining, working all over Britain, Scotland, Shetlands, couple of hundred miles out in the Atlantic, down into the Bay of Biscay. And various times I was working out of France, bought French fishing boats and delivered them back to England, and messed about with them, repaired them, worked them, sold them.

In about 1999 I met a guy in the Shetlands who was a chef off one of these big super-seismic oil-rig supply boats. I suddenly got interested in coming out of the fishing industry to go into the oil rig business. But I didn't want to go on deck of the boat, I wanted to do something else, and this guy really set me on a different track, a track I never even thought I was going to do, as the only reason I was cooking on the big trawlers was because nobody wanted to do the job. I said, 'How did you get the job?', and he said, 'You've got to have Merchant Navy qualifications.' So I said I hadn't got anything like that, me and education and college really were not suited at 49 to start doing something else. He told me to find out about it. So I was in Scalloway in the middle of the Shetlands, and I phoned up my wife and was telling her about it. Six weeks later I'm sitting in South Shields Technical College doing a Merchant Navy catering course.

It was a ship's cook and baker's certificate, so a great emphasis was put on the baking side of things, making your own bread, your cakes and everything like that. But then as the course progressed, then we went more on to the cooking side, so they could show you cooking skills. The lecturer chef, a chap called John Beale, used to do a lot of outside catering, and he used to take a team of us to do the rugby world cup, various golf tournaments, various Hampden Park events, all these football things. So that's how I got the feel for cooking ashore. That moved me on to another level – and then I was doing a bit of freelance work for catering agencies. And a very good friend, Bruce Cook, who owned trawlers in Brixham, he bought a hotel in the village, called the Cawsand Bay. And one day he phoned up and said, 'My second chef's leaving, do you fancy having a go at it?' I did 12 months there, and then he sold the business to somebody else. At the same time I was doing advanced patisserie and confectionery NVQ3 in Plymouth College, and I was talking to the chef lecturer there, and I said I'm fine doing pub grub and if I've really got to carry on doing that I will. But I just wondered how far I could go, and I really don't know how to go about this. And he said what I needed was to find a small, little exclusive hotel with about 10 or 12 bedrooms, with a restaurant that takes about 40 covers, and find a good owner-chef. And the very next day I picked up the *Western Morning News*, and it's the business property page on the Thursday morning, and there was 'top chef buys hotel in Looe' on the business property page. I thought I knew the Commonwood Manor [renamed Barclay House], because I'd been past the door hundreds of times, but I never had a clue who Nick Barclay was, or anything about him. So I just wrote to him and explained everything that I was, and for five years I worked for Nick.

When I was still on the fishing side of things it was seven- to ten-day trips, and you were catering for anything from eight hands to 15 hands on board the ship. That was always good fun. You never had a stable board to work from. Oh, I've cooked in gales of wind and everything like that, and sometimes you've got to batten down and forget about it for six, seven hours until it blows through. Long as you had one good meal during the day, and you always had a cupboard full of biscuits, crisps, all the associated rubbish that went with that. Lemonade and pop, orange juice, tea, coffee and everybody helps themselves. Chef was a secondary job, it got you out of some of the deck work. If something was wrong I could nip off and get something on to be cooked. If you think restaurant people can be food critics, you want to be stuck on board a boat with 12 people. If you don't have the best of food then everybody's moaning.

> " *There were times we've washed around the English Channel, washed around the north of Scotland and never earned a penny ...* "

I've been on boats that had drink aboard but it was never used at sea, 99 per cent of the people I've been with wouldn't drink at sea. A fisherman is committed the minute he leaves that quay. He's a different bloke, he's committed to go out there and catch fish. The ten days, seven days, whatever the trip was, until he was full up, the one sole thing was to catch fish to earn money, and that was your preoccupation. There were times we've washed around the English Channel, washed around the north of Scotland and never earned a penny, in fact been in debt. But then there were other good times when you earned a lot of money – that was part and parcel of the job.

I did it for 28 years, but there isn't so much camaraderie now as when I started fishing, because of the paperwork, the legislation. Oh you can't catch this and you can't catch that, and really being thrown to the European wolves by various governments, and civil servants who haven't got a clue what's going on. It's easy for somebody to sit in London and say, 'We'll ban the lemon sole season down in the Westcountry from January till May,' because the stocks are depleting, when that is the best time of the year for the boats to fish. The rest of the year is something different. They really don't listen, and what affects somebody in the North Sea doesn't affect down here.

Red gurnard.

I miss it from the point of view of seeing a complete new boat with new ideas that really have now come to the fore, advancement in gear technology and types of fishing that I would love to have had a go at back in the heydays, but it was harder to obtain the right gear, harder to obtain the information which gives you that chance to go and do it. But times move on, and you do something else, and I enjoy what I'm doing.

Customers are more discerning now, want to know where the fish comes from, how old the fish is. We can turn round and say the fish is 36 hours old at the most. They're quite willing to try a lot of different fish, which before they never did, so that is another good thing.

There's nothing better to me than a nice piece of pan-fried haddock, cook it slowly and then crisp it up at the end. Good pan-fried mackerel, nothing better, fresh hand-line mackerel, caught in a sustainable fishery. I used to be a cod fan, but then when I joined the Grimsby guys they wouldn't eat cod for love nor money. On the boat we did haddock. I love turbot, bass, Dover soles, I love it all. But if you have a choice keep it plain, simple, don't mess about with it, put it on a plate, sometimes with just a nice crusty bread roll, what more do you want? I detest any fish that's cooked in an oven in a liquor or in a sauce, because that's not what I want. The fish is what I want. The good old red gurnard, there isn't a better fish to eat, done simply, pan fried or grilled, seasoned well with a bit of butter on the top, nothing else, brilliant. Why complicate it?

11 Chefs and Recipes

Granny Farmer's Pan-fried Mackerel with Milk Gravy

Toby Ashworth, Managing Director
The Nare Hotel, Roseland

This recipe was a favourite of Toby Ashworth's great-great granny, Eliza Farmer. It has been passed down through subsequent generations and is still a firm family favourite. Graham Farmer, Eliza's son, was one of the pioneers of Cornish tourism, and introduced surfing on Newquay's Tolcarne beach in 1922. He leased the beach for 14 years from Sir Robert Edgcumbe. Toby Ashworth, Managing Director of the Nare Hotel, which sits in a stunning position on the Roseland peninsula overlooking Carne Beach, describes this as 'a simple, one-pan recipe that can be cooked on a beach barbecue, a Cornish range or even onboard a boat. The essential things are to have the freshest mackerel and some bacon.' The recipe uses ingredients that would mostly have been to hand in every Cornish home 100 years ago. 'In the days when pilchards and mackerel were the staple diet, there weren't the exotic ingredients we have today,' he explains. It combines the saltiness of the bacon with mackerel's unique flavour in the milk gravy (sauce), but could be served without the milk gravy if preferred.

Ingredients ... per person

- 2 slices bacon
- 1 mackerel, gutted
- plain flour
- milk

  For serving
- fresh granary bread (a 20th-century addition)
- lemons and salad leaves (optional)

Method

Dry fry the bacon in the frying pan. When the fat has run, but before the bacon browns, add the mackerel, which will cook in the bacon fat.

When the mackerel is just ready, remove fish and bacon from the pan and keep warm.

Add enough plain flour to the remaining fat in the pan to make a roux, then add enough milk to make a light milk gravy. (You may need to add a little butter or olive oil if there is not enough fat in the pan.)

If you do not have the benefit of a smoky barbecue, then cheat by using smoky bacon!

Pour milk gravy over the mackerel, and serve immediately.

Note: This would probably also work well with herring or sardines.

Sautéd Fillet of Monkfish, Quickly Marinated in Soy Sauce with Tomato, Shallot and Basil Relish

Nick Barclay, Chef-Proprietor
Barclay House Hotel, Looe

Nick Barclay has quickly made his name on the Cornish restaurant scene, winning a fistful of awards including the Cornwall Tourism award for Restaurant of the Year, and Taste of the West gold medals for three years running. A passionate fan of fresh local produce, he has taken on a new challenge – offering long, lazy lunches instead of dinners. 'Our five-year plan was to put Barclay House on the culinary map,' he said. 'Now our challenge is to target the lunch niche market, running with the trends towards healthier living and a better balanced lifestyle.' This recipe is typical of the dishes on Nick's lunch menu.

Ingredients ... serves 4

- 8 slices or pieces of monkfish – 90 g each
- 2 shallots, chopped
- 4 tomatoes
- 25 g fresh basil, finely chopped
- 60 ml balsamic vinegar
- 60 ml olive oil
- flour for dusting
- pepper
- balsamic vinegar reduction made from 60 ml balsamic vinegar reduced to 1 tbsp
- fresh basil pesto – 50 g basil and olive oil
- soy sauce

Method

To make the fresh basil pesto: Blanch basil in boiling water for 30 seconds, drain and refresh in cold water, and squeeze dry. Place in a blender with just enough olive oil to cover, and blend into a bright green liquid, which can be stored in a squeezy bottle until needed.

To make the relish: Drop the tomatoes in boiling water and remove, then skin them, and dice finely. Mix with the chopped shallots, chopped fresh basil, balsamic vinegar and olive oil, and season to taste.

To make the balsamic vinegar reduction: Reduce balsamic vinegar in a saucepan until syrupy, and store until needed. It needs to be watched carefully, so that it does not boil too fast and burn.

Dip the monkfish in soy sauce for no more than 2 minutes, then dust with a little flour, season with pepper (no salt as soy sauce is salty). Sauté in olive oil in a non-stick pan for 2 minutes on each side, until golden brown and cooked through.

Arrange on the plate with a drizzle of balsamic vinegar reduction (syrup) and a drizzle of fresh basil pesto, and serve with the relish.

This is equally good without the relish.

Note: As an alternative to monkfish you could use brill, turbot, John Dory or line-caught sea bass.

Cornish Fish Chowder

Gerry Boriosi, Lecturer
Cornwall College, Camborne

Gerry Boriosi has been a lecturer at Cornwall College for 28 years. After training in Switzerland and Italy, and working in a number of top London hotels and restaurants, including Boodles Club, what started as a temporary job at the college in Camborne, filling time while waiting for a visa to work in America, has become a lifetime's passion for all things Cornish. Among Gerry's alumni are Rick Stein, and many others who have gone on to be senior chefs or executives in hotels and restaurants all over the world

Ingredients ... serves 4

- 150 g smoked haddock, small dice
- 150 g monkfish, small dice
- 500 ml fish stock
- 500 ml chicken stock
- 200 g leeks, cut into very fine strips
- 200 g carrots, cut into very fine strips
- 200 g potatoes, small dice
- 60 g shallots, finely sliced
- 0.25 g (pinch) saffron
- 50 g butter
- chives for garnish

Method

Sweat sliced shallots in butter, and add saffron. Add stocks, and simmer gently for 15 minutes. Add leeks, carrots and potatoes, and cook for a further 8–10 minutes.

Add diced fish, and cook for 2 or 3 minutes. Serve in bowls, garnished with a chive blade.

Hot, Smoked Red Mullet, with Creamed Chive and Tarragon Potato, White Wine Sauce and Tomato Sauce

Gerry Boriosi, Lecturer
Cornwall College, Camborne

Ingredients ... serves 4

Hot, smoked red mullet
- 2 red mullet, filleted, trimmed and seasoned
- 2 tbsp olive oil
- 30 g jasmine tea
- 200 g Demerara sugar
- 200 g rice

Creamed chive and tarragon potato
- 500 g potatoes, peeled and cut into chunks
- 60 ml milk, warmed
- 60 ml double cream
- 10 g chives, finely chopped
- 10 g tarragon, finely chopped
- 50 g butter

White wine sauce
- 100 g shallots, peeled and diced
- 60 ml white wine
- 60 ml fish stock
- 200 ml double cream
- seasoning

Tomato dressing
- 1 tin plum tomatoes
- 60 g shallots, peeled and sliced
- 2 cloves garlic, finely chopped
- 200 ml tomato juice – a small tin or mixer bottle
- 50 g butter
- seasoning

Garnish
- aubergine skin, peeled into long strips
- chives

Method

The tomato sauce: Sweat sliced shallots in butter for a couple of minutes, add garlic, plum tomatoes and tomato juice, and reduce down slowly for 20 minutes. Check seasoning and consistency and pass through a fine sieve.

The potato: Steam or boil potatoes until soft, mash and add warm milk, cream and butter. Mix well to a smooth consistency, add chopped chives and tarragon.

The mullet: Lightly oil the flesh side of the red mullet fillets.

Combine smoking ingredients – tea, brown sugar and rice, and mix well.

Line a wok or other suitable container with foil, add smoking mix and place a wire mesh over this. Place wok over heat until mixture starts to smoke.

Place oiled fish on the wire mesh and cover with a lid. Cooking will take 6–8 minutes, depending on the size of the fish.

The white wine sauce: Put diced shallots, white wine and fish stock in a pan, reduce down, add double cream, and season. Cook for 2–3 minutes.

The garnish: Cut aubergine skin into very fine strips. Deep fry until crisp – approximately 1–2 minutes.

To serve: Pipe potato on to a plate. Place red mullet next to potato and dress with aubergine skin strips on top of the fish. Spoon around the white wine and tomato sauces.

Cornish Crab Bake
Billy Bunn, Fisherman

Billy Bunn was born and brought up in West Cornwall. After many years crewing on fishing boats in Newlyn and St Ives – on trawlers, gill-netters, and handlining for mackerel – he left the industry in 2000. He now works as a first mate on supply vessels supporting gas rigs in the North Sea, sailing out of Immingham or Lowestoft. Many of his fellow crew members are also former Cornish fishermen. When not at sea, he returns to his home in St Ives, and occasionally helps out on local fishing boats.

Ingredients ... serves 4

- 450 g crab meat, or the meat from one large crab – preferably a hen crab
- 1/2 large onion, finely diced
- 1 large clove garlic, finely diced
- 1/2 red pepper, finely diced
- 1/2 green pepper, finely diced
- 50 g butter
- 600 ml milk
- 300 ml double cream
- 45 g plain flour
- pinch of sea salt
- freshly ground black pepper
- good pinch of saffron
- 150 g mature cheddar, or other strong-flavoured cheese, grated
- 75 g fresh white breadcrumbs
- lemon for garnish
- watercress or parsley for garnish

Method

In a heavy-based saucepan, melt the butter and gently fry the onion and garlic, then add the diced peppers and cook until just cooked. Stir in the flour, followed by the milk and cream (or milk only – about 900 ml – for a less rich sauce), to make a white sauce, adding the pepper, salt and saffron to season. When the sauce is ready, add the crab meat and stir it in. Then add half the breadcrumbs to the mixture, stirring them in. Remove from the heat.

Spoon the mixture into an ovenproof dish, and sprinkle the remaining breadcrumbs on top. Finish with a good covering of grated cheese.

Place in a pre-heated oven, 180°C (350°F, gas 4), for about 20 minutes, or until the top has browned.

Garnish each serving with lemon, and either some parsley or a sprig of watercress. *Bon Appétit.*

Note: As an alternative to brown (or common) crab, you could use spider crab, lobster, crawfish or langoustines. *If you have a whole crab, and plan to dress it yourself, be sure to remove the gills, or 'dead men's fingers', which are poisonous.*

Wild Garlic Bastard Sole, with a Creamy Parsnip Purée, Paprika Roast Potatoes and Carrots

Paul Drye, Catering Development Manager St Austell Brewery

Despite having been a chef for 25 years, Paul Drye still gets a buzz of excitement when he finds new ingredients. On a recent tour of Newlyn fish market, with fish merchant Matthew Stephens as his guide, he came across a new flat fish that was a cross between megrim sole and lemon sole. According to Matthew, these are known in the trade as 'bastards'. Determined to see these unusual fish on his menu, he paired them with some warm, pungent, wild garlic. 'Wild garlic grows in great abundance in many parts of Cornwall, and is easy to find in summer,' he says. 'Just go for a walk in the countryside and follow your nose – the aroma is unmistakable.'

Ingredients ... serves 4

- 8 skinned bastard sole fillets (also known as Devon or witch sole)
- 30 good sized wild garlic leaves (also known as ramsons)
- 150 g Cornish butter
- 1 kg parsnips
- 50 ml double cream
- 600 g potatoes
- 400 g carrots
- 50 ml olive oil
- 1 tsp paprika
- a little salt and black pepper

Method

Wash your wild garlic leaves, and chop coarsely. Soften 100 g of the butter and stir in half the chopped leaves to make a garlic butter. Set aside.

Wash, peel, and cut the potatoes into neat pieces, and par-boil for 8 minutes. Drain and place in a roasting tin. Mix the paprika into the olive oil with a good pinch of salt, and using a pastry brush coat the surface of the potatoes. Roast in a pre-heated oven at 200°C (400°F, gas 6) for 20–25 minutes, or until nicely brown and crisp.

Wash and peel the parsnips, and boil in lightly salted water until tender. Drain, and return to the heat for a few seconds to dry out a little. Add the rest of the butter, the cream, and a generous twist of black pepper, and mash thoroughly.

Peel and cut the carrots into neat batons, or similar shapes to the potatoes. Boil in lightly salted water until just tender, but still with a bite to them.

Lay the sole fillets with what was the skin-side facing down, and sprinkle with a little salt and a twist of black pepper. Then take the remaining garlic leaves and spread on top of the fish fillets. Roll up each one quite tightly. Cook in a steamer for 12 minutes.

Melt the wild garlic butter in a small pan.

To serve, put some parsnip purée in the centre of each plate, topped with the steamed fish – two rolls per person, but cut in half to produce four rounds. Place the potatoes and carrots around the fish, and drizzle the melted garlic butter over the top of the sole. Serve immediately.

Chef's note: If you can't find wild garlic, use chives rolled up in the fish, and an ordinary garlic butter.

Note: Alternative fish could include lemon sole, megrim sole, plaice or any similar flat fish.

Mexican-style Cornish Spider Crab Salad, with Guacamole and Tortillas

Gareth Eddy, Green's Bar and Restaurant, Rosarrow Golf and Country Club, St Minver

Gareth Eddy grew up in Cornwall and is passionate about Cornish produce. After a short career fishing he cooked in several top Cornish kitchens, making his name at the St Austell Brewery's Pescadou in Padstow. In 2006 he took over running Green's Bar and Restaurant at Rosarrow Golf and Country Club, St Minver.

Ingredients ... serves 4

- 800 g white spider crab meat
- 400 g brown spider crab meat

Guacamole
- 2 avocados – firm, finely chopped
- 1 green chilli
- 5 spring onions, chopped
- 2 tbsp (30ml) Greek yoghurt
- 1 tbsp chopped coriander (optional)
- juice of 1 lime

Coriander oil
- 1 bunch coriander
- 140 ml olive oil, blended with the coriander until smooth

Tortillas
- 250 g unbleached white flour
- 1 1/2 tsp sea salt
- 1 1/2 tsp baking powder
- 50 g lard or duck fat
- 227 ml hot water

Pickled cucumber
- 1 cucumber cut into long, thin slices
- 284 ml malt vinegar
- 2 chopped red chillies

Garnish
- 284 ml sweet chilli sauce (optional)
- 8 lime wedges
- 1 bowl of peppery salad leaves

Method

The tortillas: Combine the flour, salt and baking powder in a bowl, and rub in the lard or duck fat. Add hot water, and mix lightly to a soft but not runny dough. Leave to rest in the fridge for 20 minutes.

Divide the dough into 20 pieces, then shape into balls, cover and rest. Once rested, roll out each ball on a floured surface to a 20 cm disc.

Heat a dry griddle over a high heat, and cook the tortillas on both sides, turning over as soon as the surface begins to bubble. Store between warm cloths.

The guacamole: Peel and stone the avocados, and put the flesh in a food processor. Add chopped spring onion, coriander (if used), green chilli, yoghurt and lime juice. Blend to preferred consistency.

The pickled cucumber: Put the sliced cucumber in the vinegar with the chopped chillies, and leave for only 3–4 minutes.

Heat the plates, and place 5 tortillas on each, then put a nest of salad leaves in the middle, and three slices of cucumber on top. Put quenelles of brown and white crab meat on the plate, and top with guacamole. Decorate with the coriander oil, and add a couple of wedges of lime. Serve with the chilli sauce.

Note: This could also be made using brown and white meat from a brown (common) crab.

Parmesan and Thyme Glazed Brill with Cauliflower Purée and Purple Sprouting Broccoli, served with a Warm Tomato and Red Onion Vinaigrette

Chris Eden, Chef
Marina Hotel, Fowey

Chris Eden grew up in Cornwall and, like many ambitious youngsters, went away and cooked in top London restaurants before returning. One key attraction was the rapidly improving quality of Cornish ingredients, available all year. So it is not surprising that his menu is based on fresh Cornish produce with plenty of fish, mostly supplied by local day boats.

Ingredients ... serves 4

The fish
- 4 brill fillets, skinned – each weighing approx. 150–160 g
- 300 g spinach
- 4 heads purple sprouting broccoli
- 200 g bread
- 10 g thyme leaves
- 30 g melted butter
- 50 g grated Parmesan cheese
- 1 cauliflower
- 10 g butter
- 100 ml milk
- seasoning

Tomato and red onion vinaigrette
- 5 tomatoes, deseeded and diced
- 2 red onions, chopped
- 100 ml groundnut (peanut) oil
- 20 ml olive oil
- 35 ml white wine vinegar
- 20 g chopped chervil
- 20 g chopped leaf parsley
- 20 g chopped chives
- seasoning

Method

Put bread, thyme and Parmesan in a food processor and pulse to chop and mix. Add 30 g melted butter to make a paste. Roll the mixture between two sheets of greaseproof paper, to about 5 mm thick. (It is probably easiest to roll it out on a baking sheet, and then chill on the baking sheet until set.) Cut to size to cover the brill.

Finely slice the cauliflower, and sweat slowly in remaining butter in a covered pan until soft. Add milk and seasoning and bring to the boil. Purée until smooth.

For the vinaigrette, emulsify the oils and vinegar, add the remaining vinaigrette ingredients, and gently warm.

Wilt the spinach, and steam the purple sprouting broccoli until tender.

Place brill under hot grill until perfectly cooked and golden brown. Cooking time will depend on the thickness of the fish – use a cocktail stick to test for doneness.

Circle purée around centre of a warm plate. Add spinach inside the purée and put fish on top. Arrange broccoli, and drizzle the warm vinaigrette around and on top of the dish. Chris suggests serving with a dish of boiled new potatoes, in season.

Note: Other flat fish – megrim sole, plaice, lemon sole or turbot – can be used in place of brill.

Whole Baked John Dory with Lemongrass and Chilli

Gill Faiers
Bangors Organic, Poundstock

Gill Faiers of Bangors Organic recommends this as a seasonal recipe for winter months. She has chosen John Dory for its good flavour and special texture.

Bangors started as an organic tearoom, serving totally certified organic produce, much of it grown in the Faiers' garden. The business has expanded, and now comprises accommodation, a restaurant and tearoom. This dish was developed by chef Ian Shute, who cooks menus that follow the seasons, using either fruit and vegetables just picked from their garden, or locally grown, organic produce.

Ingredients ... serves 4

- 4 whole John Dory
- 4 stalks lemongrass
- 1/2 hot chilli per serving – fresh or dried, we use Alberta – finely chopped
- knob of butter
- white wine
- sea salt
- 4 lemon wedges
- olive oil

Method

Heat oven to 200°C (400°F, gas 6). Brush an ovenproof dish with olive oil, bruise the lemongrass and place in the dish.

Place the fish on top, and add the finely chopped chilli, a splash of white wine, and a knob of butter. Season with a pinch of sea salt.

Bake for about 20 minutes.

Serve with sautéed potatoes, stir-fried chard, and a wedge of lemon.

Note: In place of the chard, any seasonal greens can be used. New potatoes may also be used, when in season. The recipe could be simplified, and be just as successful using a knob of butter and splash of white wine, again serving with whatever green vegetables are in season.

Note: Small flat fish, such as plaice, sole or dabs, or fillets of round white fish, such as pollack, could also be used.

From left: Gill Faiers, chef Ian Shute, Neil Faiers.

Rosemary-skewered Scallops, Bread and Pancetta

Neil Haydock, Head Chef Fifteen Cornwall

Neil Haydock is Head Chef at Fifteen Cornwall, which opened in 2005. He came to Cornwall after cooking at prestigious venues including the Sandy Lane in Barbados and Terence Conran's Bluebird and Mezzo restaurants in London. Based on the model set up by Jamie Oliver, each year the Fifteen Cornwall Foundation helps 20 students from disadvantaged backgrounds to build new careers in the restaurant industry. Neil Haydock is passionate about the Fifteen concept, and about working with local farmers, growers and fishermen to make the best use of the expanding range of distinctive Cornish products. The menu at Fifteen has been designed to highlight fresh fish, meat, vegetables, fruit and salads, bringing a Cornish interpretation to the Fifteen style of fresh, seasonal and Mediterranean-inspired dishes.

Ingredients ... serves 4

- 2 loaves rustic-style white bread
- 24 shelled and trimmed scallops
- 8 fresh rosemary stems, approx 30 cm long
- 16 slices pancetta
- 200 ml extra virgin olive oil
- sea salt and black pepper

Method

Strip the rosemary stems, by placing your thumb and forefinger at the top of the stem and pulling downwards to remove all the leaves to make skewers. Reserve the stems. Put the rosemary leaves into a pestle and mortar, and pound lightly to crush them. Then add the olive oil.

Cut the bread into 2 cm cubes, and toss them in the olive oil and rosemary mixture. Next, toss the scallops in the olive oil.

Take one of the rosemary stems and use it to skewer a scallop, followed by a piece of bread. Repeat until there are three scallops and three pieces of bread on each skewer.

Wrap two slices of pancetta around each skewer. Place them on an oven-proof tray, drizzle with the remaining olive oil/rosemary mixture, and season with sea salt and black pepper. Place in a hot oven (220°C, 425°F, gas 7) for 8 minutes, or until the scallops feel firm to the touch and the bread is crisp.

I like to serve the skewers with an Italian bread salad made of roughly chopped fresh tomatoes, cucumber, fresh marjoram, red onion and day-old rustic bread (which soaks up the juices), dressed with good olive oil and red wine vinegar.

Note: As an alternative to scallops, you could use chunks of monkfish or rock salmon.

Smoked Haddock Topped with Wholegrain Mustard and Cornish Cheese Rarebit, with Crushed Swede and Carrot and Mixed Leaves
Stuart Hayler, Chef
Five Degrees West, Falmouth

Stuart Hayler joined Five Degrees West in Falmouth early in 2006. This popular bar is a relaxed place to enjoy good food in a stylish setting. It offers formal meals, or shared dishes on a comfy sofa, and Stuart sources many key ingredients in Cornwall, or from Cornish suppliers. Salad leaves and herbs are grown in the gardens behind the elegant town house that has won several regional and national awards, including Cornwall Tourist Board's Pub of the Year award in 2004, and the 2006 national award for Premium Bar of the Year. Stuart trained in Cheltenham, but found Cornwall's laid-back lifestyle hard to resist. Before moving to Falmouth he cooked at the Bedruthan Steps near Newquay, and in Truro at Indaba.

Ingredients ... serves 4

- 4 fresh-smoked haddock fillets
- 450 g swede
- 450 g carrots
- Cornish butter to mash with swede and carrots
- salt and pepper to season

   The rarebit
- 1/4 bottle St Austell Tribute Ale
- 150 g bread
- 75 g grated Cornish cheddar
- 1 tbsp Worcestershire sauce
- 1 tbsp wholegrain mustard
- 1 tbsp chopped parsley

   To serve
- mixed salad leaves
- crusty bread
- lemon and lime wedges

Method

To begin: Peel swede and carrots, and cut into small dice of about 1 cm. Place in a pan of boiling, salted water, and cook until medium soft.

While the vegetables are cooking, put the rarebit ingredients in a blender and blend to a smooth, thick paste, adding more ale if necessary.

The haddock: Wash the smoked haddock, and place on a lightly oiled tray, skin side down.

Spread the rarebit over the haddock, but avoid using too much as this makes the dish very rich.

Place the fish in the oven at 220°C (425°F, gas 7) for 6–8 minutes, or until golden brown.

While the haddock is cooking, drain the swede and carrot, and lightly mash with butter. Add salt and pepper to taste.

To serve: Place mashed vegetables in the centre of a plate, and place haddock on top.

Serve with the fresh, crisp salad leaves, and garnish with lemon and lime wedges.

Note: Instead of smoked haddock try smoked pollack or any other smoked white fish.

Pan-fried Cornish Turbot, Buttered Leeks and Glazed Beetroot

Peter Hingston, Estate Head Chef Tresco, Isles of Scilly

Peter Hingston is the Estate Head Chef on the island of Tresco, taking an overview of the kitchens of both the Island Hotel and the New Inn (left) on Tresco, and the Hell Bay Hotel on Bryher. Although he is a Devon boy, growing up in Teignmouth and getting his first job in a professional kitchen in Torquay's Imperial Hotel, he came to Tresco in 1993, and has not looked back. After a couple of years at the New Inn, he moved to the Island Hotel, and has a new role working in the three kitchens, working with the three head chefs to develop new dishes. He chose turbot because it has a good meaty texture, which goes well with the earthy tastes of the beetroot and the leeks. 'It is a fantastic fish to work with, and of course we cook a lot of fish here, visitors expect it when they come to the islands.'

Ingredients ... serves 4

- 8 turbot fillets – 160 g fillets
- 2 medium leeks, washed, cut into 1 cm thick slices
- 250 g butter
- salt and pepper
- 450 g raw beetroot, unpeeled
- 250 ml water
- 250 ml cider vinegar
- 225 g caster sugar
- 1 uncooked beetroot – for crispy vegetable decoration
- 1/2 leek – for crispy vegetable decoration
- oil for frying

Method

Peel and grate 225 g raw, unpeeled beetroot. Put in a pan with the water, vinegar and sugar. Simmer for 10 minutes. Push the beetroot through a fine sieve. Catch the juice in a clean pan, and reduce until syrupy.

Cook the remaining unpeeled beetroot in boiling, salted water until tender. Strain, peel and cut into 1 cm cubes, and add to the syrup.

Melt 125 g of butter in a large saucepan. Once bubbling, add the leeks with 2 tablespoons of water, season and place the lid on top. Stir occasionally, until the leeks are tender – about 5–6 minutes.

Add the remaining butter to a warm frying pan. Season the turbot fillets on both sides, place them in the bubbling butter, and cook until golden and cooked halfway through, then turn and repeat.

Crispy vegetables: Peel, slice and cut the beetroot into very thin strips. Cut the leek in half, then into 5 cm pieces, and cut into very thin strips.

Deep-fry the leeks and beetroot separately in very hot oil (at least 160°C). They will cook at different speeds. Remove when slightly golden, turn on to kitchen paper, and season with salt.

To serve, arrange the leek slices and beetroot cubes on the plate to the same size as the fish. Place the turbot on top, then the crispy vegetables, and decorate with the beetroot syrup.

Note: Instead of turbot, you could use brill or any other white fish, such as cod, lemon sole, megrim sole or sea bass.

Millefeuille of Fish and Shellfish, with Coriander and Herb-infused Oil

Greg Laskey, Head Chef
New Yard Restaurant, Trelowarren

Greg Laskey was brought up and trained in Cornwall before working in several restaurants, including his own, in various UK locations. The opportunity to work at Trelowarren, where the majority of his ingredients come from within ten miles of the estate, was too good to miss. Fish and shellfish are from local day boats, complemented by seasonal, local goodies such as samphire and wild sea spinach.

Ingredients ... serves 4

Poaching liquor
- 2 shallots
- 1 large carrot
- 2 cloves garlic
- 1/2 tsp crushed black pepper
- pinch of salt
- handful of parsley stalks
- 1 litre water

The fish
- 120 g fish per person + shellfish: choose the best seasonal fish – e.g., a mix of scallops, mussels, clams, lobster, bream, sole, bass, mullet or cod
- 400 g puff pastry, cut into 8 squares
- 1 tbsp coriander seeds
- 150 ml olive oil
- handful of basil leaves
- 2 tomatoes, skinned, seeded and diced
- 2 cloves garlic, chopped
- squeeze of lemon juice
- salt and black pepper
- 2 leeks, braised in olive oil
- 8 stalks asparagus (in season, or more leeks), briefly cooked
- 150 g samphire (in season), washed liberally in cold water, briefly poached and drained – or a mix of seasonal vegetables: courgettes, fine beans, mangetout or sugar-snap peas

Method

The poaching liquor: Poach all the ingredients in the water for 20 minutes on a low heat; season to taste.

The fish: Poach the skinned fish in the simmering (not boiling) poaching liquor for 10 minutes.

Bake the puff pastry squares till golden brown.

Dry roast the coriander seeds until they change colour, and add olive oil, basil, tomatoes, lemon juice, salt, pepper and garlic. Warm slightly.

Prepare the vegetables and keep warm.

Put one pastry square on each plate. Place the plain fish on top; garnish with braised leeks, asparagus and samphire, and pour the herb-infused oil liberally over. Top with the second pastry square. Serve.

Note: The fish can be changed according to the seasons and availability – a mix of white, oily and shellfish, and bivalves such as mussels or scallops.

Sea Bass with Saffron Sauce and Tomato *Concassé*

Ben Lightfoot, Chef
The Sticky Prawn, near Flushing

Ben Lightfoot (below right) has been cooking at the Sticky Prawn, which he owns with his father, Paul (below centre), for five years. Set in a superb position on Flushing quay, the Sticky Prawn is ideally placed to make the most of fresh Cornish fish. Cornish-born, Ben is passionate about using as much local, organic and Cornish produce as possible – fish, tomatoes, cream, butter, cheese, game, meat and vegetables.

Ingredients ... serves 4

The fish
- 4 fresh sea bass fillets – line-caught
- 600 g fresh baby leaf spinach – washed
- 4 spring onions, finely chopped
- fresh nutmeg
- freshly ground salt and pepper
- butter or oil for cooking
- 2 large beef tomatoes, or 4 tomatoes

The sauce
- 600 ml fish stock
- 300 ml Noilly Prat or dry vermouth
- 300 ml white wine, Cornish if possible
- 300 ml double cream
- 4 shallots finely diced
- butter or oil for cooking
- pinch of saffron

Method

The sauce: Sauté the shallots in butter or oil, then add the white wine and Noilly Prat (or vermouth), and reduce to one-third of original volume. Add fish stock, and reduce again to one-third. Add double cream, and as the sauce gets to boiling point add a pinch of saffron. You can reduce the sauce further if you wish. It can be made in advance and reheated.

The tomato concassé: Skin the tomatoes – either by grilling or dipping briefly in boiling water. Deseed the skinned tomatoes, and dice into very small pieces.

The fish: Briefly fry the spring onions in oil in a hot pan, then add the spinach and allow it to wilt. Season with freshly grated nutmeg, salt and pepper.

Meanwhile, put the bass on a buttered baking tray or grill pan, skin side up, and place under a very hot grill for 3–5 minutes (depending on thickness of the fish, and the heat of your grill), until the skin is crispy.

Place fish on the spinach mixture, serve with tomato *concassé* and the saffron sauce.

Pan-roasted Lemon Sole

Ian Murray, Chef
The Devonport Inn, Kingsand

Ian Murray started fishing as a young boy, and turned to cooking some 40 years later. He cooked on board trawlers and many other boats before opting for a kitchen on dry land. He spent five years at the award-winning Barclay House Hotel in Looe, and is now cooking at the Devonport Inn in his home village of Kingsand in South East Cornwall. At the Devonport Inn he has developed a menu that is simple and light in style, using lots of local fish supplied by Bluesail Fish in Looe.

Ingredients ... per person

- 1 whole lemon sole, gutted
- 30–40 g butter
- olive oil
- sea salt and freshly ground black pepper
- flour for dusting
- lemon juice (optional)
- lemon, parsley or dill for serving

Method

Season the whole lemon sole and set the oven at 200°C (400°F, gas 6).

Heat a little olive oil in a large, ovenproof pan.

Lightly dust the lemon sole with flour and put in the pan.

Cook gently for about 2 minutes on each side, then transfer the pan to the oven and cook for a further 6–8 minutes, until the fish is cooked right through.

While the fish is cooking, melt the butter in a small pan and heat until it becomes frothy and then golden brown. At this stage you could add a squeeze of lemon juice to the butter.

Place the fish on a large plate, pour over the brown butter and garnish with a sprig of parsley or dill, and some lemon.

Serve with a salad, simple green vegetables and new potatoes, or chips if desired.

Note: Lemon sole is considered the fish that represents Looe. It comes from a non-pressure stock and is not subject to quotas. Alternatives could be plaice, megrim sole, turbot, brill or any other flat fish. Ian Murray suggests leaving the fish whole and serving with the head on, but the fish can be trimmed, if preferred, before cooking.

Newlyn-landed Ray Wing Stuffed with Black Olive Tapenade, Char-grilled Vegetables and Herb Oil

Ben Reeve, Chef
The Bay Restaurant, Penzance

Stephen and Yvonne Hill opened the Bay Restaurant at the Mount Prospect Hotel in 2002, designing it to showcase the freshest local produce. Chef Ben Reeve uses fish from Newlyn and Looe, produce from nearby farms and gardens, and herbs from dedicated local growers. The menu changes with the seasons.

Ingredients ... serves 4

The fish
- 1.5 kg ray wing, filleted and skinned, or 4 ray wings, filleted and skinned
- butter and olive oil for roasting

Tapenade
- 250 g stoned black kalamata olives
- 50 g anchovies
- 25 g capers
- 1 1/2 cloves garlic
- 2 tsp olive oil
- pinch of black pepper

Herb oil
- 25 g flat-leaf parsley
- 10 g coriander
- 10 g tarragon
- 25 g chervil
- extra virgin olive oil to blend

Char-grilled vegetables
- a mix of seasonally available vegetables such as: sliced sweet peppers; fennel – cut in half or quarters, according to size; plum tomatoes, halved; courgettes, sliced; Cornish new potatoes, cooked

Method

The tapenade: Blend all tapenade ingredients for approximately one minute – the mix should still be fairly chunky.

The herb oil: Roughly chop the herbs, add a little extra virgin olive oil and season.

The ray: Place the filleted ray wing clean side down (the upside, skin side will have a pink look).

Spread the tapenade thinly over the fish, roll up and secure with a cocktail stick.

Roast in a hot oven with a little butter and olive oil for approximately 10 minutes. Leave to rest for two minutes before serving.

While the fish is cooking, brush the vegetables with olive oil and quickly char grill. Alternatively, roast the vegetables in olive oil in a hot oven.

Arrange the ray on a plate, with some vegetables, and decorate with the herb oil.

Note: This recipe could be made using fillets of other flat fish such as megrim sole, plaice or lemon sole.

Right: Ben Reeve, chef at The Bay.

Herring Recheado, Katchumber Salad and Pilau Rice

Rick Stein
The Seafood Restaurant, Padstow

Rick Stein needs no introduction: his restaurants, television programmes and books all promote Cornish fish. This recipe is from *Rick Stein's Seafood*.

Ingredients ... serves 4 as starter

The fish
- 4 x 225 g herrings, filleted, heads off
- 1 tsp Goan masala paste per fish

The rice
- sunflower oil, for frying
- 6 large shallots, peeled and thinly sliced
- 3 whole cloves
- 3 green cardamom pods
- 5 cm piece of cinnamon stick
- 1 bay leaf
- 275 g basmati rice
- 1/2 tsp salt
- 600 ml boiling water

The katchumber salad
- 450 g vine-ripened tomatoes, thinly sliced
- 1 medium red onion, quartered and thinly sliced
- 2 tbsp roughly chopped coriander
- 1/4 tsp ground cumin
- 1 tbsp white wine vinegar
- 1/4 tsp salt

The Goan masala paste
- 1 tsp cumin seeds
- 2 tsp coriander seeds
- 2 tsp black peppercorns
- 1 tsp whole cloves
- 1 tsp turmeric powder
- 110 g medium-hot red chillies, stalks removed and chopped roughly
- 1 tsp salt
- 6 cloves garli c, chopped roughly
- 1 tsp light muscovado sugar
- 1 tsp tamarind paste (optional)
- 5 cm fresh root ginger, peeled, chopped roughly
- 2 tbsp red wine vinegar

Method

If you are cooking the herrings on the barbecue, light it 40 minutes before you are ready to cook.

The Goan masala paste: Grind the cumin seeds, coriander seeds, peppercorns and cloves to a fine powder. Transfer to a food processor and add the other ingredients. Blend to a smooth paste.

The fish: Spread the cut face of one fillet with a teaspoon of masala paste. Place another fillet on top, reshape the fish and tie in two places with string.

The rice: Heat 1 cm of oil in a large frying pan. Add the sliced shallots and fry them, stirring occasionally until crisp and golden. Lift out with a slotted spoon on to plenty of kitchen paper, and leave to drain.

Heat 2 tablespoons of oil in a large pan, add the whole spices and the bay leaf and cook for a few seconds until they start to smell aromatic. Stir in the rice, salt and water, bring to the boil, then cover and cook over a low heat for 10 minutes. If you are cooking the herrings under the grill, pre-heat it to high.

The katchumber salad: Layer all the ingredients together in a shallow dish.

Remove the rice from the heat, and leave for 5 minutes. Barbecue or grill the herrings for 3 minutes each side until crisp and lightly golden. Lift on to warmed plates. Toss the fried shallots with a little salt, and stir into the cooked rice. Serve with herrings and salad.

Note: Mackerel is a good alternative. The fishmonger can fillet the fish and remove the heads.

Starry Gazey Pie

Richard Stevenson, Chef
The Ship Inn, Mousehole

Mousehole is home of starry gazey pie. According to legend, Tom Bawcock bravely set sail in appalling weather after days of storms had left the village on the verge of starvation. He returned with seven sorts of fish, which were baked in a pie with the heads and tails above the pastry crust (gazing at the stars), to prove there were fish in the pie. The pie is recreated each year on 23 December in the Ship Inn – an occasion for drinking, feasting and singing, including the traditional song, *Tom Bawcock's Eve*.

Ingredients ... serves 6

Pastry
- 300 g plain flour
- 150 g butter
- cold water to mix
- milk or melted butter for pastry glaze

Filling
- 400 g undyed smoked haddock fillets
- 200 g pollack fillets
- 200 g whiting fillets
- 200 g ling fillets
- 6 herrings or pilchards/sardines for presentation
- 3 hard-boiled eggs, chopped
- sea salt and freshly ground black pepper
- 1 litre milk (or half milk and half water)
- 1 small onion, peeled
- 3 cloves
- small bunch parsley – separate the stalks and leaves, finely chop the leaves
- 50 g butter
- 45 g plain flour

Method

Make the pastry by rubbing the butter into the flour, and then adding enough water to bind the ingredients together. Chill in the fridge until required.

Cut the heads and tails off the herrings (or pilchards/sardines), and put aside. The cuts must be angled so that on the finished pie the fish look upwards. The remaining herring can be filleted, skinned, and added to the fish mixture if desired.

Poach fish fillets in the milk (or milk and water), with the onion, cloves and parsley stalks, until just yielding to a knife. Drain off poaching liquor and reserve, and flake the fish.

Make a béchamel sauce, using the butter, flour and poaching liquid. Season, and add the flaked fish, and the chopped parsley. Put this mixture into a large pie dish, and add the hard-boiled eggs.

Roll out the pastry, and use it to cover the pie. Arrange the herring heads and tails to look as if they are swimming through the pie. Cover the eyes with pieces of pastry during cooking, to keep them bright.

Glaze the pastry with milk or melted butter, and cook in a hot oven at 200°C (400°F, gas 6) for 10 minutes, then at 180°C (350°F, gas 4) for about 50 minutes, depending on the size of the pie.

Note: According to one version of the legend, the original pie used sand eels, horse mackerel (scad), herrings, pilchards, dogfish and ling. Try a mix of white fish – pollack, smoked haddock, cod, whiting, ling – and herrings or pilchards, according to availability.

Grilled Fillet of Hake with Two-colour Pasta, Asparagus, Langoustine Tails and a Red Pepper Jus

Nigel Tabb, Chef-Proprietor
Tabbs Restaurant, Truro

Tabbs moved to Truro in 2005. Nigel Tabb is passionate about working with the growing number of specialist producers in Cornwall, and makes everything from bread to ice cream and chocolates. 'Hake is a lovely fish, readily available from Cornish boats,' he says. 'It is quite soft, so get your fishmonger to fillet, scale, gut and pin bone it, and ask for some bones to make your fish stock. You can freeze any surplus.'

Ingredients ... serves 4

- 1kg hake fillet
- 12 langoustine or langoustine tails
- 2 minced onions
- 2 cloves garlic, crushed

  Pasta
- 250 g pasta flour
- 2 eggs
- 2 egg yolks
- pinch salt
- 1 tsp virgin olive oil
- 1 tsp squid ink or paprika, depending on the colour you prefer

- 8 asparagus spears
- 1 clove garlic finely chopped
- 1 tbsp double cream or crème fraiche
- butter for frying
- red pepper, finely chopped
- 2 shallots, finely chopped
- a little dry sherry
- 3 tsp crème fraiche or double cream

Method

Mix the pasta flour, eggs and egg yolks, salt, olive oil and colouring into a dough, or two doughs of different colours. Pass through a pasta machine six times, folding and turning each time. Reduce further with a couple more passes through the machine, then cut to the thickness you want. Simmer in salted, boiling water, with a little oil, for 2–3 minutes until just tender. Drain and refresh in cold water. Alternatively, use 400 g bought fresh pasta, and follow the instructions.

Cook the langoustine for 3–5 minutes in boiling, salted water, refresh and gently peel off the shell and pull out the tail. Keep the shells and add to the washed fish bones. Just cover with water, and add minced onions and crushed garlic. Bring to the boil and simmer for 20 minutes, strain and you have fish stock.

For the red pepper jus: Gently fry the shallots; add the red pepper, cook for a further 2–3 minutes, then add about 285 ml of fish stock, reduce by half to two-thirds, and add a little dry sherry. Bring back to the boil and add crème fraiche, boil again and check seasoning. Cover until serving.

To assemble the dish: Season the hake, and grill it skin side up. While the fish is cooking, gently stir fry the asparagus and langoustine tails in a little butter. If the asparagus is thick, split it down the length of the stalk. Add a little crushed garlic and the pasta, stir gently then add a tablespoon of cream and heat for about a minute. Arrange on plates, top with the grilled fish, and dress with the red pepper jus.

Use leeks or courgettes if asparagus is not in season.

Note: You could try black bream, haddock or pollack.

Red Gurnard and Braised Fennel with Orange Dressing and Pickled Kale

Nik Tinney, Chef-Proprietor Saffron, Truro

Nik Tinney is a Truro boy. After cooking in top London restaurants he returned to Cornwall, to cook good food at Saffron. He is passionate about using Cornish suppliers, and sources vegetables, salads and herbs as locally as possible. Fish comes from Newlyn and Penryn, oysters from Falmouth.

Ingredients ... serves 4

Braised fennel
- 1 kg fennel
- 2 sprigs rosemary
- 1 level tbsp sea salt
- good grind of black pepper
- zest and juice of 1 large orange
- 250 ml extra virgin olive oil
- 250 ml fish or vegetable stock

Dressing
- 1/2 red onion, roughly sliced
- 2 cloves garlic, sliced
- 1 tbsp balsamic vinegar
- zest and juice of 2 oranges
- cooking liquor from the braised fennel
- butter
- salt
- cayenne pepper

Fish
- 4 gurnard fillets – each 160–180 g, trimmed, scaled and pin-boned
- 2 tbsp extra virgin olive oil
- sea salt and freshly ground black pepper

Kale
- 1 bunch washed purple kale
- 25 g unsalted butter
- 2 tbsp balsamic vinegar

Method

Braised fennel: Preheat oven to 240°C (475°F, gas 9). Quarter the fennel lengthways, and place in an ovenproof dish with all the other ingredients. Bring to the boil, cover and braise in the oven for 1 hour. When cooked, remove the fennel and set aside to cool. Strain the cooking stock, and use the liquid to make the dressing. *Note:* this can be done the day before.

Dressing: Sweat off the red onion and garlic in a small saucepan with a little butter. Add the orange juice, zest and balsamic vinegar. Bring to the boil and reduce by half. Cool slightly and blend to purée the mixture. Slowly add the fennel liquor to form an emulsion. Sieve, adjust seasoning with salt and cayenne pepper.

Fish: Season gurnard with salt and black pepper. Heat a heavy frying pan to a medium, gentle heat. Add olive oil, warm and then add the fish fillets, skin side down. Cook for 4 minutes, until flesh starts to turn pale white halfway through the fillet, then turn. Reduce heat and cook for 1 minute. When the fish is cooked, it should be slightly firm but not spongey.

Warm the fennel in the oven. Remove fish fillets from pan and keep warm.

Melt the butter in the pan until gently foaming. Add the purple kale, season and quickly stir fry, adding balsamic vinegar to wilt the kale.

Place the warm fennel on a plate, with the fish on top, kale to the side, and a small pool of dressing.

Crawfish Lasagne

Ben Tunnicliffe, Chef-Proprietor
Abbey Restaurant, Penzance

Ben Tunnicliffe is one of Cornwall's top chefs. His commitment to using as much fresh, local and seasonal produce as possible is almost unequalled in Cornwall. It goes without saying, he says, that it is the quality of Cornish produce that has made his business what it is. Fish always features strongly on his menus – bought from Newlyn market each day if possible. It was his arrival in Cornwall in late 2000 to work at the Abbey Restaurant that really set him on his way to winning his first Michelin star in 2003. A change at the end of 2005 put Ben and his wife Kinga in control of the restaurant in their own right, turning away from Michelin stardom to concentrate on a more informal, relaxed setting for his food.

The key to this dish, he says, as with all his cooking, is the quality of the ingredients.

Ingredients ... serves 4

- 2 courgettes, approximately 20 cm long, 4 cm wide, washed and cut into small dice
- 2 carrots, approximately 20 cm long, 4 cm wide, peeled, cut into small dice
- 250 ml fish stock
- 125 ml double cream
- 1 cooked crawfish, about 1kg in weight
- 25 g basil leaves
- 12 sheets pasta – either bought lasagne or home-made – cut into 8 cm squares. (If making your own, you could roll the squares through the pasta machine with a parsley leaf in-between the squares, to use as the top sheet for garnish.)

Method

If cooking the live crawfish, drop it into boiling water for 10 minutes, remove and cool quickly in iced water.

Blanch the carrots and courgettes separately in salted, boiling water for 20 seconds, till just cooked but slightly crunchy. Refresh in cold water. Reserve until needed.

Remove meat from crawfish shell, including legs and claws.

For the sauce: Reduce the fish stock by half, or until a good gutsy base is achieved. Add cream and bring back to the boil; simmer until a good sauce consistency. Check seasoning and remove from heat.

Cook the pasta sheets.

Bring sauce back to the boil, add vegetables and crawfish meat and finely shredded basil. Check seasoning again.

Build the lasagne on each plate, starting with a pasta square, alternating with the sauce, finishing with a pasta square.

Note: As an alternative to crawfish, lobster could be used – or any other fish with a good meaty texture, such as monkfish, cod, halibut or hake.

Newlyn Fish Market – or Ling Turbot the Fish Opera 6 am

Early morning scales glitter
Silver ingots hoisted from the deep
Shunted around, in boxes
At high speed, the bidding war
Ice like confetti
Scattered over the wet floor
Conger curled up asleep
Skate wings it, flying low,
Megrim sole, Lundy, Fastnet
Copper green mackerel,
Monkfish, nod and a wink
Bass, playing the sea's orchestra,
With a herring aid
Pilchard in need of salt,
Squid, inked out
Lobster clawing its way back
Your plaice or mine?
Gurnard's head
Coley, Dab and Pollack
Mullet over,
Bream of Gerontius
Hake and John Dory
Ray, Cod and Haddock
In leading roles,
Ling Turbot for a tenner
The Fish Opera, Brill.
Shark, Fin Macool
Was it not
Who taught St Piran
To make crab soup?
With scallops for eyes.
Seaweed in hand.
Whiting to go.
It rains
Gutters work overtime.

James Crowden, 2005

Right: Landing boxes of fish packed in ice at Newlyn.

Bibliography and Websites

Barber, R. (2002), *Tresco Times: The Last Piece of England*. Tiverton: Halsgrove.

Barton, R.M. (ed.) (1972), *Life in Cornwall in the Late Nineteenth Century*. Truro: D. Bradford Barton.

Berry, C. (1963), *Portrait of Cornwall*. London: Robert Hale.

Borlase, W. (1758), *The Natural History of Cornwall*. Oxford, printed for the author.

Bowley, R.L. (1957), *The Fortunate Islands: The Story of the Isles of Scilly*. Reading: Bowley Publications. Paperback 2004.

Carew, R. (2000), *Survey of Cornwall 1602*. Launceston: Tamar Books.

Clover, C. (2004), *The End of the Line: How Overfishing is Changing the World and What We Eat*. London: Ebury Press.

Corin, J. (1988), *Fishermen's Conflict: The Story of Newlyn*. Newton Abbot: David & Charles, Tops'l Books.

Davidson, A. (1979), *North Atlantic Seafood*. London: Macmillan. Totnes: Prospect Books, 2002.

Fox, H. (2001), *The Evolution of the Fishing Village: Landscape and Society along the South Devon Coast, 1086–1550*. Oxford: Leopard's Head Press.

Halliday, F.E. (2001), *A History of Cornwall*. Thirsk: House of Stratus. (Duckworth, 1959.)

Hamilton Jenkin, A.K. (1932), *Cornish Seafarers*. London: J.M. Dent & Sons.

Harris, K. (1983), *Hevva! Account of the Cornish Fishing Industry in the Days of Sail*. Redruth: Dyllansow Truran.

Kurlansky, M. (1999), *Cod: A Biography of the Fish that Changed the World*. London: Vintage.

MacGarvin, M. & Jones, S. (2000), *Choose or Lose: A recovery plan for fish stocks and the UK fishing industry*. Godalming, WWF-UK.

Noall, C. (1972), *Cornish Seines and Seiners: History of the Pilchard Fishing Industry*. Truro: D. Bradford Barton.

Paston-Williams, S. (2005), *Fish Recipes from a Busy Island*. London: National Trust Books.

Payton, P. (2004), *Cornwall: A History*. Fowey: Cornwall Editions. (Alexander Associates, 1996.)

Smart, D. (1992), *The Cornish Fishing Industry: A Brief History*. Redruth: Tor Mark Press.

Smith, J. & Stevens, J. (2005), *North-East Sole, or Thereabouts*. St Martin's, Isles of Scilly: Scilly Books.

Smylie, M. (2004), *Herring: A History of the Silver Darlings*. Stroud: Tempus, 2004.

Stevenson, W. (2001), *Growing Up with Boats*. Newlyn: W.S. & S.

Various reports of Cornwall Sea Fisheries Committees, courtesy of the Cornwall Sea Fisheries Committee.

Websites and other information

Cornish Fish Producers' Organisation, to find out about the region's largest fishermen's representative body, www.cornishfpo.org.uk

Cornish Sardine, for information about buying Cornish sardines, www.cornishsardine.com

Duchy Fish Quota Company, to find out how Cornish fishermen are being supported, www.duchyfishquota.co.uk

Invest in Fish South West, for options on regional fisheries management, www.investinfishsw.org.uk

Seafood Cornwall, all about Cornish seafood, including where to buy, eat and recipes to try, www.seafoodcornwall.co.uk

South West Handline Fishermen's Association, for information about handline-caught mackerel and sea bass, www.linecaught.org.uk

Suppliers and Outlets

The fishmonger may be a disappearing species on most high streets, but not in Cornwall. Here is a selection that sells Cornish fish, shellfish or smoked fish either direct, online or by mail order. Also listed are the producers and processors featured in *Cornish Fishing and Seafood*, and others that there was no room to include. Those that do not sell direct to consumers are not listed.

Arwenack Fisheries, 29 Arwenack St, Falmouth TR11 3JE, T: 01326 312235

Atlantis Smoked Fish, Fore St, Grampound, Truro TR2 4SB, T: 01726 883201,
W: www.atlantisfoods.co.uk

Bodmin Seafoods, 1 Bell Yard, Bell Lane, Bodmin PL31 2JL, T: 01208 77117

Bude Shellfish, 5 Lansdown Rd, Bude EX23 8BH, T: 01288 354727

The Cornish Collection (mail order only), M. Stevens & Son Ltd., Back Rd West, St Ives TR26 3AR, T: 01736 799392,
W: www.mstevensandson.co.uk

Cornish Cuisine (smoked fish, retail and mail order), The Smokehouse, Islington Wharf, Penryn, T: 01326 376244,
W: www.smokedsalmon-ltd.com

Cornish Fish Direct (mail order only), Newlyn, T: 01736 332112, W: www.cornishfish.co.uk

Falmouth Bay Oysters (mail order only), The Docks, Falmouth, T: 01326 316600,
W: www.falmouthoysters.co.uk

The Fishy Plaice, Biscombes Lane, Callington PL17 7LB, T: 01579 382843

Fowey Fish (and mail order), 37 Fore Street, Fowey PL23 1AH T: 01726 832422,
W: www.foweyfish.com

Fruits of the Sea, Market Place, St Ives TR26 1RZ, T: 01736 794979

W. Harvey & Sons (and mail order), The Coombe, Newlyn, Penzance TR18 5HF, T: 01736 362983,
W: www.crabmeat.co.uk

Isles of Scilly Shellfish (mail order only; closed Jan–March), T: 01720 423898,
W: www.scillyshellfish.co.uk

Jeffersons Seafoods, Unit 1, Buller Quay, East Looe PL13 1DX, T: 01503 269076
W: www.jeffersonsseafoods.co.uk

Dennis Knight, 1 Azime Court, Rock Rd, St Minver, Wadebridge PL27 6PW, T: 01208 862422

Dennis Knight Fish Merchants, The Fish Cellars, 1 Fore St, Port Isaac PL29 3RB T: 01208 880498

Martins Seafresh (mail order only), Barn Lane, St Columb TR9 6BU, T: 01637 889168,
W: www.martins-seafresh.co.uk

Mevagissey Wet Fish, The West Quay, Mevagissey PL26 6QU, T: 01726 843839

Newlyn Fish Company, 15 Stable Hobba, Newlyn, Penzance TR20 8TL, T: 01736 369814

Pengelly's Fish Shop (and mail order), The Quay, East Looe PL13 1DX, T: 01503 262246, and 2 The Arcade, Fore St, Liskeard PL14 3JB, T: 01579 340777

Quayside Fish Centre (and mail order), Fore St, Porthleven, Helston TR13 9HJ, T: 01326 562008,
W: www.quaysidefish.co.uk

St Martin's Bakery, Moo Green, St Martin's, Isles of Scilly, Toby Tobin-Dugan, T: 01720 423444
W: www.stmartinsbakery.co.uk

Scillonian Shellfish Company, 25 Sally Port, St Mary's, Isles of Scilly, T: 07748 805273

Scales, Unit 1, Lemon St Market, Lemon St, Truro TR1 2LS, T: 01872 277797

Seabourne Fish, Unit T, Islington Wharf, Penryn TR10 8AT, T: 01326 378478

Seafayre Cuisine, Unit E, St Erth Industrial Estate, Hayle TR27 6LP

Matthew Stevens & Son, Back St East, St Ives, TR26 3AR, T: 01736 799392,
W: www.mstevensandson.co.uk

W. Stevenson & Sons, Harbour Road, Newlyn, Penzance, T: 01736 362982, Market Place, St Ives, T: 01736 794979, Wharfside, Wharf Rd, Penzance, T: 01736 331459,
W: www.wstevensonandsons.co.uk

Tregida Smokehouse (and mail order), Trelash,

Warbstow, Launceston PL15 8RL, T: 01840 261785, W: www.tregidasmokehouse.co.uk

Trelawney Fish (and mail order), 78 The Strand, Newlyn, Penzance TR18 5HW, T: 01736 361793, or 0800 5877894 for mail order

J.H. Turner (retail and wholesale), The Coombe, Newlyn, Penzance TR18 5HS, T: 01736 363726, W. www.jhturner.co.uk

Wing of St Mawes (mail order), T: 01726 861666, www.cornish-seafood.co.uk

Chefs

Chefs, restaurateurs and hotel owners who have contributed recipes to *Cornish Fishing and Seafood* are listed below. Note that contact details are for hotels, restaurants and pubs.

Toby Ashworth, The Nare Hotel, Carne Beach, Veryan-in-Roseland TR2 5PF, T: 01326 501111, W: www.thenare.com

Nick Barclay, Barclay House Hotel, St Martins Rd, East Looe PL13 1LP, T: 01503 262929, W: www.barclayhouse.co.uk

Gerry Boriosi, Cornwall College, Trevenson Rd, Pool, Redruth TR15 3RD, T: 01209 616161, W: www.cornwall.ac.uk/cpr

Billy Bunn, fisherman, St Ives

Paul Drye, St Austell Brewery Co. Ltd., 63 Trevarthian Rd, St. Austell PL25 4BY, T: 01726 74444, W: www.staustellbrewery.co.uk

Chris Eden, Marina Villa Hotel & Waterside Restaurant, Esplanade, Fowey PL23 1HY, T: 01726 833315, W: www.themarinahotel.co.uk

Gill Faiers, Bangors Organic, Bangors House, Poundstock, Bude EX23 0DP, T: 01288 361297, W: www.bangorsorganic.co.uk

Neil Haydock, Fifteen Cornwall, On The Beach, Watergate Bay TR8 4AA, T: 01637 861000, W: www.fifteencornwall.co.uk

Stuart Hayler, Five Degrees West, Falmouth TR11 4AU, T: 01326 311 288

Peter Hingston, Tresco Estate, Isles of Scilly TR24 0QQ, T: 01720 424110

Greg Laskey, New Yard Restaurant, Trelowarren, Mawgan, Helston TR12 6AF, T: 01326 221595

Ben Lightfoot, The Sticky Prawn, Flushing Quay, Flushing, Falmouth TR11 5TY, T: 01326 373734, W: www.thestickyprawn.co.uk

Ian Murray, The Devonport Inn, The Cleave, Kingsand, Torpoint PL10 1NF, T: 01752 822869

Ben Reeve, The Bay Restaurant, Britons Hill, Penzance TR18 3AE, T: 01736 366890, W: www.bay-penzance.co.uk

Rick Stein, The Seafood Restaurant, Padstow, T: 01841 532700, W: www.rickstein.com

Richard Stevenson, The Ship Inn, South Cliff, Mousehole, Penzance TR19 6QX, T: 01736 731234

Nigel Tabb, Tabbs Restaurant, 85 Kenwyn St, Truro TR1 3BZ, T: 01872 262110

Nik Tinney, Saffron, 5 Quay St, Truro TR1 2HB, T: 01872 263771

Ben Tunnicliffe, The Abbey, Abbey St, Penzance TR18 4AR, T: 01736 330680, W: www.theabbeyonline.com

Sponsors

We should like to thank all our sponsors, without whose generosity this book would not have been published. They are: Abbey Hotel, Bangors House, Bay Restaurant/Mount Prospect Hotel, Bluesail Fish, Cornish Fish Producers Organisation, Cornish Ice Co. Ltd., Cornwall Enterprise, John Collins of Dennis Knight Fish Merchants, Duke of Cornwall's Benevolent Fund, Fal Fish, Fifteen Cornwall, Invest In Fish South West, Marina Villa Hotel, Nare Hotel, Newlyn Fish Industry Forum, Pengelly's fishmongers, Penwith DC (Rural Economy), Penwith DC, Sustainable Tourism, Saffron, Seafood Cornwall, South West Regional Development Agency, St Austell Brewery, Tabbs, The Seafood Restaurant, The Sticky Prawn Bar & Restaurant, Trelowarren, Tresco Estate, W. Harvey & Sons, YEQT Ltd., and one who wished to remain anonymous.

Acknowledgements

None of this book would have been possible without the help and time of many people in the Cornish fishing industry, including many fishermen. To all of them we say thank you for giving up your time and for your patience, for taking us to sea, and for helping us to better understand what you do and why.

Particular thanks also go to: Eddy Derriman and his staff at the Cornwall Sea Fisheries Committee, and the crew of *St Piran*; David and Alec Stevens; Dave Bond; Stefan Glinski; Nathan de Rozarieux and Jon Lansley at Seafood Cornwall; Clare Leverton and Nicky Harrison at South West Pesca; Alan Qualtrough, Editor in Chief at the Western Morning News, for allowing me time off to write the book; Guy Crowden (for maritime research); James Crowden (for historical research); John Forster at Penwith Farm Business Centre; Elwyn and Mo Jones; Freya Laughton; Linda Maclean (for food styling); John McWilliams at the St Ives Trust Archive Study Centre; Ian Mitchell; David Muirhead; Mark Pender; Rob Poole at Penwith District Council; Jennie Raiment (for recipe testing); Stephen Nowell; Heather Squires, Spike Searle and Jennifer Storemski at Invest in Fish; Steve Watt of the Isles of Scilly Sea Fisheries Committee; Andy Wheeler; Douglas Williams; Tony Woodhams at the Newlyn Fish Industry Forum; all the chefs and restaurateurs who generously gave us recipes and cooked them for us; all those who took part in verbatims.

The recipe for Rick Stein's Herring Recheado is taken from *Rick Stein's Seafood*, published by BBC Worldwide Ltd © Rick Stein 2001. The drawings on pages 201–3 are by Tony Knight of Brixham, reproduced with permission from the Living from the Sea Museum, Looe. The photograph of Carol Trewin is by Neil Palmer, and that of Adam Woolfitt is by Donna Woolfitt. All other colour photographs were taken by Adam Woolfitt, mostly in 2005–6.

Archival paintings and photographs are reproduced by permisssion of: EMPICS (page 65); Gibsons of Scilly (page 37, top); Andrew Lanyon (pages 36, 37, bottom, and 39); Board of Trustees of the National Museums & Galleries on Merseyside (Walker Art Gallery, Liverpool) (page 33); Tyne & Wear Museums/ Laing Art Gallery (page 35). Paintings of fish (pages 197–9) are reproduced courtesy of the Sea Fish Industry Authority. We have been unable to trace the copyright holder of the photographs on page 64.

Newlyn Fish Market – or Ling Turbot the Fish Opera 6am is copyright James Crowden, and appears with kind permission of Tom Jaine. It was first published by Prospect Books in *Open-Mouthed*, 2006.

Special thanks from Adam to his long-suffering wife Penelope, and from Carol to James for his encouragement, impromptu text editing. Without his support, and encouragement from Adam, this book might not have been finished. But it was and their part in this deserves a special thank you.

Carol Trewin and Adam Woolfitt

First published in 2006 by
Alison Hodge, Bosulval, Newmill, Penzance, Cornwall
TR20 8XA, UK

www.alison-hodge.co.uk   info@alison-hodge.co.uk

© Text: Carol Trewin, 2006

© Photographs: Adam Woolfitt, 2006

© This edition: Alison Hodge, 2006

ISBN-13 978-0-906720-42-4
ISBN-10 0-906720-42-7

British Library Cataloguing-in-Publication Data

A catalogue record for this book is available from the British Library.

Edited, designed and originated by
BDP – Book Design and Production, Penzance, Cornwall

Cover design: Christopher Laughton

Printed and bound by Butler & Tanner Ltd., Frome, Somerset

To order a print of a picture in this book contact Adam Woolfitt via email at adampix@dircon.co.uk